# THE GREEK ORATORS

# THE GREEK ORATORS

THE BEGINNINGS OF ORATORY—ANTIPHON
Thrasymachus—ANDOCIDES—LYSIAS—ISAEUS
ISOCRATES-Alcidamas-Polycrates—AESCHINES
DEMOSTHENES—Phokion—DEMADES—Pytheas
LYCURGUS—HYPERIDES—DINARCHUS-Demetrius of Phalerum—MINOR ORATORS.

BY

## J. F. DOBSON, M.A.

TRINITY COLLEGE, CAMBRIDGE,

PROFESSOR OF GREEK IN THE UNIVERSITY

OF BRISTOL

ARES PUBLISHERS INC.

CHICAGO        MCMLXXIV

Unchanged Reprint of the Edition:
London, 1918.
ARES  PUBLISHERS  INC.
150 E. Huron Street
Chicago, Illinois 60611
Printed in the United States of America
International Standard Book Number:
0-89005-050-3
Library of Congress Catalog Card Number:
74-77869

# PREFACE

THE object of this book is to provide a reasonably short account of the works of the Orators and to give a general idea of the style of each.   It seemed to me at the outset that this object could be best attained, not by applying methods of scientific analysis, but by giving numerous quotations from the speeches to emphasise the points which I wished to bring out. I have therefore avoided as far as possible the technicalities of criticism, and illustrated my remarks by translations of characteristic passages, hoping thus to make my work easily accessible not only to classical students, but also to others who, while generally interested in the Classics, have not the time or the capacity to study them in the original.

I have no idea of superseding the standard works on the subject, such as Jebb's *Attic Orators* and Blass' *Attische Beredsamkeit*, which deal with the subject more fully and from a somewhat different point of view. No student of the Orators can afford to neglect the works of these scholars, but though I have frequently consulted them, I have by no means considered myself bound by their opinions; in fact, my chief claim to consideration is that my own judgments are entirely independent of authority, and are based directly upon a first-hand study of the extant writings of the Orators.

The chief work, in addition to the two above mentioned, to which I am indebted is Croiset's *Histoire de la Littérature Grecque*.

I have to thank Balliol College and the Clarendon Press for permission to print extracts from Jowett's *Plato*.

J. F. DOBSON

BRISTOL, *July 1919*

# CONTENTS

# THE GREEK ORATORS

## CHAPTER I

## THE BEGINNINGS OF ORATORY

### § 1

ORATORY is one of the earliest necessities of society; as soon as men were organised on terms of equality for corporate action, there must have been occasions when opinions might differ as to the best course to be pursued, and, if there were no inspired king whose unquestioned authority could impose his will, the majority must decide whether to flee or to fight, to kill or to keep alive. Thus different plans must be discussed, and, in cases where opinion was evenly balanced, that side would prevail which could state its views most convincingly; and so the need for deliberative oratory arose.

With the Greeks oratory was instinctive; in the earliest semi-historical records that we possess, eloquence is found to be a gift prized not less highly than valour in battle; the kings and princes are not only 're-nowned for their power,' but are 'leaders of the people by their counsels, . . . wise and eloquent in their instructions'; strength and courage are the property of all, but the real leaders must be the counsellors, βουλήφοροι ἄνδρες. Nestor, who is almost past the age for fighting, is honoured among the first for his

A

eloquence, and whereas Achilles shares with many other warriors the glories of the *Iliad*, Odysseus, fertile in counsel, is the chief subject of an entire poem. The speech of Phœnix in the ninth book of the *Iliad* shows us the ideals which were aimed at in the education of a prince. He tells how he trained the young Achilles to be a 'speaker of words and a doer of deeds';[1] and Achilles, as we know him, well justified this training. The leading characters in the Homeric poems are already fluent orators, able and ready to debate intelligently on any concrete subject, and, moreover, to seek guidance from general principles. Nestor makes frequent appeals to historical precedent; Phœnix introduces allegorical illustration;[2] many speakers refer to the sanctity of law and custom; though the particular case is foremost in the mind, generalisations of various kinds are by no means infrequent. The Homeric counsellor can urge his own arguments and rebut those of his opponent with a natural facility of speech and readiness of invective which even a polished wielder of personalities like Demosthenes might envy.

From the spontaneous outpourings of Achilles and his peers to the studied artifice of Lysias and Demosthenes is a long journey through unknown country, and it is obvious that no definite course of development can be traced; but a reference to Homer is of twofold importance. In the first place, it may indicate that Greek oratory was obviously of native growth, since the germs of it are to be found in the earliest annals; secondly, Homer was studied with such devout reverence not only by the Athenian orators

---

[1] *Iliad*, ix. 443.

[2] *Ibid.*, ix. 502 *sqq.*

themselves but by their immediate literary predecessors, the cosmopolitan Sophists and the rhetoricians of Sicily, that his influence may have been greater than would at first sight seem probable.

## § 2

The records of eloquence may be studied from various points of view, which may be roughly classified under the headings ' literary ' and ' practical,' though it is not always easy to keep the elements distinct. A stylistic study of the writings of the Athenian orators must find a place in any systematic work on the development of Attic prose, but in a work like the present, which professes to deal with orators only, such a study cannot be carried out with any attempt at completeness ; thus, while it may be possible to discuss the influence of Thucydides or Plato on Demosthenes, there will be no room to consider how far the historian himself may have been influenced directly by Antiphon, or the philosopher by Gorgias, though a cursory indication may be given that such influences were at work. When, however, we regard rhetoric not for its literary value but as a practical art, our task becomes more feasible ; in literature there are many eddies and cross-currents, but in oratory, especially of the forensic type, there is more uniformity of flow. Antiphon and Demosthenes had, to a great extent, similar ground to traverse, similar obstacles to overcome or circumvent ; and a study of their different methods of approaching like problems may give some reasonable and interesting results which will be a contribution to the history of the ' Art of Persuasion.' Even here we shall find difficulties, for one who is reckoned among the greatest orators, Isocrates, is known not to have been practical at all in the sense in which Demosthenes was ; his so-called speeches were never meant to be delivered, and depended for their efficacy far more on their literary style than on their practical characteristics. There is, perhaps, only one great factor which is common to all orators alike ; they all give us, both directly and indirectly, invaluable materials for the study of Athenian history, information with regard both to public and private life and national character. While the speeches before the assembly and in public causes increase our historical knowledge in the wider sense, the private speeches, often dealing with matters of the utmost triviality, provide a miscellaneous store of information on domestic matters only comparable to that more recently recovered from the *papyri* of Egypt.

§ 3

It would seem that constitutional liberty and a strong civic feeling are indispensable as a basis for the growth of oratory. Such a statement must be made with caution, as it leaves out of account a thousand influences which may have been operative ; but we have no records of oratory at Athens before the establishment of the democracy, and after the limitation of Athenian influence due to the spread of Hellenism under Alexander, oratory very rapidly declined.

The imagination of Herodotus gives us, in the debates of the Persian court, some idea of what he conceived the oratory of an earlier age to be; but as he transferred the ideas of his own country to another, without any serious attempt at realism, such speeches are of little value to us. Thucydides again inserted speeches freely into his history, but these, he candidly admits, are not authentic records but imaginary reconstructions. Nevertheless, it is chiefly on Thucydides that we must draw for information about the eloquence of the early statesmen of the democracy.

Themistocles has left behind him some reputation as a speaker. Herodotus indicates how he harangued the Greeks before the battle of Salamis;[1] Thucydides commends him for ability in explaining his policy,[2] and the author of the pseudo-Lysian *Epitaphios* names him as 'equally capable in speech, decision, and action.'[3] Beyond these meagre notices, and a reference to his eloquence in Cicero,[4] we have nothing earlier than Plutarch,[5] who tells us that from early youth he took an interest in the practice of speech-making, and that he studied under a Sophist, Mnesiphilus, who apparently taught him something of the science of statesmanship. Plutarch records his answer to Eurybiadas, who had taunted him in the council of allies with being a man without a city—since Athens was evacuated—and therefore not entitled to the right of speech :

' We, villain, have left our houses and our walls, disdaining to be slaves for the sake of these lifeless things ; but still we have a city—the greatest of Greek cities—in our fleet of 200 triremes, which now are ready to help you if you care to be saved by their aid ; but if you go away and betray us a second time, the Greek world shall forthwith learn that the Athenians possess a free city and a country no worse than the one they have lost.'[6]

---

[1] Herod., viii. 83.　[2] Thuc., i. 138.　[3] § 42.
[4] *Brutus*, § 28.　[5] *Themistocles*, ch. ii.　[6] *Ibid.*, ch. xi.

Another fragment is preserved by Plutarch, an address to Xerxes in quite a different vein, containing an elaborate metaphor which may have been thought suited to the Oriental mind :

‘ The speech of man is like to a piece of cunning embroidery, for both when unrolled display their patterns, but when folded up conceal them.’[1]

Many others of his sayings are chronicled ; they are more or less apocryphal, as his retort to the man of Seriphos, who hinted that Themistocles owed his greatness to the fact that his city was great. ‘ You, Themistocles, would never have been famous if you had been a Seriphian ’—‘ Nor would you, if you had been an Athenian.’[2]   His interpretation of the oracle, explaining ‘ wooden walls ’ as ships, shows the man ready at need like Odysseus; and the impression that we form of him from the very slight indications which we possess, is of a man always clear and plausible in his statements, never at a loss for an explanation, and perhaps rather a good debater than an orator.

Of Pericles, who represents the following generation, we have a clearer picture.  We know more about his private life and the associates who influenced his opinions.  His earliest instructors were the musicians Damon and Pythoclides, of whom the former remained his intimate friend through life,[3] and, if we believe Plutarch, was capable of giving him advice even on questions of statesmanship.[4]   The friendship of Anaxa-

---

[1] Ch. xxix.    [2] Plato, *Republic*, i. 330 A.
[3] Plato, *Alcibiades*, I., 118 c.
[4] Plut., *Pericles*, ch. iv., who quotes Plato (comicus) : σὺ γάρ, ὥς φασι, Χείρων ἐξέθρεψας Περικλέα.

goras was doubtless a powerful influence, as Plato affirms in a well-known passage of the *Phaedrus* : [1]

'All the arts require discussion and high speculation about the truths of nature ; hence come loftiness of thought and completeness of execution. And this, as I conceive, was the quality which, in addition to his natural gifts, Pericles acquired from his intercourse with Anaxagoras. . . . He was thus imbued with the higher philosophy . . . and applied what suited his purpose to the art of speaking.'

He is said also to have been acquainted with Zeno of Elea, an accomplished dialectician, and with the great Sophist Protagoras.

Plutarch represents him as amusing himself by discussing with Protagoras a question which is the theme of one of Antiphon's tetralogies—a man in a gymnasium accidentally kills another with a javelin : who is to blame ? [2] In Xenophon's *Memorabilia* [3] we find him engaged in sophistical discussion with his young nephew Alcibiades, who, fresh from the rhetorical schools, was apparently his superior in hair-splitting argument.

Thucydides puts three speeches into the mouth of Pericles ; though the language is that of the historian, some of the thoughts may be those of the statesman. We seem to recognise his high intelligence, developed by philosophical training, and the loftiness and effectiveness of which Plato speaks. [4]

The comic poet Eupolis gives us a picture from a different point of view :

A. 'Whenever at Council he rose in his place
That powerful speaker—so hot was the pace—
Could give other runners three yards in the race.'

---

[1] p. 270 A, Jowett's translation.
[2] Antiphon, *Tetral.* ii.　　　[3] I. 2. 40.　　　[4] Plato, *l.c.*

B. 'His speed I admit ; in addition to that
   A mysterious spell on his lips ever sate :
   He charmed ; and alone of the orators he
   Left something behind, like the sting of a bee.' [1]

We know from Thucydides the extent of his influence over the people. He was no demagogue in the vulgar sense ; they knew him to be sincere and incorruptible. He was never deterred by the unpopularity of his policy ; he would lead the people rather than submit to be led by them ; he could abase their spirits when they were unduly elated, or raise them to confidence when unseasonably disheartened.[2] At the height of his career his eloquence was the more effective because it was rarely displayed ; minor matters in the assembly were transacted by his subordinates ; when Pericles himself arose to speak it was a signal that a matter of national importance was to be debated, and his appearance roused a confident expectation that the treatment would be worthy of the subject.[3] The epithet ' Olympian,' applied to him originally in sarcasm, was felt to be more truly applicable than its originator, perhaps, intended. His eloquence was a noble exposition of the fine intelligence and high character which first claimed a hearing.

Though we have no verbal record of his speeches, a few of his phrases stuck in the memory of chroniclers. Aegina was to him ' the eye-sore of the Piraeus '—it spoiled the view from the Athenian harbour.[4] The Samians, who submitted very reluctantly to the bless-

---

[1] Bothe, *Comic Frag.*, i. 162. See also Aristophanes, *Acharn.* 530.
   ' Then Pericles the Olympian in his wrath
    Lightened and thundered and confounded Greece.'
[2] Thuc., ii. 65.              [3] Plut., *Pericles*, ch. vii.
[4] Arist., *Rhet.*, iii. 10. 7 D.

ings of Athenian civilization, are like ' babies that cry when you give them their pap, but take it all the same ' ;[1] and Boeotia, disintegrated by civil war, is like an oak split by oaken wedges.[2]  His finest simile —not, perhaps, original, since Herodotus attributes a similar phrase to Gelon, when Greece refused his invaluable assistance—occurred, according to Aristotle, in a funeral speech :

' The city has lost its Youth ;  it is as though the year had lost its Spring.'[3]

§ 4

The eloquence of these earlier statesmen, though significant of the tendency of the Attic genius, is an isolated phenomenon.  It has no bearing on the development of Athenian oratory.  We have now to consider two direct influences, that of the Sophists and that of the early rhetoricians of Sicily.

In the middle of the fifth century B.C.,—when in turn the unrestricted imagination of the Ionian philosophers had failed to explain the riddle of existence on physical grounds, the metaphysical Parmenides had denied the possibility of accurate knowledge, and Zeno, the dialectician of Elea, had reduced himself to dumbness by the conclusion that not only knowledge is impossible but even grammatical predication is unjustifiable, for you cannot say that one thing is another, or like things unlike,—Philosophy fell somewhat into disrepute.  A spirit of scepticism spread

---

[1] Thuc., i. 115-117 ; Arist., *Rhet.*, iii. 4. 3.
[2] Arist., *ibid.*
[3] Herod., vii. 162 ; Arist., *Rhet.*, i. 7. 34.  In a later age the orator Demades borrowed it.  (Athenaeus, iii. 99 D.)

over the Greek world, and the greatest thinkers, foiled in their attempts to discover the higher truths, turned their attention to the practical side of education. In various cities of Greater Greece there arose men of high intellectual attainment, conveniently classed together under the title of *Sophists* (educators), who, neglecting abstract questions, undertook to prepare men for the higher walks of civic life by instruction of various kinds. The greatest of these, Protagoras of Abdera, expressed his contempt for philosophy in the well-known dictum, ' Man is the measure of all things—of what is, that it is ; and of what is not, that it is not.' He therefore devoted himself to the study of literature, and, in particular, of Homer. He attained great popularity ; in the course of long travels throughout the Greek world, he made several visits to Athens, where he knew Pericles. Plato, in the dialogue named after him, gives us some idea of the fascination which his personality exercised over the young men of Athens, and, indeed, ' Sophistry ' as a whole had a tremendous popularity. All young men of good family and position, who aspired to political life, flocked to hear the lectures of the Sophists. Alcibiades, Critias, and others undoubtedly owed to this movement much of their political ability.

The morality of sophistry has been much discussed. The comic poets represent it as the chief instrument for the destruction of the ancient ideals of conduct. Plato, though he recognized its humanistic value and spoke with appreciation of several individual teachers, blamed their teaching as a whole. Certainly the claim of Protagoras, that he could make the worse cause appear the better, laid him particularly open to attack.

Protagoras made some elementary studies in grammar, presumably as a basis for logic.   His method of teaching was apparently by example.   In the dialogue of Plato he gives a demonstration of how a given subject should be discussed : his discourse consists first of a ' myth,' then a continuous speech, finally a criticism on a poetical quotation.   We may suppose that this is a reasonable imitation of his methods.   His pupils committed to memory such speeches, or summaries of them, on various subjects, and were thus moderately well equipped for purposes of general debate.

Prodicus of Ceos, who seems to have been many years younger than Protagoras,[1] was more concerned with moral philosophy than with dialectical exercises. He paid the greatest attention in all his teaching to ὀρθοέπεια, the correct use of words, *i.e.* the distinction of meaning between words which in the popular language have come to be treated as synonymous.[2] This precision may have been carried to the point of pedantry, but as the correct use of terms is an important element in prose style, his studies deserve consideration.

Hippias of Elis is of less importance.   He was ready to discourse on any subject under the sun, and could teach his pupils a similar glibness ; abundance of words was made to conceal a lack of ideas.

§ 5

Cicero has preserved, from Aristotle, a statement that forensic rhetoric came to its birth at Syracuse, when, after the expulsion of the tyrants in 465 B.C.,

---

[1] Plato, *Protag.*, 317 C.
[2] Plato, *Protag.*, 337 A-C, where Plato parodies his style.

many families, whose property had been confiscated by them, tried to re-establish their claims.[1]  Certainly Corax, the founder of rhetoric, was teaching about the year 466 B.C., and composed a τέχνη, or handbook of rhetorical principles.[2]  He was followed by his pupil Tisias, who also wrote a treatise which Aristotle pronounced to be better than his master's, and was in turn soon superseded by a better one.[3]  Both Corax and Tisias attached great importance to εἰκός (probability) as a means of convincing a jury.  A sample of the use of this argument from the work of Corax is the case of the man charged with assault, who denies the charge and says, ' It is obvious to you that I am weak in body, while he is strong ; it is therefore inherently improbable that I should have dared to attack him.'  The argument can of course be turned the other way by the prosecutor—' the defendant is weak in body, and thought that on that account no one would suspect him of violence.'  We shall find that this argument from εἰκότα is very characteristic of the orator Antiphon ; it occurs in his court speeches as well as in his tetralogies, which are model exercises. It seems, indeed, that he almost preferred this kind of argument to actual proof, even when evidence was available.[4]  Tisias improved on the theme of Corax ; supposing that a feeble but brave man has attacked a strong one who is a coward, he suggests that both should tell lies in court.  The coward will not like to admit his cowardice, and will say that he was attacked by more than one man.  The culprit will prove this to be a lie, and will then fall back on the argument of

---

[1] Cicero, *Brutus*, § 46.  [2] Arist., *Rhet.*, ii. 24. 11.
[3] *Soph. Elench.*, 183 p. 28 *sqq.*  [4] *Vide infra*, p. 36.

Corax, ' I am weak and he is strong ; I could not have assaulted or robbed him,'—and so on.[1]

An anecdote of these two rhetoricians further indicates the slipperiness of the ground on which they walked.[2] Tisias took lessons from Corax on condition that he should pay the fee only if he won his first case in court. After some lapse of time Corax grew impatient for his money, and finally brought an action—the first case, as it happened, on which Tisias was ever engaged. Corax asserted, ' If I win the case, I get my money by the verdict ; if I lose it, I claim payment by our contract.' ' No,' said Tisias, ' if I win, I don't pay, and if I lose I don't pay.' The court dismissed the case with the remark, ' A bad *crow* lays bad eggs ' ; [3] and this was obviously to the advantage of the younger man, who had nine points of the law on his side.

Though no writings of either are preserved, we can form an idea of their methods. They were wholly immoral or non-moral, and perversely sophistical. The plausible was preferred to the true, and the one object was to win the case. Their method of teaching was, according to Aristotle, ' quick but unscientific,' [4] and consisted of making the pupil learn by heart a large number of ' commonplace ' topics and standard arguments suitable to all kinds of legal processes. They do not appear to have paid any attention to style on the literary side.

## § 6

Gorgias of Leontini, a contemporary of Protagoras, started out, like the Sophist, from the position that

---

[1] Quoted by Plato, *Phaedrus*, 273 B-C.
[2] Schol. on Hermogenes ; also Sext. Empir. *adv. Mathem.*, ii. 96.
[3] κακοῦ Κόρακος κακὰ ᾠά.      [4] *Soph. Elench.*, 184 a. 1.

nothing can be known, and the pursuit of philosophy is a ploughing of the sand. He is said to have been a pupil of Tisias, and occupies a place between the early rhetoricians and the Sophists usually so-called. Like the former, he studied and taught oratory, but whereas they were only concerned with the struggle for mastery in debate, he entertained, like Protagoras, a broad view of education, and, while continuing to regard rhetoric as the art of persuasion,[1] attached more attention to the artistic side than any other educator had done. He became the first conscious artist in prose style.

Like the other Sophists he travelled from town to town giving displays of his art, and gained riches which he spent freely.[2] In 427 B.C. he came to Athens as an ambassador from his native city,[3] and produced a remarkable impression on his hearers, not only the multitude before whom he spoke, but the highly educated class who could appreciate his technique. Thucydides owed something to him, and the poet Antiphon showed traces of his influence.[4] We hear of his sojourn at Larissa, where the Thessalians, in admiration, coined from his name the word which Philostratus uses to express his exuberant style.[5]

His first work is said to have been a sceptical treatise on Nature, or the Non-existent.[6] This was followed by a

---

[1] Cf. Plato, *Gorgias*, 453 A ; *Phaedr.*, 259 E.

[2] Isocr., *Antid.*, § 155.

[3] If it is true, as Philostratus, *Ep.* ix. says, that Aspasia ' sharpened the tongue of Pericles ' in Gorgian style, he must have visited Athens in a private capacity at an earlier date, unless his *Olympiac* and other speeches were widely circulated and read.

[4] Πολλαχοῦ τῶν ἰάμβων γοργιάζει, Philost., *Lives of the Sophists*, ix. 493.

[5] Plato, *Meno*, 70 B ; Philost., *Epist.* ix. 364.

[6] περὶ φύσεως ἢ τοῦ μὴ ὄντος, Sext. Emp., vii. 65. Cicero (*Brut.*, § 46) mentions also a collection of *communes loci* made for instructional purposes.

certain number of speeches, the most famous of which was the *Olympiac*, in which, like Isocrates at a later date, he urged on the Greeks the necessity of union. The *Funeral Oration*, to which we shall recur, is supposed to have been delivered at Athens, but this can hardly have been the case, as such speeches were regularly delivered by prominent Athenian statesmen, and there would be no occasion for calling in a foreigner. A *Pythian* speech and various *Encomia* are recorded ; some on mythical characters, which may be regarded as mere exercises, some on real people, as the Eleans.[1] He seems not to have written speeches for the law-courts ; his tendency, as in his personal habits, so in his speech, was towards display, and so he originated the style of oratory known as epideictic, which Isocrates in a subsequent age was destined to bring to perfection. Though an Ionian by birth, he instinctively recognized the great possibilities of the Attic dialect, and chose it as his medium of expression ; it was not, however, the Attic of everyday life, but a language enriched by the exuberance of a poetical imagination.  We possess of his actual work only one noteworthy extract from the *Funeral Speech* ; but from this, joined to a few isolated criticisms and phrases preserved by commentators, as well as from the language ascribed by Plato to his imitator Agathon,[2] we can form some idea of his pompous exaggerations.

He was much addicted to the substitution of rare expressions—γλῶτται, as the Greek critics called them —for the ordinary forms of speech.  His language

---

[1] Arist., *Rhet.*, iii. 14. 12.

[2] *Symposium*, 194 E, *sqq.*, 197 D ;  the latter contains some excellent examples : πραύτητα μὲν πορίζων, ἀγριότητα δ' ἐξορίζων· φιλόδωρος εὐμενείας, ἄδωρος δυσμενείας, etc.

abounded in archaic and poetical words, striking metaphors and unusual compounds. He frequently employed neuter adjectives and participles in preference to the corresponding abstract nouns ; he liked to use a verbal noun accompanied by an auxiliary in places where a simple verb would be naturally employed. Finally, though he could not aspire to composition in elaborate periods like Isocrates or Demosthenes, he developed the use of antithesis, word answering to word and clause to clause, pointing his antithetical style not only by the frequent use of μὲν and δέ, but by the use of assonance at the ends of clauses, corresponding forms of verbs in similar positions, and by some attention to rhythm and equality of syllabic value in contrasted clauses.

His chief fault was excess ; he was a pioneer in expression, and did very valuable work ; but he lacked a sense of proportion. The result is that the page of his genuine work which we possess reads like a parody of style, as every characteristic is carried to extreme. But the teacher must indulge in exaggeration, or the pupil will not grasp his points, and the work of Gorgias has a considerable value. It was the first attempt to form a style, and his followers learned partly by imitation, partly by avoiding the faults which were too prominent. The very fact that the fragment preserved is possibly not in his best style makes it the easier to observe his influence on his successors— Antiphon, Thucydides, and many subsequent writers of artistic prose.

In addition to the speeches already mentioned we possess two *encomia* on Helen and Palamedes, which are attributed to him. Their authenticity is very doubtful, but Blass, who discussed the question very thoroughly in his *Attic Orators* without coming to a conviction, has since decided in favour of their genuineness.[1] This is entirely a matter of personal opinion; but, even if not genuine, they are probably able imitations of the Gorgian style and method.

The fragment from the *Epitaphios* can hardly be translated in a way that will give a proper idea of its affectations, but as some notion of its most striking faults may be formed from an English version, some extracts are added. In the Greek in some places there seems to be very little sense, and what there is has been entirely subordinated to the sound:

'What quality was there absent in these men which ought in men to be present? And what was there present that should not be present? May I have the power to speak as I would, and the will to speak as I should, avoiding the jealousy of gods and escaping the envy of men. For these were divine in their valour, though human in their mortality; often preferring mild equity to stern justice, and often the uprightness of reasoning to the strictness of the laws, considering that the most divine and universal law is this—to speak, to omit, and to do the proper thing at the proper time. Two duties above all they practised, strength of mind and strength of body; the one in deliberation, the other in execution; tenders of those who by injustice were unfortunate, punishers of those who by injustice were fortunate. . . . And accordingly, though they have died, our yearning died not with them, but immortal over these bodies not immortal it lives when they live no more.'

Contrast and parallelism are rampant throughout this incredible piece of bombast, which in addition to

[1] Introduction to the Teubner edition of Antiphon (1908), p. xxviii.

B

the curious jingles produced by such words as γνώμην καὶ ῥώμην ; δυστυχούντων, εὐτυχούντων, shows a poetical vocabulary in such phrases as ἔμφυτος ῎Αρης, 'the Mars that is born in them,' ἐνόπλιος ἔρις, ' embattled strife,' and φιλόκαλος εἰρήνη, ' peace that loves the arts.' Antiphon and Thucydides suffered severely from the contagion of this style, and a conscious imitator, the author of the pseudo-Lysian *Epitaphios*, has reproduced its florid monotony.

# CHAPTER II

## ANTIPHON

### § I

ANTIPHON is said to have been almost contemporary with Gorgias, but a little younger.[1] He was born about 480 B.C. He took no part in public life, perhaps disdaining to serve the democracy owing to his strong aristocratic prejudices. He wrote many speeches for others, but himself never spoke in the assembly and very rarely in the public courts. Most of his speeches were written for private individuals, but we have a record on one '*about the tribute of Samothrace*,' apparently composed on behalf of that community when appealing against their assessment. Having lived in comparative obscurity all his life, he stepped suddenly into brilliant light in 411 B.C., the year of the revolution of the Four Hundred. According to Thucydides his was the brain which had planned all the details of this anti-democratic conspiracy. The historian pays a striking tribute to his ability as an organiser :

'It was Pisander who proposed this motion and in general took the most active steps for the subversion of the democracy ; but the one who contrived the whole plot and the details of its working and who had given his attention to it longest was Antiphon, a man who

---

[1] Ps.-Plut., *Lives of the Orators*, Antiphon, § 9.

must be placed in the first rank for his character, his ingenuity, and his powers of expression. He never put himself forward in the assembly, nor appeared, from choice, at any trial in the courts, but lay under the people's suspicion owing to a reputation for cleverness. He was, however, more capable than any other man of giving assistance to anybody who consulted him with regard to a case either in the courts or the assembly. Eventually, when the Four Hundred suffered reverse and were being harshly treated by the democracy, he was himself brought to trial, for participation in the revolution, and is known to have made the finest defence ever on record as having been delivered by a man on trial for his life.' [1]

During the short rule of the Four Hundred he seems to have been one of the leaders of the extreme party, as opposed to the followers of Theramenes, who advocated measures of conciliation. He went, with Phrynichus and eight other envoys, to negotiate peace with Sparta in the hope of thus securing the oligarchical government. Shortly after the failure of this embassy came the murder of Phrynichus and the fall of the Four Hundred, and the democracy was ready for revenge. Most of the ringleaders fled to Deceleia ; Antiphon and Archeptolemus remained, were prosecuted for treason to the people, condemned and executed. Their property was confiscated, their houses razed to the ground, their descendants disfranchised for all time, and their bodies refused burial in the soil of Athens or any of her allies.

On the occasion of his trial the orator, who had spent the best years of his life in pleading by the lips of others

[1] Thuc., viii. 68.

in causes which did not interest him, justified his renown and far surpassed all expectation, delivering what was, in Thucydides' opinion, the finest speech of its kind ever heard up to that time. Aristotle preserves an anecdote telling how the poet Agathon congratulated the condemned man on his brilliant effort, and Antiphon replied that ' he would rather have satisfied one man of taste than any number of common people'—οἱ τυγχάνοντες, a fine aristocratic term for great Athenian people.[1]

§ 2

At the time when Antiphon composed his speeches, Attic prose had not settled down into any fixed forms. The first of the orators was therefore an explorer in language ; he was not hampered by traditions, and this freedom was an advantage ; but on the other hand, the insufficiency of models threw him back entirely on his own resources.

Of his predecessors in prose-writing, the early historians were of no account as stylists. Herodotus wrote in a foreign dialect and a discursive colloquial manner which was unsuited to the needs of oratory ; Gorgias, indeed, used the Attic dialect, but had hindered the growth of prose by a too copious use of florid poetical expression. Antiphon, therefore, had little to guide him, and we should expect to find in his work the imperfections which are natural in the experimental stage of any art.

So few of his works remain that we cannot trace any development in his style ; it is only possible to guess

---

[1] *Eth. Eudem.*, iii. 1232 b. 7.

at certain influences which may have helped to form it.

He must have been familiar with the methods of the best speakers in the assembly and the law-courts of the Periclean age ; without great experience of procedure in both he could not have hoped for any success as a speech-writer. He must have been versed in the theories of the great Sophists, such as Protagoras and, more particularly, Gorgias ; and the model discourses which they and others composed for their pupils' instruction were, no doubt, accessible to him. The general influence of Sophistry is, however, to be traced more in the nature of his arguments than in his style.[1]

## § 3

As regards vocabulary, we are struck at once by the fact that Antiphon uses many words which, apart from their occurrence in these speeches, would be classed as rare or poetical ; words, that is, which a maturer prose-style was inclined to reject. This was partly the result of circumstances ; as has been noted, there was no canon of style and vocabulary, and the influence of Gorgias had been rather to confuse than to distinguish the dictions of prose and poetry, while the great importance attached to poetry in the sophistical education of the time increased the difficulties for any experimental writer who was unwilling to resort to the colloquial language. In many cases, however, we may give Antiphon credit for intention in the deliberate use of poetical words : the ' austere ' style ' is wont to

---

[1] The Sophistical element is very prominent, especially in the tetralogies. Like Tisias he makes great use of arguments from probability.

expand itself,' says Dionysius, ' by means of big spacious words ' ;[1] and a store of such words is to be found in the poets, notably Aeschylus.[2]

Antiphon is not singular among prose writers in introducing poetical words ; Plato, the greatest master of Attic prose, is in some cases more poetical than the poets themselves, though his genius is sufficient to obviate any sense of harshness or incongruity. But to an orator such harshness might on occasion be a positive advantage for producing a particular effect ; an unusual word must, at the worst, attract attention ; at the best it lends dignity to an otherwise pedestrian sentence. Dionysius classed Antiphon and Aeschylus together as masters of the ' austere ' style, and some of the orator's words and phrases, quite apart from his treatment of his subjects, have a certain touch of Aeschylean majesty.

Besides poetical words—words which may, as we see, have been used intentionally, in preference to their ordinary equivalents in everyday speech—he employs, for the same reasons, a certain number of unusual words and forms not necessarily poetical. Every conscious stylist makes experiments : some of his innovations may become current coin ; others may never pass into general circulation, but remain unused until, perhaps, after many generations an archæologist discovers and uses the hoard.[3] A few familiar words

---

[1] *De comp. verborum*, ch. 22.

[2] Such words are, for instance, ἀνατροπεύς ; μήνιμα and ἀλιτήριος, separately, as μήνιμα ἀκέσασθαι, δεινοὺς ἀλιτηρίους ἕξομεν, or together, μήνιμα τῶν ἀλιτηρίων προστρίψομαι ; θεία κηλίς, γεγωνεῖν, ὀπτήρ, ἀείμνηστος.

[3] Rare but not poetical words are, *e.g.* ὑπῆρκτο, χωροφιλεῖν, καταδοχθείς, ἐπίδοξος, and, from lost speeches, μοιρολογχεῖν, τριβωνεύεσθαι, ἀστοργία, and many others quoted by lexicographers for their peculiarity.

occur in unusual forms which are generally regarded as un-Attic; unless they are to be removed by emendation, we must suppose that they were used intentionally to give an archaic tone.[1]

Another noticeable characteristic of Antiphon's language is the frequent employment of circumlocutions both for verbs and nouns; a neuter participle or adjective in combination with the definite article does duty as a substantive, while a verbal noun joined to an auxiliary takes the place of a verb. Thus, by an artifice which becomes very common in later writers, ' the beautiful ' is used as a synonym for the abstract noun ' beauty,' and to ' be judges of the truth ' is substituted for ' judge the truth.' These artificialities are often to be noticed in Thucydides, especially in the speeches, and are probably derived from Gorgias, who seems to have instituted the fashion.[2]

## § 4

Aristotle and subsequent critics distinguish, in prose, the running style (εἰρομένη λέξις) and the periodic (περιοδική). The characteristic of the former is that a sentence consists of a succession of clauses loosely strung together (εἴρω), like a row of beads; generally by τε, δέ and other copulae; the sentence begins and ends with no definite plan, and may be of any length. In the word *period* (circuit) the metaphor is rather that of a hoop; the sentence does not stretch out indefinitely in a straight line, but after a certain time

---

[1] *E.g.* οἴδαμεν, ἤδεις, and the remarkable εἰκότερον.

[2] *Vide supra*, p. 16. A striking example of the verbal periphrasis is in Antiphon, *Herodes*, § 94: νῦν μὲν οὖν γνωρισταὶ γίνεσθε τῆς δίκης, τότε δὲ δικασταὶ τῶν μαρτύρων· νῦν μὲν δοξασταί, τότε δὲ κριταὶ τῶν ἀληθῶν,

bends back on itself so that the end is joined to the
beginning. It must, according to Aristotle,[1] be of
limited length, not longer than can be taken in at a
glance or uttered in one breath, and have a definitely
marked beginning and end.[2]

Aristotle finds the loose, running style tedious,
because it has no artistic limit of length, and never
gets to an end until it has finished what it has to say.
To us it seems to have this slight advantage, that it
can always stop when it has said what it means, and
has no temptation to plunge itself into antithesis or
lose ·its way at the cross-roads of chiasmus before it
arrives at its destination ; for though, in the periodic
style, the end of the sense should ideally coincide with
the end of the period, there are in practice many
instances where the sense is fully expressed and the
sentence might end before the ' circuit ' is artistically
complete.

The baldest examples of the ' strung together ' style
must be sought in the fragments of the early historians ;
but Herodotus is sufficiently near to them to provide
us with an object-lesson.

Take, for instance, the following :

' When Ardys had reigned forty-nine years, Sadyattes
his son succeeded him, and he reigned twelve years, and
Alyattes succeeded Sadyattes. And he made war on
Cyaxares, the descendant of Deioces, and the Medes, and
drove the Cimmerians out of Asia and took Smyrna, a
colony of Colophon, and attacked Clazomenae. Here he
had not the success he desired, but met with grave disaster.

---

[1] *Rhet.*, iii. 9. 1-2.
[2] *Rhet.*, iii. 9. 3 : λέξιν ἔχουσαν ἀρχὴν καὶ τελευτὴν αὐτὴν καθ᾽ αὑτὴν
καὶ μέγεθος εὐσύνοπτον. *Ibid.*, 5 : εὐανάπνευστος.

And during his reign he did other noteworthy deeds, as follows.  He fought with the Milesians . . .' etc., etc.[1]

Yet even Herodotus, the most obvious exponent of the loose style, shows a tendency towards the greater compression of periodic writing ; this tendency is at times strongly marked, *e.g.* in the speeches of the Persian nobles in debate.[2]  Here there is a continual movement towards the balance of clauses ; it is very far from the harmonious structure of Isocrates, and is perhaps unconscious, but the elements of the periodic style are there.

The particular faculty of this latter style is that it can be more emphatic and precise than the other.  It must be concentrated (κατεστραμμένη) [3] if the sentence is to be of moderate length ; it tries, as Dionysius says, ' to pack the thoughts close together, and bring them out compactly.' [4]

These qualities, concentration of thought and preciseness of expression, are essential for a pleader in the courts, and so it was not unnatural that the development of the periodic style should coincide at Athens with the rise of forensic oratory.  Antiphon, the first practical pleader on scientific lines, is also the earliest of extant writers known to have been a careful student of periodic expression.

It must not be supposed that all his work consisted of periods carefully balanced : on the one hand, perfection could not be attained at the first onset ; many of the sentences are crude ; in some cases there is a

---

[1] Herod., i. 16-17.      [2] *Id.*, iii. 80-81.
[3] Arist., *Rhet.*, iii. 9. 3.
[4] Dion., *de Lysia*, 6 : ἡ συστρέφουσα τὰ νοήματα καὶ στρογγύλως ἐκφέρουσα λέξις.

weakness of emphasis due to imperfect mastery of the form ; on the other hand, there are cases where the style is freer and more analogous to the simple fluency of the *εἰρομένη λέξις*.    The plain fact is that the method of Herodotus is the most appropriate for telling a straightforward narrative from one point of view only ; while the periodic style comes spontaneously into being for purposes of criticism, or where we contrast what is with what might have been ; or of debate, where we put up alternatives side by side with the object of choosing between them.

The first object of history, to the mind of Herodotus, is to tell a story ; and Herodotus mostly keeps this end in view.    Thucydides in some parts of his narrative does the same, but whereas he has a greater tendency to consider each event not by itself but in relation to other circumstances, such as the motives for the action, its effects and influences, he is often periodic even in narrative.    He is still more so in speeches.    The object of a deliberative speech is not usually to tell a plain story but to produce a highly-coloured one ; it mentions facts chiefly with the object of criticizing them and drawing an inference or a moral.

If this is true of the speeches in Thucydides, it must be still more applicable to those of a forensic orator. In Antiphon we find short passages in the simple narrative style—for instance, in the statement of facts in the *Herodes* case ; but a short section of this nature is followed by criticism and argument expressed in the more artificial period.    This is inevitable ; there is no time to spend on long narratives.

Closely connected with the desire for a periodic style is the tendency to frequent use of verbal antithesis, an artistic figure which provides a happy means of completing the period and the sense.  It is useful because the second part of the antithesis supplies the reader or hearer with something which he is already expecting.  It is the application in practice of a familiar psychological law of association by contrary ideas.  Such contrast is emphasized in Greek by the common use of the particles μέν and δέ, and is of unnecessarily frequent occurrence in Athenian writers. All readers of Thucydides will remember that author's craving for the contrast between ' word and deed.' In judicial rhetoric this kind of opposition must inevitably occur very often.  From the nature of things each speaker will want to insist on his own honesty and the dishonesty of his opponents ; the truth which he is telling as opposed to their lies, and to contrast the appearances, which seem so black against him, with the transparent whiteness of his character as revealed by a true account of the case.  But Antiphon, like the speakers in Thucydides, carries this use of antithesis too far, for a sentence which contains too many contrasted ideas is difficult to follow, and so loses force.

A fair example may be taken from the third speech of the second tetralogy :

' I, who have done nothing wrong, but have suffered grievously and cruelly already, and now suffer still more cruelly not from the words but the acts of my adversary, throw myself upon your mercy, Gentlemen—you who are avengers of impiety but discriminators of piety—and implore you, in view of plain facts, not to be over-persuaded by a malicious precision of speech, and so consider the true explanation of the deed to be false ; for his statement has been made with more plausibility than truth; mine will be made without guile, though at the same time without force.'

This outburst is part of a sentence in which the prosecutor expresses his indignation that the opponent whom he has accused of murder has had the audacity to defend himself at some length.

One more example—from the speech on the charge of poisoning—is almost ridiculous.

'Those whose duty it was to play the part of avengers of the dead and my helpers, have played the part of murderers of the dead, and established themselves as my adversaries.'

## § 5

All speakers must consider the sound of their sentences as well as their grammatical structure, and among all careful writers we find that attention is paid to the balance of clauses. Some orators go further than this; they emphasize contrasts or parallels by the repetition of similar sounds and even show a preference for certain rhythms, it being a maxim of late rhetoricians that prose, though not strictly metrical in the same way as verse, should possess a characteristic rhythm of its own.

Some authors go so far as to change the natural order of words for the purpose of escaping hiatus of open vowels, which are necessarily awkward to pronounce in rapid speech. This is familiar from the pages of Demosthenes, and what the later writers did systematically, Antiphon, and even Thucydides, seem to have done at times instinctively.

As regards the balance of clauses, a good example may be found in the opening of the *Herodes* speech :

τοῦ μὲν πεπείραμαι πέρα τοῦ προσήκοντος,
τοῦ δ' ἐνδεής εἰμι μᾶλλον τοῦ συμφέροντος,

where the correspondence of the two clauses in equal numbers of syllables is noticeable. The next sentence shows the same sort of correspondence, though not quite so precise ; but here the structure is more elaborate, since we have two clauses, each of two parts, contrasted both in whole and part :

A.    οὗ μὲν γάρ μ' ἔδει κακοπαθεῖν τῷ σώματι μετὰ τῆς αἰτίας τῆς οὐ προσηκούσης,

a. ἐνταυθοῖ οὐδέν μ' ὠφέλησεν ἡ ἐμπειρία,

B.    οὗ δέ με δεῖ σωθῆναι μετὰ τῆς ἀληθείας εἰπόντα τὰ γενόμενα,

β. ἐν τούτῳ με βλάπτει ἡ τοῦ λέγειν ἀδυναμία.

Though there is no rhythmical correspondence here, and the syllabic lengths only correspond roughly, the ' antistrophic ' structure is obvious.

Gorgias, if we may condemn him on the evidence of a single short fragment, seems to have affected rhyme —at any rate his collocation of γνώμην and ῥώμην cannot have been accidental—and the similar sound of the endings of the two clauses in the first passage quoted above proves that Antiphon at any rate took no pains to avoid such natural assonance. In an inflexional language, where there is always a strong probability that a rhyme will occur wherever we have to use an adjective agreeing with a noun, or two verbs in the same tense and person, some ingenuity has to be employed at times to avoid a rhyme, and

Antiphon here, at any rate, did not choose to avoid it.
The use of rhyme in verse seems to have been offensive
to the Greek ear;[1] perhaps for that very reason it
may have been at times desirable in prose, its harshness
producing the same kind of effect which Antiphon elsewhere attains by the use of uncommon words.

Hiatus is of fairly common occurrence in Antiphon,
and I cannot point to any certain instance of an attempt
to avoid it by a change from the natural order of words.

Antiphon draws little from common speech ; perhaps
his dignity prevented him from enforcing a point by
the use of those γνῶμαι—proverbial maxims—which
Aristotle recommends ; and he seldom has recourse
to colloquialisms. We are inclined, however, to put
in this class such a phrase as περιέπεσεν οἷς οὐκ ἤθελεν
—'he got what he didn't want'—used of an unfortunate who has been accidentally killed through
his own negligence.

Metaphors are rare, but telling when they do occur, as
δίκη κυβερνήσειε—'May justice steer my course';
ζῶντες κατορωρύγμεθα—'I am buried in a living tomb,'
used by a man who lost his only son; or, again, the
appeal of the prisoner to the jury not to condemn him
to death—ἀνίατος γὰρ ἡ μετάνοια τῶν τοιούτων ἐστίν—
'Repentance for such a deed can never cure it.'

Some exaggeration of language is permitted to an
orator. The defendant in the first tetralogy thus
appeals for pity—'An old man, an exile and an out-
cast, I shall beg my bread in a foreign land.'
The so-called 'figures of thought' (σχήματα διανοίας)
such as irony and rhetorical questions, so frequent in

[1] See Verrall, *Rhyme and Reason*, in *The Bacchants of Euripides*.

Demosthenes, are scarcely used by Antiphon. There is no instance either of the hypocritical reticence (παράλειψις), also common in later orators, which by a pretence of passing over certain matters in silence hints at more than it could prove.

Greek oratory was much bound by conventions from which even the greatest speakers could not altogether escape. To some extent this may be attributed to the evil influence of the teachers of rhetoric, but by far the greater part of the blame must rest upon the Athenian audiences.

The dicasts, with a curious inconsistency, seem to have demanded a finished style of speaking, and yet to have been suspicious of any speaker who displayed too much cleverness. It was, in fact, the possession of this quality which made Antiphon himself unpopular.[1] A pleader, therefore, who felt himself in danger of incurring such suspicion, must apologize to his audience in advance, stating that any strength which his case might seem to possess was due to its own inherent justice, not to his own powers of presenting it. He must compliment the jury on their well-known impartiality, and express a deep respect for the sanctity of the laws. The early rhetoricians made collections of such ' topics ' or ' commonplaces,' and instructed their pupils how to use them. The process became merely mechanical; any speaker could obtain from the rhetorical handbooks specimens of sentences dealing with all such requirements, but only a man of rare genius could, by originality of treatment, make them sound at all convincing. Aristotle at a later date made a practically exhaustive collection of such topics.[2]

---

[1] *Supra*, p. 20.　　　　　[2] Arist., *Rhet.*, i.

Antiphon, in his Tetralogies, showed by example how some of these commonplaces might be employed. In his real speeches he uses them freely, and with so little care that he repeats his own actual words even within the limits of the few extant speeches.[1]

In the introduction of these devices, however, he shows some skill. The speech on the murder of Herodes is quite subtle in places. Compliments are paid to the jury, but the flattery is not too open. It is sometimes achieved rather by suggestion than by statement. ' Not that I wished to avoid a trial by your democracy,' says the defendant ; and again, ' Of course I could trust you quite without considering the oath you have taken ' ; or once more, in parenthesis, ' On the supposition that I had no objection to quitting this land for ever, I might have left the country.' Here, and in other cases, there is little more than a hint which an intelligent juror may grasp.

The most prominent of all the topics used by Antiphon is the appeal to the divine law by which guile meets with punishment ; the murdered man, if unavenged by human justice, will find divine champions who will not only bring the homicide to book, but will punish the guilty city which has become polluted by harbouring him. So much stress is laid upon this conception of divine justice that some writers have believed that Antiphon held firm religious views which he thus expressed. This opinion may reasonably be held, but it must not be pressed. We know from external sources that Antiphon was not in

---

[1] *E.g.*, on the laws, *Herodes*, § 14, and *Choreutes*, § 2, where the same passage of about eight lines occurs with only the alteration of two or three unimportant words.

C

sympathy with the existing government, yet the speakers of his orations express or imply admiration for the democracy; the speech-writer, in fact, wrote what he thought would be acceptable to the judges rather than what he himself believed. Arguing, in Antiphon's own way, from probabilities, we may say it is more likely that a highly educated contemporary of Anaxagoras and Pericles should in private life profess a moderate scepticism than an unquestioning belief in the sort of curse that destroyed the house of Atreus, even though Antiphon may be Aeschylean in style.

The argument of the defendant in the *Herodes*, ' Those who have sailed with me have made excellent voyages, and sacrifices at which I have assisted have been most favourably performed, and this is a strong argument for my innocence,' does not appeal to us, who do not believe in the accidental blood-guiltiness of the community which unknowingly harbours a guilty individual. It may or may not have had some weight with Antiphon himself, but it certainly would have some influence on the common people of Athens, who believed that the whole city was polluted by the sacrilege of the mutilation of the Hermae. The fact that it must impress the jury was a good reason for inserting it, whether Antiphon had any religious feeling or not.[1]

§ 6

It remains to consider Antiphon's manner in the treatment of his subjects.

---

[1] Jebb (*Attic Orators*, vol. i. pp. 40-41) insists that the prominence given to this kind of argument points to a deep religious feeling in the orator's heart. However, we meet with the same type of argument in Aeschines, to whom no such depth of feeling is usually imputed.

His personal dignity is as remarkable in his manner as in the formalities of style. As we turn back to him from Demosthenes or Aeschines, who lowered the tone of forensic pleading to suit contemporary taste, we are surprised to find that he hardly ever condescends to ridicule, never to scurrilous invective. His judicial adversaries are not necessarily persons of discreditable parentage, immoral character, and infamous occupation. They may perhaps be liars, for one's own statement of the case must be assumed to contain the whole truth, and consequently the other side must depend on falsehood; but even here the orator is prepared to admit, with almost un-Attic generosity, that his adversaries have been misled and are not acting up to their true character. Take the opening of Tetralogy II. 3:

' The behaviour of my adversary shows, better than any theory could, that necessity constrains men to speak and act contrary to their better nature.

Up to the present he has never spoken shamelessly or acted desperately; but now his misfortunes have constrained him to use language which, knowing him, I should never have expected him to utter.'

Antiphon's method of constructing his speeches is simple : a conventional preface, of the kind which every rhetorician kept in stock,[1] is followed by an introduction describing and criticizing the circumstances under which the action has been brought.[2] The facts, or a selection of facts of the case, are then narrated,[3] and are followed by arguments and proofs.[4] The evidence of witnesses may be interspersed through

---

[1] Cf. the Demosthenic collection of προοίμια.
[2] προκατασκευή.    [3] διήγησις.    [4] πίστεις.

the narrative, taken point by point ; or, if the narrative is short and simple, all the testimony may be reserved for the end. A peroration,[1] reviewing the situation and containing a final appeal to the court, normally ends the speech.

The speeches in the Tetralogies, which are only blank forms composed for practice or as specimens for study, contain only preface, argument, and peroration ; there being no actual facts to deal with, there is no introduction or narrative.

It is a peculiar weakness of the extant speeches that they rely so much more on arguments from general probability (εἰκότα) than on real pleading on the basis of evidence.[2]

Thus the defendant in the *Herodes* mentions quite casually that he never left the ship on the night when the murder was committed on shore, but he produces no evidence for the *alibi* and treats it as of quite secondary importance.[3] He insists more on the point that the slave who gave evidence against him was probably induced to bear false witness by the prosecutors. Another piece of evidence against him is the assertion that he wrote a letter to Lycinus, stating that he had committed the murder. ' Why,' he asks, ' should I have written a letter, when my messenger would know all the facts ? '

It may be, in this instance, that the defendant's case was a very weak one, and that he was obliged to rely on generalities : but the First Tetralogy affords an interesting parallel. There the defendant, in his *second*

---

[1] ἐπίλογος.

[2] This is another characteristic of the earlier rhetoricians ; *vide supra*, p. 12.

[3] *Herodes*, § 26.

speech, the last speech of the trial, affirms, what he has apparently forgotten to mention before, that he never left his house on the night of the murder.

The most serious artistic defect in the extant speeches is the lack of that realism which the Greeks called ἦθος, characterization. The language of the defendants in the *Herodes* and the *Choreutes* is very similar, though the former is a young Lesbian and the latter a middle-aged Athenian. Moreover, the young Lesbian apologizes for his inexperience and lack of capacity for speaking, and does so in polished periods elaborated with all the devices of rhetorical art—antithesis of words and ideas, careful balance of the length of clauses, and judicious employment of assonance.

A perusal of Antiphon's introduction to the speech *de Caede Herodis* will help, better than any detailed criticism, to an understanding of his methods of composition. We must note the disproportionate length of this introduction, to which the pleader evidently attaches more importance than to the disproof of the charge itself.[1] A study of it leads us to believe that the guilt or innocence of the party would have little to do with the verdict if he had once succeeded in impressing the jury favourably. He apologizes in artistic periods for his incapacity in public speaking, and enlarges on the commonplace that truth has often been stifled through lacking the power of expression.

He makes no appeal for impartiality, since he can trust the jury—another brazen commonplace (§§ 1-7).

The procedure of his adversaries is as shameless as it is unjust (§§ 8-9); it is even sacrilegious (§§ 10-12), so that they merit indignation, while the defendant,

---

[1] The Introduction amounts to one-fifth of the whole speech.

who respects the laws of God and man as he loves his country, deserves every indulgence (§§ 13-15). The prosecutors' brutality can be explained by their distrust in the justice of their case and the uprightness of the jury (§§ 16-17). Finally, they have had ample time to work up their case, while the victim of their intrigues is called upon at a moment's notice to answer the most serious charges (§§ 18-19).

' 1. I could wish, Gentlemen, that I possessed a capacity for speaking and an experience of the world on a scale corresponding to the misfortune and sufferings that have befallen me ; as it is, my experience in the latter is as much beyond my deserts as my deficiency in the former falls short of my requirements.

' 2. When I had to suffer in my own person under an undeserved charge, I had no experience to help me on ; now, when my salvation lies in a plain statement of the facts as they occurred, I am thwarted by my incapacity in speaking.

' 3. In many instances men with no capacity in speaking have been disbelieved because they only told the truth, and have owed their ruin to the fact that they could not demonstrate the truth ; many, on the other hand, who possess the capacity for speaking, have been believed on account of their lies, and owed their salvation to the fact that they lied well. So one who has not the necessary experience of procedure in the courts must inevitably be at the mercy of the speeches of the prosecution ; he cannot rest secure upon a true statement of the facts of the case.

' 4. Now, most parties in such causes as this make a request for a fair hearing—implying a mistrust of themselves and a conviction that you are not impartial. I shall make no such request, for it is only reasonable that honest men should grant a hearing to the defendant, even though he has not asked for it, just as the prosecutor has been granted a hearing without asking.

' 5. But my prayer is, firstly, that if my tongue leads me into error, you will be merciful, and consider that my error is due to inexperience rather than guilt ; and secondly, that if I should in any point express myself well, you will attribute such expression not to any cleverness of mine but to the inherent power of truth ; for justice demands that a man guilty in his actions should not win salvation by his speech, and, equally, that one righteous in his actions should not for his speech be brought to ruin ; for an error in speech is the tongue's fault—an error in action is a fault of the heart.

' 6. A man who realizes that his personal safety is en-dangered is bound to err sometimes ; he has to think not only of the defence he is making, but of its possible results ; for the issue of all matters yet undecided depends on chance rather than on forethought.

' 7. Such considerations cannot fail to cause anxiety to one whose life is in danger ; indeed, I observe that people who have a thorough experience of the courts fail to do justice to their powers when in danger themselves, but are far more successful in cases which involve no personal danger. Thus, Gentlemen, my request is both lawful and righteous ; it is as just for you to grant as for me to prefer it ; and I now proceed to answer in detail the charges which have been brought against me.

' 8. First, I would draw attention to the illegality of the methods by which I have been forced into this trial, not that I wish to avoid judgment by this democratic court— for even if you had taken no oath, and were bound by no law, I should be ready to leave in your hands the decision about my life, confident as I am that I have done no wrong in this matter, and that your verdict will be a just one— but in order that my enemies' violent and illegal action against me in this case may help you to realize their con-duct towards me on other occasions.

' 9. My first point is this : Contrary to all precedent at Athens, though I am on trial for murder, I was indicted for " criminal violence." Now my enemies themselves have testified that I neither belong to the class of " violent criminals," nor am subject to the law which covers such cases. It applies to such offences as stealing and highway robbery, and they have shown that no such charge can attach to me.

' Thus their conduct in the matter of my summary arrest has made it in the highest degree legal and just for you to acquit me.

' 10. They say, indeed, that the taking of life is in itself an aggravated form of " criminal violence." I admit that it is a most serious kind, and so is sacrilege or treason ; but you have laws which deal with each of these charges specifically.

' And, to begin with, they have brought me to trial in the Agora, the very place which a defendant in a charge of murder is ordinarily warned to avoid ; secondly, they have proposed a penalty of their own choosing, whereas the law ordains that the man who has taken another's life shall lose his own in return.

' This they have done, not for my benefit, but for their own convenience, and herein they have failed in that respect for the dead which the law prescribes.

' 11. Again, as I imagine you all know, all the courts concerned with murder trials sit in the open air, with this particular object, that the jurors may not have to enter the same building with those who have blood on their hands, and that the prosecutor in a trial for murder may not find himself under the same roof with him who committed the act.

' But you, Sir, have acted contrary to all precedent in transgressing this law ; and not only this : It was incumbent on you to take the most solemn and binding oath, to invoke destruction upon yourself and your family and your house if you failed in its conditions, namely, that you would not bring any charges against me except such as referred to the murder and my complicity in it.

'Had this obligation been observed, however great crimes I had committed I could not be found guilty except in view of the one fact of blood-guiltiness, and on the other hand, however many good deeds I had to my credit, these good deeds could not save me.

' 12. All this regular procedure you have violated ; you have invented laws for your own use ; you who prosecute me have taken no oath ; your witnesses who bear witness against me have taken none, though they ought first to take the same oath as yourself ; they should lay their hands upon the sacrifice while they are bearing witness against me.

' Further, you ask the court to dispense with the oath ; to give credence to your witnesses and bring in a verdict of Guilty, though you yourself have made them disinclined to credit you by transgressing the established laws, and by imagining that your own illegal conduct should in their consideration have precedence over law itself.

' 13. You say, however, that if I had been set at liberty I should not have remained here, but should have gone away and disappeared—as if you had compelled me against my will to enter the country.   I answer that, on your supposition that I should not have minded saying farewell to Athens, it was open to me either not to appear in obedience to the summons, and so incur judgment by default, or to go away after replying to the opening speech of the prosecution ; for this privilege is open to all.   But you, by legislating in your own interest, are trying to withhold in my case alone this privilege which belongs to all of Greek race.

' 14. Yet I think we must all agree that the laws which govern such procedure are the best laws in the world, and most in accordance with divine sanction.   They have a double claim to respect ; they are the most ancient laws in this land, and they are unchangeable as the offences with which they deal ; and this is the strongest indication that a law is well framed ; for time and experience teach mankind to recognize what is not well done.

' So you do not require to learn from the speeches of the prosecution whether the laws were well framed or not, as he implies ; but you do require to learn by the aid of the laws whether the speeches of the prosecution are urging a righteous and lawful action, or the reverse—as I assert.

' 15. The laws, then, which relate to the charge of murder, are excellently framed, inasmuch as no one has ever ventured to disturb them ; you alone have ventured to legislate anew, and for the worse. You would set aside justice as you have transgressed law in your attempt to bring me to ruin. But your illegal procedure is in itself the strongest evidence in my favour ; for you knew well enough that nobody who had taken that solemn oath would have borne witness against me.

' 16. Again, you did not rely on the facts sufficiently to allow the question of facts to be settled indisputably by a single trial ; you reserved for yourself the right to dispute the judgment, and reopen the case, implying a distrust in the verdict of the present court. The result is that even if I am acquitted I am no better off, since it is open to you to say that I was acquitted on the charge of criminal violence but not on the charge of murder ; whereas, if you secure my condemnation you will demand my death on the ground that I have been found guilty of murder.

' What can surpass the cruelty of such a device by which you, if you can once convince the jury, have attained your object ; while I, if I escape your clutches once, find the same danger awaiting me again ?

' 17. Again, my imprisonment was a monstrous illegality. I consented to produce three sureties as required by law, but they contrived that I should not be allowed to do so. There is no other instance on record of the imprisonment of a non-Athenian who consented to produce sureties.

' Yet the officers who have custody of criminals are subject to this same law, so that this is another privilege common to all men which was withheld from me alone.

' 18. Of course, it suited my accusers, firstly, that I should be as unprepared as possible, through being unable to attend to my own business in person, secondly, that I should suffer personal ill-usage, and in consequence of this personal ill-usage find my own friends more ready to bear false witness in support of my accusers than true witness in my support. And so they inflicted a life-long disgrace on me and my family.

' 19. Thus I have been brought to trial handicapped in many ways in relation to your laws and to justice; but even with these disadvantages I shall try to demonstrate my innocence.

' But it is a hard task to refute at a moment's notice a number of deliberate falsehoods long-prepared; for it is impossible to be forearmed against unexpected attacks.'

After this long preamble, the speaker at last discusses the accusation (§§ 19 *sqq.*), and to some extent deals satisfactorily with the evidence—entirely circumstantial—which has been brought against him. It has already been noticed that, though he casually leaves it to be inferred that he could prove an *alibi*, he lays no stress on the assertion, and is far more concerned with showing that it is ' improbable ' that he should be a murderer. The final and, apparently, the most important argument is drawn from the absence of divine signs which might have pointed to the speaker's guilt. He makes no attempt, like the defendant in the First Tetralogy, to suggest other explanations of the crime; many crimes, he says, have before now baffled investigation, and he is only concerned with denying the charge against himself.

## § 7

In the *Life of Antiphon*, falsely ascribed to Plutarch,[1] we read that sixty speeches were extant under the orator's name, but of these twenty-five were considered spurious by the critic Caecilius of Calacte. We have now fifteen, viz. the three Tetralogies, or sets of four speeches ; the speeches on the Murder of Herodes, the Death of the Choreutes, and the Charge of Poisoning. All of these deal with homicide, the department in which Antiphon, presumably, showed especial skill. Blass has collected besides the titles of twenty-three other speeches on miscellaneous subjects.[2]

The Tetralogies, each consisting of four short speeches on the same imaginary case—two for the prosecution, and two for the defence—have this peculiar interest, that they stand on the border-line between theory and practice. They differ from the exercises composed by other early rhetoricians and from the declamations of the Roman Empire in that they are not concerned with historical or mythological personages in possible or imaginary positions, but treat cases which, although fictitious, are of the kind which might arise in every-day life at Athens. Thus these skeleton-speeches give a clear idea of the lines on which either side might plead its case in an actual trial. The professional advocate must be ready to plead on either side in any cause, and here we find Antiphon composing speeches in turn suitable for both sides. As has been noted, there is very little detail given. No narrative

---

[1] Ps.-Plut., *Lives of the Ten Orators.*
[2] *Attische Beredsamkeit,* vol. i. pp. 104-105.

of facts occurs ; the actual circumstances presupposed
can only be gathered from the arguments employed ;
and the result is that the outlines of the speeches
both in accusation and defence are very clearly marked.

The argument of the First Tetralogy is as follows :—
A certain citizen has been murdered on his way home
from a dinner party. His slave, who was mortally
wounded at the same time, deposed that one of the
murderers was a certain enemy of his master, against
whom the latter was on the point of bringing a serious
law-suit. The case comes before the Areopagus.

*a.* The accuser argues that the deceased cannot
have been murdered by robbers, since he was not
plundered ; nor in a drunken brawl, which was impossible considering the time and place. Therefore
the crime was premeditated, and the motive was
revenge or fear. The accused had both these motives,
and moreover the slave identified him.

*β.* The defendant argues that the murder may have
been done by robbers who were scared away before they
had robbed the corpse, or by some criminal who feared
the dead man's testimony, or by some other enemy,
who felt secure because he knew suspicion would fall
on the accused. The slave may have been mistaken
or perhaps suborned. If probability is to decide the
case, it is more probable that the defendant would
have employed some one else to do the murder than
that the slave would be certain of having recognized
the criminal. The danger of losing a law-suit could
not have seemed so serious as the present danger of
losing his life.

*γ.* The accuser in his second speech ingeniously
meets the arguments of *β* point by point ; and

δ. The defendant criticizes and disposes of the arguments of γ, and incidentally mentions that he could prove an *alibi*—though he does not seem to lay any stress on this.

With the exception of the evidence of the slave, now dead, the whole case rests on a discussion of probabilities.

The Second Tetralogy deals with the death of a boy accidentally killed by a javelin with which another youth was practising in the gymnasium. The question to decide was, who was to blame—the accuser maintained that it was a case of homicide, the defendant suggested unintentional suicide ! [1]

The Third Tetralogy supposes that an old man has been brutally beaten by a young man, and died of his injuries a few days later. The defendant attempts to put the blame first on the dead man, since he struck the first blow, secondly on the surgeon ; and, finding this not plausible enough, goes into exile : the second speech for the defence is spoken by a friend of the accused.

The extant speeches composed for real cases may be taken in the order of their importance.

*On the Murder of Herodes.*—Herodes, an Athenian citizen who had settled at Mitylene, made a voyage to Aenus in Thrace to receive the ransom of some Thracian captives. He sailed with the accused, a Mitylenean whose father lived at Aenus. They were driven by a storm to shelter at Methymna, and there exchanged from their open boat into a decked vessel.

---

[1] In the similar case discussed by Pericles and Protagoras, the third possibility was considered—the guilt of the javelin. (Plut., *Pericles*, ch. 36.)

They fell to drinking to pass the time, and Herodes, going ashore one night, was never heard of again. His companion continued the voyage, and on returning to Mitylene was charged with murder. It was asserted that a slave had confessed to having assisted in the murder, and that a letter had been discovered from the defendant to one Lycinus, supposed to be the instigator of the crime.

By the laws of the Athenian League such a trial must take place at Athens ; ordinarily a case of murder would come before the Areopagus, but actually the accused was indicted as a ' *malefactor*,' [1] was arrested and brought before an ordinary court. He contends that this is a grievance, for if the prosecution fails he may still be brought before the Areopagus. Further, he was kept in prison, all bail being refused. This was, apparently, illegal.

The trial took place probably about 417 or 416 B.C. The introduction to the speech has been quoted.[2] The narrative gives first the facts up to the defendant's arrival at Athens (§§ 19-24), and shows that probability is against the prosecution (§§ 25-28) ; next, the return of one of the ships to Mitylene, and the confession of the slave under torture (§§ 29-30). The slave's evidence is proved to be worthless (§§ 31-41). The alleged letter to Lycinus is discussed, and the defendant proves that he himself had no motive for the murder, and cannot be expected to know who is the real culprit (§§ 42-73). Odium has been unjustly stirred against him by the assertion of his father's disloyalty (§§ 74-80). The absence of signs of divine anger is a further proof of his innocence (§§ 81-84). Finally, he appeals for another

---

[1] ἔνδειξις κακουργίας.    [2] *Supra*, p. 38 *sqq.*

chance at least, since, if acquitted now, he may be tried again by the Areopagus (§§ 85-95).

The speech *On the Choreutes* refers to the death of a boy Diodotus, who was being trained to sing in a choir at the Thargelia, and was accidentally poisoned by a drug given him to improve his voice. The *choregus* or choir-master was accused of poisoning before the Areopagus.

The extant speech is the second for the defence; the date is probably about 412 B.C. The speaker comments on the disingenuous action of his adversaries, who refused to have slaves examined, and introduced much irrelevant matter. He contrasts the openness of his own conduct. The epilogue is lost.

The speech *Against a Stepmother on a Charge of Poisoning* is sometimes regarded as a mere exercise, but, in striking contrast to the Tetralogies, this speech contains full and detailed narrative. Its authenticity has been further questioned, but we have so little material for judging of the style of Antiphon that it is impossible to pronounce definitely against the supposition that this speech was composed by him. It may be that it was an early work ; it is certainly less powerful than the other two genuine speeches.

*The Argument.*—A young man accuses his stepmother of having poisoned his father by the help of another woman, a slave. The father was dining with Philoneos, a former lover of this woman, and she was persuaded to administer a love-philtre to the two. Both men died, the woman was put to death, and the prosecutor now urges that his stepmother, who instigated the crime, should be punished for her guilt.

Of the speeches known to us only by name or by short fragments, it is probable that some at any rate were the work of Antiphon the Sophist, with whom the orator is often confused. A work on rhetoric and a collection of proemia and epilogues were also current under the orator's name.

D

# CHAPTER III

## THRASYMACHUS—ANDOCIDES

### § I

A NEW period begins with Thrasymachus of Chalcedon, who adopted Athens as his home. He is placed by Aristotle between Tisias, one of the founders of rhetoric, and Theodorus of Byzantium,[1] who was a contemporary of Lysias. According to the chronology of Plato's *Phaedrus*, he was already at the height of his powers when Isocrates was only a youth of promise.[2] The dramatic date of the dialogue being 410 B.C., we may suppose him to have been born between 460 and 450 B.C., though there is no clear indication.

He seems to have followed the lines of his predecessors. He composed a τέχνη or handbook of rhetoric, and composed or compiled a collection of passages to serve as models for his pupils, called by Suidas ἀφορμαὶ ῥητορικαί (*oratorical resources*). This probably included the *exordia* and *epilogues* mentioned by Athenaeus.[3] Aristotle mentions a work called Ἔλεοι (*appeals to pity*),[4] and a book with the mysterious title ὑπερβάλλοντες completed his educational output.[5] He composed also

---

[1] *Soph. Elench.*, 183 b. 32.  [2] 267 C.
[3] x. 416 A.  [4] *Rhet.*, iii. 1. 7.
[5] The word seems to mean *powerful* or *convincing* ; whether τόποι (*commonplaces* or *passages*) or λόγοι (*arguments*) is the word to be supplied, we cannot even conjecture.

some epideictic speeches, which, as Suidas calls them
παίγνια, were probably of the mythological type, of
which we possess examples in the *Helen* and *Palamedes*
of Gorgias.   Dionysius says that he left no deliberative
or forensic speeches, and this statement agrees with
the known fact that he was an alien, and therefore
could not appear in the courts or the assembly.[1]   On
the other hand, Suidas mentions public speeches, and
Dionysius has himself preserved a fragment of what
appears to be a deliberative speech.[2]   The probability
is that this was composed only as a model for his
pupils, and it is, in fact, of a vagueness which would
be appropriate to almost any circumstances.

He excelled in the 'pathetic' style: 'For the
" sorrows of a poor old man," ' says Socrates, ' or any
other pathetic case, no one is better than the Chalce-
donian giant ; he can put a whole company of people
into a passion and out of one again by his mighty
magic, and is first-rate at inventing or disposing of
any sort of calumny on any grounds or none.'[3]   These
gifts seem to have been the natural expression of his
impetuous and passionate character represented in the
*Republic*.[4]

The loss of his works is much to be regretted, since
he was the inventor of a style—the *tempered* style,
as it was called by Dionysius—which, standing between the austerity of Antiphon and Thucydides, and
the elaborate simplicity perfected by Lysias, combined
the best qualities of both.   He was thus a forerunner
of Isocrates.   In the fragment which is preserved, we
find no trace of rare or poetical words or audacious

[1] *de Isaeo*, ch. xx.
[3] *Phaedrus*, 267 c (Jowett).
[2] *de Demosthene*, ch. iii.
[4] Book I., 336B.

compounds such as Gorgias used ; none of the complicated sentences of Thucydides, and no forced antithesis ; the diction is flowing, and the expression clear.  He seems to have been the first writer to make a careful study of metrical effect, and is mentioned for his frequent use of the *paeon* by Aristotle, who apparently classed him with those writers to whom diction is more important than ideas.[1]

The fragment already mentioned purports to be the *exordium* of a political speech :

' I could have wished, men of Athens, that my lot had been cast amid those ancient times and conditions when the younger men were content to be silent, since circumstances did not force them to speak in public, and their elders were able administrators of the state. . . .'

This is a conventional opening ; a similar phrase of regret (ἐβουλόμην) begins the speech of Antiphon on the murder of Herodes,[2] and Aeschines has elaborated the same theme of the superiority of political life in the time of Solon in a way which leads us to suspect that he had the *prooemium* of Thrasymachus in mind.[3]

Of the works of Theodorus of Byzantium not a sentence remains.  A contemporary of Lysias, he taught rhetoric and composed certain works on the subject.[4]  He concerned himself with the proper divisions of a speech, adding a section of ' further narrative' (ἐπιδιήγησις) to the usual narrative, and ' further proof' (ἐπιπίστωσις) to proof.[5]  It is for

---

[1] *Rhet.*, iii. 8. 4 ; iii. 1. 7.   The *paeon* = – ◡ ◡ ◡ or ◡ ◡ ◡ –.

[2] Cf. Aristoph., *Frogs*, 866 : ἐβουλόμην μὲν οὐκ ἐρίζειν ἐνθάδε.

[3] Aesch. *in Ctes.*, § 2.

[4] The reference by Arist., *Rhet.*, ii. 23. 28 to ἡ πρότερον Θεοδώρου τέχνη—the *earlier* treatise of T.—implies others.

[5] Cf. Arist., *Rhet.*, iii. 13. 4 : διήγησις, ἐπιδιήγησις, προδιήγησις ; ἔλεγχος, ἐπεξέλεγχος.

this over-subtlety that Plato ridicules the ' cunning artificer of speeches ' from Byzantium.[1]

§ 2

Andocides was born about 440 B.C., a member of a family which had been distinguished for three generations.

His great-grandfather, as he tells us, fought against the Pisistratidae ; his grandfather Andocides was one of the envoys for the peace with Sparta in 445, and was twice subsequently a *strategus* ; his father, Leogoras, is mentioned by Aristophanes as rearing pheasants.[2] The orator himself was a member of a ἑταιρεία or club —probably a social rather than a political club, as the only meeting mentioned was purely for convivial purposes.

In 415, on the eve of the sailing of the Sicilian expedition, Athens was startled and horrified by a remarkable act of sacrilege. The images of Hermes which stood everywhere in the town were, all but one, mutilated and defaced in a single night. The superstitious citizens, with a deep feeling that the whole community must suffer for the guilty action of some of its members, considered this an evil omen for the fortunes of the Syracusan expedition, and, less reasonably, took it as an indication of impending revolution and an attempt to subvert the democracy. Their anxiety was increased by rumours that a profane parody of the Eleusinian mysteries was being celebrated in certain private houses. Such acts of impiety were likely to bring upon Athens the wrath of the gods who had hitherto protected her.

[1] *Phaedrus*, 266 c, λογοδαίδαλος.        [2] Aristoph., *Clouds*, 109.

It will be remembered how Alcibiades, one of the leaders of the expedition, was accused of complicity in the plot, and how this accusation brought about his recall from Sicily and his estrangement from his native city, which led to the utter failure of the great enterprise of conquest, and ultimately, through the total loss of her best armies and fleets, to the downfall of Athens herself.

Andocides was accused of complicity both in the profanation of the mysteries and the mutilation of the Hermae. Of the former charge he apparently succeeded in clearing himself, but he confesses to a knowledge of the affair of the Hermae.

A certain Teucrus denounced eighteen persons as guilty of the mutilation of the busts. Of these some were put to death, the rest went into exile. The list included some members of the club to which Andocides belonged. Another informer, Dioclides, came forward with a tale that about three hundred persons were implicated, and he named forty-two of them, including Andocides and twelve of his near relations. Athens was in a panic, and eager for instant vengeance. The informers' victims were at once imprisoned, and their situation was grave indeed. Andocides describes how, to save his father and other innocent persons, he at last resolved to tell what he knew. He gave his information under a promise of immunity from punishment, but in accordance with the terms of a subsequent decree he suffered ' *atimia*,' comprising exclusion from the market-place and the temples ; and being thus debarred from a public career he decided to go abroad.

In the *de Reditu*, delivered in 410 B.C., five years after the outrage, Andocides implies that he was him-

self concerned in the deed, and asks pardon for his
'youthful folly' (§ 7). The language of Thucydides [1]
and others also implies that he accused himself along
with others. The language of the *de Reditu* is not,
however, explicit, and does not necessarily disagree
with the statement made twelve years later in the
*de Mysteriis*.

Andocides there affirms that he knew of the plot
and opposed its execution, but it was carried out
without his knowledge. In proof of this he points out
that the Hermes opposite his own house was the only
one not mutilated.

'So I told the Council that I knew the culprits, and I
declared the facts—namely that Euphiletus suggested the
plot while we were drinking, and I spoke against it, and for
the moment prevented it. Some time later I was riding a
colt I had in Cynosarges, and had a fall, and broke my
collar-bone and cut my head, and was carried home on a
stretcher. Euphiletus, hearing of my condition, told the
others that I had been persuaded to join them, and had
agreed to take a hand in the work and mutilate the Hermes
beside the shrine of Phorbas. In this statement he deceived them, and this is the reason why the Hermes which
you all see in front of our house, the one erected by the
Aegeid tribe, was the only Hermes in Athens not to be
mutilated, because it was supposed that I would do it, as
Euphiletus said. The conspirators, when they heard of it,
were highly indignant, considering that I knew of the
affair, but had taken no part in it. On the next day Meletus
and Euphiletus came to me and said :

' " We have done it, Andocides, and it 's all over. If you
care to keep quiet and hold your tongue, you will find that
we are as good friends to you as ever ; if not, our enmity

---

[1] Thuc., vi. 60.

will count much more than any friendship you could form by betraying us."

' I answered that, from what had occurred, I considered Euphiletus a scoundrel; but that they had much more to fear from the fact of their guilt than from my knowledge of it.' [1]

This story is at least a plausible one. The only suspicious detail is the orator's own candid admission that all of those whom he accused—with the exception of four—had already been named by Teucrus and punished, some by death, the rest by exile, so that his ' confession ' could do them no further harm. The four others whom he included were not yet in prison, though they were known to be associates of those who had already paid the penalty. They had time to escape into exile (§ 68). We may suspect that they received from the informer due notice of his intentions. Thus, at the expense of driving four men, who were probably guilty, into exile, Andocides undoubtedly saved the lives of himself, his father, his brother-in-law, and the rest of the forty-two prisoners. The informer Dioclides now recanted, and said that he had been compelled by Alcibiades and Amiantus to lay false information. He was brought to trial and put to death (§ 66). Andocides, suffering from partial disfranchisement, was for many years away from Athens. He engaged in commerce in many countries, and made money, sometimes by discreditable means. He had dealings with Sicily, Italy, the Peloponnese, Thessaly, Ionia, the Hellespont, and finally, Cyprus, where Evagoras, King of Salamis, bestowed a valuable property on him.[2]

---

[1] *de Myst.*, §§ 61 *sqq.*

[2] *Ibid.*, § 4.

In 411 B.C. he made an attempt to recover his rights. He procured oars for the Athenian fleet at Samos, and returned to Athens to plead his cause. Unfortunately the Four Hundred had then just usurped the government, and they rejected his plea on the ground that he had helped their enemies. Later, in 410 or 408 B.C., he made another attempt, and delivered the speech *de Reditu*, but was again unsuccessful. It was only after the amnesty of Thrasybulus (403 B.C.) that he resumed his full citizenship, and henceforward took an active part in public life, figuring now as an ardent democrat, speaking in the assembly and performing liturgies. In 399 B.C. old enmities burst into flame, and he was accused of impiety on two counts— as having taken part in the Eleusinian mysteries at a time when he was legally disqualified from doing so, and as having deposited a suppliant's branch on the altar at Eleusis during the time of the mysteries— which was a profanation. The penalty for either offence was death, and the *de Mysteriis* is his successful answer to these charges.

In 391 B.C., as one of the envoys delegated to bring about a peace with Sparta, he delivered the *de Pace*. The peace was not concluded. This is the last mention of this interesting adventurer, though the pseudo-Plutarch affirms that he went into exile again. If that is true, we know that he had comfortable places to retire to, in Cyprus and elsewhere.

§ 3

Ancient critics dealt severely with Andocides. Though Alexandrine criticism included him in the list of the ten standard orators, Dionysius barely mentions him ; [1] Quintilian disparages his work,[2] and Herodes Atticus modestly hopes that he himself is at least superior to Andocides ; [3] Hermogenes sums up his defects as an orator as follows :

' He aims at being a statesman, but does not quite succeed.  He lacks proper articulation and distinctness in his " figures," he lacks order in connecting his sentences and rounding them off, losing distinctness by the use of parentheses, so that he strikes some as ineffectual and needlessly obscure.  He has very little finish or arrangement and little vigour.  He has a small, but very small, portion of cleverness in systematic argument, but practically none of any other kind.' [4]

It is with some hesitation that I give this tentative translation of a difficult passage.  It seems to mean that Andocides, though he uses ' figures,' such as antithesis, rhetorical question and irony, does not attain ' precision ' or make them distinct enough. His sentences are sometimes deformed because a parenthesis overpowers the main clause.  His diction is unpolished and unconvincing.  The only credit which he deserves is for his $\mu\epsilon\theta o\delta o\varsigma$—his system of stating his case ; wherein Hermogenes was perhaps thinking of the way in which the orator arranges his material, giving only part of the narrative at a time, and criticizing it as he goes along, rather than keeping narrative and arguments quite separate.  Later and more practised orators have been commended for this method.  By general cleverness, Hermogenes probably

---

[1] Dion., *de Lysia*, ch. 2.   [2] Quint., xii. 10, 21.
[3] Philostratus, *vita Her. Att.*, ii. 1, § 14.
[4] Hermogenes, περὶ ἰδεῶν, ch. xi. p. 416.  Spengel (*Rhetores Graeci*).

means skill in the use of the usual sophistries of the rhetorician.

The Pseudo-Plutarch is less severe on the orator:

' He is simple and inartificial in his narratives, straight-forward and free from " figures." ' [1]

It must at once be granted that many of the criticisms aimed at Andocides hit their mark ; but it is open to doubt whether they can penetrate deep enough to deal a vital blow at his reputation. The ancient critics were academic and tended to lose sight of practical details. They were, as a rule, more concerned with the impressions that a speech produced on the reader than with its effect on the hearers ; they laid great emphasis on the artistic side, and in examining a speech looked carefully to see how closely the orator had followed the artificial rules of the rhetorician. But this kind of estimate may lead to injustice, for not only must the critic refer to an artificial standard established by convention, a standard which might not have been recognized by the orator's contemporaries, but, even granting that certain rules of rhetoric should generally be followed, we may maintain that particular circumstances justify a speaker in departing from them. Rhetoric is a practical art, whose object, as Plato tells us, is persuasion ; and though most people who practise it will do best to move on the accustomed lines, there may be some who can succeed without following the beaten track.

Andocides is not to be compared to his predecessor Antiphon in the points which are the latter's chief characteristics—dignity of manner, balance of clauses

[1] Ps.-Plut., *Lives of the Ten Orators.*

and verbal antithesis ; but, on the other hand, he has command of a fairly lucid style, and a gift for telling a straightforward narrative of events, two matters in which the older orator was not conspicuously successful. Again, Andocides starts with one signal advantage. If we read the tetralogies of Antiphon, excellent as they may be in showing the writer's grasp of the technique of his trade, and turn from them to one of the real speeches, the *Herodes*, for instance, we feel at once how great a gain it is to have the human interest before us. A speech in which real persons are concerned must always have this advantage over a declamatory exercise. But we still feel that the personal element is not so prominent as it might be, simply because the orator is not giving voice to his own thoughts on an occasion where his own interests are deeply concerned, but stringing together sentences which an obscure young man from Mitylene may clumsily stumble through without, perhaps, in the least comprehending their cleverness. But Andocides is a real live man speaking in his own person and in his own defence on a most serious charge. He is in grave danger, and must exert himself to the utmost ; he must rise to the great occasion, or expect to pay the penalty—perhaps with his life. This is an occasion, if there ever can be one, when style may be completely put in the background, where matter is of more importance than method, where the means are of no account unless the end can be attained ; for epigram cannot temper the hemlock-cup, and the laws of Athens are stronger than the rules of oratory.

It was natural to Antiphon to pay attention to details of style, and his style is of a rather archaic tone.   Andocides, on the other hand, was not a trained orator, except in so far as every Athenian was trained in youth in the elements of speaking.   He was not either a professional pleader or a frequent speaker in public—indeed, from the fact that he lived long in exile he cannot have had many opportunities of appearing either in the law-courts or the assembly. Possessing a convenient fluency of speech and a thorough command of the language of daily life, he finds in it a satisfactory means of expression.   In most cases he seems to have by nature what Lysias obtained by art—a clear and direct way of expressing his thoughts, a simplicity of language in which nothing strained or unfamiliar strikes the ear.   On the other hand, there are inconsistencies in his style ;  there are times when, apparently without premeditation, he does use words or phrases slightly foreign to the speech of common life.   We have a feeling that this was done without affectation ;  that in the course of his fluent and rapid utterance he used just those words which naturally occurred to him as appropriate.[1]   In this he differs from Lysias, who took the common speech and perfected it into a literary form, attaining by study a refined simplicity and purity which only careful practice could produce.

[1] The following is a list of some of the poetical or unusual words and phrases occurring in the speeches—*de Myst.* : § 29 ταῦτα τὰ δεινὰ καὶ φρικώδη ἀνωρθίαζον.   § 67 πίστιν . . . ἀπιστοτάτην.   § 68 ὁρῶσι τοῦ ἡλίου τὸ φῶς.   § 99 ἐπίτριπτον κίναδος.   § 130 κληδών.   § 146 (γένος) οἴχεται πᾶν πρόρριζον.

*de Pace* : § 7 τὸν δῆμον . . . ὑψηλὸν ἦρε.   § 8 and in three other passages κατηργάσατο (*secure, bring about*, cf. Eur. *Her.*, 646 πόλει σωτηρίαν κατεργάσασθαι).   § 18 κρατιστεύειν.   § 31 ἐκτεῖναι τὸν θυμόν, ἀρχὴν πολλῶν κακῶν.

The *de Pace* is noticeable for the recurrence of two grammatical forms which do not occur in the other speeches, the use of τοῦτο

On the whole, Andocides is most effective when he is most simple ; when he uses common words and makes no attempt at the rhetorical artifices which do not come natural to him. The following narrative will emphasize my point :

' When we had all been taken to prison, and it was night and the prison gates were shut, and one man's mother had come, and another's sister, and another's wife and children, and sounds of lamentation were heard as they wept and bewailed our miserable state, Charmides spoke to me—he was a cousin of mine, of the same age as myself, and he had been brought up in our home from childhood.

' " Andocides," he said, " you see what serious trouble we are in ; and though I did not want to say anything, or to annoy you at all before, I am now forced to do so on account of the misfortune we are come to.

' " Your other friends and associates, apart from us who are your relations, have some of them already been executed for the charges on which we are being done to death, while others have admitted their guilt by fleeing from the country.

' " If you have heard anything about this affair, tell the truth, and by doing so save both yourself, and your father, who must be very dear to you, and your brother-in-law, who is married to your only sister, and finally, all the rest of your family and friends, not to mention me—for in all my life I have never caused you annoyance, but am devoted to you and ready to do anything I can to help you." ' [1]

μὲν, τοῦτο δέ after the manner of Herodotus for the simple μέν and δέ ; and the repetition of δέ with a resumptive force, as, *e.g.*, § 27 ἃ δὲ πρὸς τούτους μόνους ἐκεῖνοι συνέθεντο, ταῦτα δ' οὐδεπώποτ' αὐτούς φασι παραβῆναι.

The illogical use of the plural of οὐδείς in the same sense as the singular (*de Myst.*, § 23 οὐδένας, § 147 οὐδένα) is perhaps colloquial. There are many instances of the use of this plural in the later orators, a point which Liddell and Scott did not observe, or, at any rate, failed to make clear. Another phrase which may be colloquial is τῇ γνώμῃ καὶ ταῖν χεροῖν ταῖν ἐμαυτοῦ (*de Myst.*, § 144).

[1] *de Myst.*, §§ 48-50.

His exposure of Dioclides is simple and effective ; he repeats the informer's statement, and with a very few words of comment makes it appear ridiculous :

' Encouraged by his country's misfortunes Dioclides laid information before the Council.   He asserted that he knew the persons who had mutilated the Hermae, and that there were about three hundred of them.   He proceeded to relate how he had come across the matter.

' He said that he had a slave working at Laureion, and had to go there to get the man's wages.   He rose very early, having mistaken the time, and started on his way.   The full moon was shining, and as he passed the gateway of Dionysus, he saw a number of men coming down from the Odeum into the Orchestra.   He was afraid of them, and so went into the shadow and sat down between the pillar and the pedestal on which the bronze statue of the General stands.

' He estimated the number of the men he saw at about three hundred, and they were standing round in groups of five or ten, or, in some cases, twenty.   He could recognize most of them, as he saw the moonlight shining on their faces.

' Now he made this monstrous statement in the first place in order that it might be in his power to say that any citizen he liked was or was not a member of that company.

' After seeing all this, he said, he went on to Laureion, and on the next day heard of the mutilation of the Hermae. So he knew at once that it was the work of the men whom he had seen.[1]

The opening of the speech shows a reasonable use of the sort of commonplaces which custom demanded as a preface to argument—the malignity and ingenuity of the speaker's enemies and the perplexity caused

[1] *de Myst.*, §§ 37-39.

by the number of their accusations which makes it difficult to know where to begin.

' Nearly all of you know, Gentlemen, with what persistency my enemies have contrived to harm me in every possible way, by fair means or foul, from the time when I first came to Athens, and there is no need for me to dwell upon the subject ; but I shall ask you only for just treatment, a favour which is as easy for you to grant as it is important for me to gain.

' First, I would have you bear in mind that I have now appeared before you without having been in any way forced to await my trial ; I have neither surrendered to bail, nor have I suffered the constraint of imprisonment. I appear because I have put my trust above all in the justice of my cause, and secondly, in your character ; feeling as I do that you will give a just decision, and not allow me through a perversion of justice to be ruined by my enemies, but that you will much rather save me by allowing justice to take its course in accordance with the laws of the city, and the oaths which you have sworn as a preliminary to the verdict which you are about to record.

' It is reasonable, Gentlemen, that, in the case of men who voluntarily face the danger of a trial, you should take the same view of them as they do of themselves.  Those who refuse to await their trial practically stand self-condemned, so that you may reasonably pass on them the sentence which they have passed on themselves ; but as for those who wait to stand their trial in the confidence that they have done no wrong, you have a right to hold the same opinion about them which they have held about themselves, and not decide, without a hearing, that they are in the wrong. . . .

' I am considering, therefore, from which point I ought to begin my defence.  Shall I begin with the last-mentioned plea, that my indictment was illegal ? or with the fact that the decree of Isotimides is not valid ? or shall I appeal to

the laws and the oaths which you have taken ? or, lastly,
shall I start by relating the facts from the beginning ?

' My greatest difficulty is that the various counts of the
indictment do not stir you all equally to resentment, but
each of you has some point which he would like me to
answer first.   It is impossible to deal with them all at once,
and so it seems to me the best course to relate the whole
story from the beginning, omitting nothing ;  for if you
thoroughly realize what actually occurred, you will easily
recognize the lies which my accusers have told to my
discredit.' [1]

The peroration is simple and vigorous in its direct-
ness :

' Do not deprive yourselves of your hopes of my help,
nor deprive me of my hopes of helping you.   I now request
those who have already given proof of the highest nobility
of feeling towards the democracy to mount the platform
and advise you in accordance with what they know of my
character.   Come forward, Anytus and Cephalus, and you
members of my tribe who have been chosen to plead for
me—Thrasyllus and the rest.' [2]

Reference has already been made to the vitality of
his speech.   Compared with his life-like vigour, the
' austerity ' of Antiphon becomes dull and pompous.
The most striking feature of his work is the ease with
which, in reporting conversations or explaining motives,
he breaks into direct quotation, recalling his own words
or putting words into the mouths of others to express
what they said or thought.  We recognize in this
something of a Homeric quality ;  it is comparable
to the Epic use of ὧδε δέ τις εἴπεσκε and καὶ ποτέ τις
εἴπῃσι.
The following extract shows how the main thread

---

[1] *de Myst.*, §§ 1-3 and 8.          [2] *Ibid.*, § 150.

of the sentence may be lost in a tangle of such parenthetical quotations :

' From the first, though many people informed me that
my enemies were saying that I should never await my
trial—" For what could induce Andocides to await his trial,
when he may leave the city and still be well off ?   If he
sails to Cyprus, where he comes from, there is waiting for
him a large and flourishing farm of which he has the free-
hold ;  will he prefer to put his neck into a halter ?   With
what end in view ?   Cannot he see which way the wind
blows here ? "   I, Gentlemen, disagree entirely with this
view.   I would not live and enjoy the utmost prosperity
somewhere else at the price of losing my fatherland ;  and
even if the wind did blow here as my enemies say it does,
I would rather be a citizen of Athens than of any other
city ;  prosperous, for the present, as such other cities may
seem to me to be.   Holding such views as these I have
committed to you the decision about my life.' [1]

It has been noted that Andocides is not addicted
to the use of verbal antithesis such as Thucydides and
Antiphon have made too familiar.  We do not find
him playing upon the contrasts between ' word and
deed,' ' being and seeming ' with such recurrent
monotony.

There is, however, one kind of antithesis to which he
is somewhat partial—an antithesis of thought rather
than language.  He is fond of explaining a difficulty
of choice by putting it in the form of a dilemma.

As far as his own personal conduct was concerned,
he must often have had to face dilemmas.  From the
part which he had played in the sacrilege, and the
awkward positions in which consequently he found
himself placed, it must often have been equally difficult

<hr>

[1] *de Myst.*, §§ 4, 5.

and dangerous for him to lie and to speak the truth.
So it is not unnatural that we should often find sentences like the following :

' How would each of you have acted, Gentlemen, if you
had had to choose either to die nobly, or to owe your life
to a disgraceful action ?
' Some may say that what I did was base, but many
would have chosen as I did.'[1]

This appeal to the individual feelings, especially the
request by which it is prefaced, that they will judge
' by human standards ' ($\dot{a}\nu\theta\rho\omega\pi\acute{\iota}\nu\omega\varsigma$), is effective in
its boldness. The speaker must have felt sure of
his audience before he ventured to appeal to the lower
nature which every one would like to repudiate.

In marked contrast to the dignity of Antiphon,
Andocides from time to time lapses into scurrility,
dragging into his speech discreditable anecdotes relating
to his opponents which are quite irrelevant to his proper
subject and merely serve to raise a laugh at the moment.
Thus the long recital about the domestic affairs of
Callias (§§ 123-130) has no bearing at all on the trial.
A man whose father has been three times unhappily
married may still be a trustworthy witness. The
introduction of the irrelevant story is then quite
unjustifiable, but, since such examples of bad taste
were freely tolerated at Athens, it was worth while
to make a score by such foul hitting, especially if one
could deliver the blows as neatly as in the following
passage :

' At the mother's request, the relations took the child
to the altar at the time of the Apaturia.  They brought

---

[1] *de Myst.*, § 57.

a victim, and requested Callias to perform the sacrifice. He asked who was the father of the child. " Callias, the son of Hipponicus."—" But I'm Callias."—" Yes, and it's your child." ' [1]

There is more to be said in justification of the attack on Epichares. To prove, or to assert violently, that his accuser was an enemy of the democracy and a person of vile character formed a presumption in favour of the defendant. Demosthenes himself made a custom of such practices, and was not less un- scrupulous or less irrelevant than Andocides :

' But Epichares, who is the worst of them all, and wants to keep up his reputation, and so acts vindictively against himself—for he was a member of the Council in the time of the Thirty ; and what is the provision in the law which is inscribed on the pillar in front of the Council room ? " Whosoever shall hold office in the city when the demo- cracy has been overthrown, may be slain without penalty, and his slayer shall be free from blood-guiltiness, and shall possess the property of the slain." Surely then, Epichares, any one who slays you now will have clean hands, according to Solon's law ? Let me have the law on the pillar read aloud ? ' [2]

But Andocides in such cases certainly violates the laws of good taste, and in the matter of this personal abuse, though less fertile in vocabulary, is a worthy forerunner of the great orators. His scurrility is hardly excused by the ingenuity of its epigrammatic form :

' You jackal, you common informer ! . . . are you allowed to live and prowl about the city ? Little do you deserve it ; under the democracy you lived by the informer's

---

[1] *de Myst.*, § 126.    [2] *Ibid.*, § 95.

**trade** ; under the oligarchy, for fear of being forced to **give**
up the money you had made by informing, you **were a**
menial of the Thirty. . . .'[1]

and again :

' One result of your decision to observe the present laws
is that he has been restored from exile to citizenship, and
from legal disability to the free exercise of the informer's
trade.'[2]

The use of parenthesis is sometimes carried by
Andocides to extremes.  An instance has been quoted
in which the grammatical construction breaks down
because the writer introduces an imaginary conversation into the middle of it.[3]  The style is sometimes
so loose and discursive that not only is the construction difficult to follow, but the argument is obscure.
The writer suffers from an inability to keep to the
point, or rather, he tries to explain several things at
once, and so makes nothing clear.  An extreme
instance is to be found in §§ 57 *sqq.* of the *de Mysteriis.*
His thoughts run too fast for his tongue, and he has
not the technical skill to guide them on their proper
courses.  Such sentences afford a practical comment
on the introduction to the same speech, in which he
states that he does not know where to begin.[4]

On the other hand, passages may be found in which
a series of short sentences, loosely combined, and
disturbed by *anacoluthon*, are really effective, since
they simulate the broken utterance of passion.  Of
such is the following :

' Then the herald inquired who had deposited the suppliant's branch, and no one answered.  Now we were

---

[1] ὦ συκόφαντα καὶ ἐπίτριπτον κίναδος, κ.τ.λ., *de Myst.*, § 99.
[2] *Ibid.*, § 93.        [3] *Supra*, p. 66.        [4] § 8.

standing close by, and Callias could see me. When nobody answered, he retired into the temple. Eucles, stepping forward—oblige me by calling him up—Now then, Eucles, first of all give evidence whether I am speaking the truth.'[1]

## § 4

I have dealt hitherto chiefly with the speech *de Mysteriis*, the best of Andocides' work. The other speeches now demand a short mention. The *de Reditu* differs remarkably from the later speech, *de Mysteriis*, but it is chiefly a difference of tone. The verbal style is much the same, though there is rather more tendency to antithetical structure. The language is simple, the sentences are less hampered with parentheses. But here Andocides is humble ; he appears as a young man without friends speaking before a critical and hostile assembly ; he is moderate in his language, apologetic in tone, careful not to give offence by any sarcastic or ill-considered utterance. In the *de Mysteriis* he is speaking with the conscious-ness not of a better cause but of increased powers and an assured position in the State. He is confident, almost arrogant at times ; he is bitter and violent in his attacks on his enemies.

The *de Pace* bears a general resemblance in style to the other speeches, except for certain grammatical peculiarities. Dionysius declared it to be spurious, but modern critics mostly regard it as genuine.

The chief grounds for suspicion are the inaccuracies of the historical narrative (§§ 3-9) and the curious fact that a very similar passage occurs in Aeschines (*de F. L.*, §§ 172-176), where even certain peculiarities

---

[1] *de Myst.*, § 112.

of phraseology[1] are reproduced.  As to history, the orators were often inaccurate about the past history of their own country.  Careless statements occur even in the *de Mysteriis*.  Demosthenes is an untrustworthy authority even for events almost contemporary.  As to the other matter, there is good reason for the belief that Aeschines plagiarized Andocides in the fact that a reference to Andocides, the grandfather of the orator, which occurs in both speeches, is in place in a speech of Andocides, while there is no particular reason why Aeschines, if he were composing the passage, should have mentioned him.  In some minor points, as Jebb has shown, Andocides is more accurate than Aeschines.  The suggestion that the *de Pace* is a spurious speech, composed by a later rhetor who plagiarized from Aeschines, is therefore hardly tenable.  There remains a third possibility, that both Aeschines and Andocides borrowed from the same semi-historical compilation, perhaps a lost rhetorical exercise.

The *de Pace* and the *de Reditu* are not enlivened by excursions into anecdote or the consequent direct quotations of speech which characterize the *de Mysteriis*.  The historical argument already mentioned is dull in itself, but the tedium of the *de Pace* is somewhat relieved by a not infrequent use of rhetorical question.

' What is there left for us to discuss ?  The subject of Corinth and the invitation of Argos.  First, I should like to be informed about Corinth : if the Boeotians do not join us in the war but make peace with Sparta, what will Corinth be worth to us ?  Remember the day, men of Athens,

---

[1] *E.g.*, the poetical ὑψηλὸν ἦρε.  Andoc., § 7 ; Aesch., § 174.  Cf. Euripides, *Supp.*, 555, and *Her.* 323.

when we made our alliance with the Boeotians ; what was our feeling in that transaction ?   Was it not that we and Boeotia in combination were strong enough to stand against all the world ?   But now our question is, if the Boeotians make peace, how shall we be able, without Boeotian help, to fight against Sparta ?   We can do it, say some people, if we protect Corinth, and have an alliance with Argos.

' But when the Spartans attack Argos, are we going to help Argos or not ?   We must definitely choose one course or the other.' [1]

An appeal for peace does not give such opportunities for oratory as a call to arms ; nevertheless, a greater orator might have made more of the subject.

The speech *Against Alcibiades* is undoubtedly spurious and belongs to a much later date.

It is based upon a complete misconception of the nature of the law about ostracism.   The speaker is represented as discussing the question whether he himself or Nicias or Alcibiades should be ostracized— a quite impossible position.   The speech is little more than a collection of some of the stock anecdotes about Alcibiades, such as occur in Plutarch.

The names of four lost speeches are preserved :— πρὸς ἑταίρους, συμβουλευτικός, περὶ τῆς ἐνδείξεως and ἀπολογία πρὸς Φαίακα.   Fragments—a few lines in each case—remain of two unnamed speeches.   One of these refers to Hyperbolus as still in Athens, and so must be placed not later than 417 B.C., the year when Hyperbolus was ostracized.   It deserves quotation as being typical of the snobbish-

---

[1] *de Pace*, §§ 24-26.

ness of the young aristocrat, not yet disciplined by misfortune.

' I am ashamed to mention the name of Hyperbolus ; his father is a branded slave, who up to the present day works in the public mint ; he himself is a foreigner, a barbarian, and a lampmaker.' [1]

[1] Frag. 5 (Blass)

## CHAPTER IV

## LYSIAS

### § 1

THOUGH we attempt a chronological arrangement
of the orators, such a treatment is apt to be
misleading, for their lives and the periods of their
activity overlap considerably.  About the year 390 B.C.
Andocides was still composing speeches, Lysias was
yet in his prime ; Isocrates had already made himself
a reputation, and Isaeus had at least begun to be
known.  It would be rash therefore to attempt to
trace in the work of any one the influence of any of
the others.  Speaking and writing as contemporaries
all may have had something to teach and something
to learn, but we can hardly say that one is in the
fullest sense the literary predecessor or the disciple
of another.

Lysias was by descent a Syracusan ; his father
Cephalus, of whom Plato gives us a charming picture
in the opening chapters of the *Republic*, was induced
by Pericles to settle in Athens, and there Lysias was
born.  The Pseudo-Plutarch gives the date as 459 B.C.,
and Dionysius gives the same year ; but this is founded
on an assumption.  He was known to have gone to
Thurii at the age of fifteen, and Thurii was founded in
443 B.C.  But there is no proof that Lysias went to

Thurii in the year of its foundation ; we only know that he cannot have been born earlier than 459 B.C. Tradition, however, made him live to the age of eighty or eighty-three, and his latest known speech is dated, probably, in 380 B.C., so that if we assume his death to have occurred shortly after 380 B.C., we shall be consistent.[1] The modern view, supported by Blass, that Lysias was born not earlier than 444 B.C., has little evidence to support it. It is based chiefly on the statement of the Pseudo-Plutarch that Lysias did not go to Thurii till after his father's death, and the belief that Cephalus was alive in 430 B.C., the date in which the scene of the *Republic* is supposed to be laid. But Blass has himself collected instances of Plato's untrustworthiness about dates, and the biographer by himself is a poor authority.

Lysias, then, went to Thurii with his brothers Polemarchus and Euthydemus. He is said to have studied under the Syracusan rhetorician Tisias. After the loss of the Athenian armies in Sicily, 413 B.C., Lysias and his brothers were among three hundred persons accused of ' Atticizing,' and were expelled from Thurii. They returned to Athens in 412 B.C. From this year till 404 B.C., the brothers lived in prosperity and happiness, making a considerable fortune as proprietors of a shield-factory, where they employed 120 slaves.

They had many friends ; they belonged to the highest class of aliens—the *isoteleis*—and the evidence of Plato and Dionysius makes it clear that they mixed

---

[1] Two lost speeches for Iphicrates, 371 B.C. and 354 B.C., were pronounced spurious by Dionysius ; but, as he accepted the date of Lysias' birth as 459 B.C., he was bound to conclude that these speeches were not by him.

with the most cultivated society. They took pride in the performance of all public services which fell to their share.

Fortune changed for the sons of Cephalus when in 404 B.C. a successful revolution brought the Thirty into power ; the orator himself gives a graphic description of the way in which their ruin was brought about.

The Thirty, he tells us, ' avowed that they must purge the city of wrongdoers, and turn the rest of the citizens towards virtue and justice.' Two of the leaders pointed out that some of the *metoeci* were discontented with the new constitution ; these *metoeci* were rich, so that their execution was not only a moral duty but a sound financial move. They easily prevailed on their colleagues, who, as Lysias neatly puts it, ' thought nothing of taking life but thought a lot of making money.' The orator's name was on the list, and he was arrested at a dinner-party in his own house. He describes what followed :

' I asked Piso whether he would save my life for money ; he said he would, if it was a large sum. So I said I was ready to pay a talent, and he agreed to the terms. I knew well enough that he regarded neither god nor man, but I thought my only chance lay in trusting him. So when he had sworn by his own and his children's hope of salvation that he would save me if he got a talent for it, I went into my strong-room and opened the chest.'

The sight of its contents, amounting to about six talents' worth of gold and silver as well as a quantity of plate, was too much for Piso's honesty. ' I begged him to allow me enough for my journey, but he said I ought to be well satisfied if I saved my skin.'

The prisoner was handed over by Piso to the keeping of Damnippus and Theognis in the former's house, and Damnippus, who seems to have been softer-hearted than the rest, agreed to speak with Theognis on Lysias' behalf. He knew his man, and 'thought he would do anything for money.' While they were bargaining, Lysias managed to slip away unnoticed through the back-door, and on the following day escaped on ship-board to Megara ; his brother Pole-marchus was arrested by Eratosthenes and put to death.[1]

During his exile, which lasted something less than a year, Lysias showed himself a true friend of the democracy. He gave two hundred shields to the army and obtained recruits and gifts of money. When the oligarchy fell in 403 B.C. the ecclesia, on the motion of Thrasybulus, passed a vote conferring the citizenship on Lysias ; but owing to some informality the decree was declared illegal, and he lost his privilege immediately. From this time till about 380 B.C. he was actively employed in writing speeches, very few of which he delivered himself. His industry must have been considerable, since Dionysius attributed to him not less than two hundred forensic speeches.

The prosecution of Eratosthenes in 403 B.C. marks, so far as we know, his only personal contact with Athenian politics. The occasion of the *Olympiacus* shows us Lysias appealing to a far wider audience at the Olympic festival of 388 B.C. He died, according to the computation of the ancients, soon after 380 B.C., at the age of about eighty years.

---

[1] *Against Eratosthenes*, §§ 5-17.

## § 2

In literature as in politics we grow tired of hearing Aristides called the Just, and so perfect writers are less admired than they should be. In Latin Terence, praised by all for the purity of his style, is less read than the ruder Plautus, and in Greek Lysias, accounted by ancient critics the standard writer of Attic prose,[1] is less appreciated than Demosthenes.

Using the everyday language as a literary medium, Lysias, by his exceptional skill and mastery over its idiom, exalted it to a simplicity and accuracy of expression never surpassed by other writers. This simplicity is deceptive :

> ' ut sibi quivis
> Speret idem, sudet multum frustraque laboret
> Ausus idem.'

It is not till we analyse a passage or try to imitate the style that we realize how great a part has been played by art in this structure which seems so natural.

The smoothness strikes us, after a time, as monotonous, and many readers will turn with relief from Lysias' polish to the more telling ruggedness of Antiphon, or the varied magnificence of Plato. Lysias, in fact, provides us with an excellent example of the purest prose, but the comparative coarseness of the average taste prefers something less refined, less carefully purged of the natural impurities which prevent insipidity, less free from the colouring matter which gives character.

So far I have considered only the broad impression produced by the language, apart from more personal elements in style.

[1] Dion., *de Lysia*, ch. 2 : τῆς ᾽Αττικῆς γλώττης ἄριστος κανών.

As an orator, Lysias is, on first acquaintance, disappointing. He seems to lack fire, and to subordinate vigour to precision.

For this apparent weakness we must make certain allowances. We must remember that he has to be judged chiefly by speeches written for others, and speeches dealing with cases which in their very nature are often unimportant, and in their details have little interest.

It would be unreasonable to ask for any other qualities than clear statement of fact in a speech for the prosecution relating to embezzlement by a trustee for a will (*Against Diogiton*), or in the indictment of Nicomachus, a magistrate who has not rendered his accounts in due course. Such speeches are of considerable importance indirectly : to the jurist, as bearing upon the peculiarities of Attic Law ; to the general reader, because they help to fill in details of the picture of public and private life at Athens. We should not pass a hasty judgment on the writer because, considered as examples of oratory, they are less attractive and impressive than some of the more famous models.

I will reserve for future consideration the only speech in which the personal feelings of Lysias are deeply involved—the accusation of Eratosthenes. Of the other speeches there is none which, taken as a whole, is comparable to the finest of the public speeches or the harangues of Demosthenes. Though Lysias had often to deal with trials of public men, these trials were never really of public importance. It was not his business to lay down a definite line of policy for his city to follow ; it was not for him to awake an apathetic nation to the need of instant and decisive action.  We cannot believe that any of his speeches would appeal, or were meant to appeal, to Athens as a whole.

Even when he is dealing with events that took place during the tyranny of the Thirty, though no doubt feeling still ran high, we have the impression that only that part of the community which had been directly concerned in promoting or thwarting the Revolution would be keenly interested in the process of punishing or rewarding those who had played minor parts : the majority had acquiesced, with greater or less unwillingness, at the time of the changes, and now that the trouble was past, were eager to make the best of the present ; political memory at Athens was short.

The position of Demosthenes was very different ; his chief activity was not after a crisis, but during a time of national danger.   He found great opportunities and he rose to them.

A great enthusiasm is required to produce really great men, whether orators or statesmen.  A gifted man under the influence of a great constructive idea may, with exceptional opportunities, become a Pericles ; an extraordinarily favourable combination of such circumstances may give birth to an Alexander.

In modern times the greatest eloquence is usually on the side of the opposition, and in all ages a losing cause has tended to produce more conspicuous men.

Demosthenes owes his great reputation partly to his exceptional ability, but in very large part also to his opportunities, to the fact that he was fighting against national apathy and foreign aggression for a noble ideal—his conception of Athenian Liberty.  A lesser intellect might have shone under such circumstances ;

and on the other hand Demosthenes, if he had had no opportunity for the speeches against Philip, might have been ranked almost in the same class with such orators as Lysias.

## § 3

Lysias is no less simple in the arrangement of his subject-matter than in his language. Practically every speech which has come down to us in entirety may be analysed into four elements—preface, narrative, proof, and epilogue. The preface or epilogue may be very slight; the narrative may be so self-evident that proof is practically unnecessary, or on the other hand, there may be hardly any facts to narrate, so that beyond the words of the indictment only an accumulation of proofs is required; but the order of the parts seems to be invariable. We have seen that Andocides instinctively divided up his narrative, where there was a long story to tell, and interspersed the parts with proofs of the details. Isocrates, who states the necessity of the divisions which Lysias tacitly adopted, himself departs from his own rules at times, while Isaeus, by a judicious subdivision and shifting of the parts, contrives, as Dionysius says, to ' outmanœuvre ' the judges.[1]

Within these limits Lysias aimed at elasticity; though the form of the speech was to be settled precisely, his artistic sense demanded a variety in the details. It is remarked by Dionysius that, though he composed two hundred speeches, he never used the same preface twice. Some orators were in the habit of using over again the opening sentences which had already served as introduction to an old speech,

[1] καταστρατηγεῖ.

F

and even borrowing such *proems* whole from the speeches of their predecessors or from rhetorical hand-books.

Lysias, with a truer instinct for what was appropriate, composed for every speech a *proem* adapted to its requirements. His versatility in this small matter is much to be admired. It is to be noticed also that there is considerable variety in his ways of ending his speeches ; though many of his epilogues practically say the same thing in different words, they nearly all succeed in saying it in a way more appropriate to the particular speech than to any other.

As there is diversity in these forms, so there is great variety in the details of expression. There are very few formal mannerisms on which we could seize if we wished to produce a parody of the style. There are indeed one or two common necessary phrases which he employed frequently, but even these are presented in different shape from time to time.[1]

## § 4

Lysias varies greatly in the structure of his sentences, at one time producing periods neatly turned, with clauses carefully balanced, at another time writing in a style by no means periodic ; again varying his form by mingling the two methods, inserting in the middle of the period a parenthesis or relative clause which keeps us in suspense, or attaching to the end of the period an extra limb which, from a technical point of view, spoils its symmetry. It is impossible without

[1] *E.g.* δεινὸν δέ μοι δοκεῖ εἶναι εἰ νῦν μὲν . . . τότε δέ, etc., and ἄξιον δ' ἐνθυμηθῆναι ὅτι . . .

quoting a large number of examples to prove these statements in detail, but we may state broadly that in speeches dealing with serious matters of public interest the style is more periodic ; in some of the private speeches on comparatively trivial subjects the style is simpler and more straightforward.

But there is often much variety within the limits of the same speech ; as Blass and others have pointed out, the narrative is usually told in a simple style,[1] while for arguments and proofs the greater elaboration of the period is employed. As I have pointed out in a previous chapter,[2] narrative and argument seem naturally to evoke different styles, and it may be supposed further that the juries trying the more serious cases looked for a more finished style of speech than the colloquial simplicity which would be admissible in minor police-court cases. But even in the unimportant private speeches Lysias has not one method only, and we feel that he varied his style of sentence-construction to suit the character of the speaker for whom he wrote. Thus the youth Mantitheus is nearly as simple in speech as he is ingenuous in thought, while the cripple, whom we feel to be a plausible rascal, glibly produces strings of neat antitheses, such as the following :

' The rich with their money can buy exemption from danger, the poor are compelled by their indigence to practise moderation. The young claim indulgence from their elders, but both young and old are equally severe on the faults of the others.

---

[1] Examples are numerous : *e.g.* the speech of Polyaenus (*For the Soldier*, §§ 4-5) shows a simplicity in narrative which Herodotus could not have surpassed.

[2] Ch. ii. pp. 26-7.

' The strong have the opportunity, without risk to themselves, of ill-treating whom they will ; the weak can neither defend themselves against an aggressor when they are ill-treated, nor overpower their intended victims when they wish to ill-treat others.' [1]

<h2 style="text-align:center">§ 5</h2>

The variation of sentence-construction is a minor help towards the delineation of character—a necessary part of the business of a professional speech-writer who tries to be realistic.  But, in order that the speech may seem appropriate to the speaker, it is necessary that not only his words and phrases but his sentiments should be consonant with his character.  This effect Lysias attempted to produce, and he is credited with having attained great success.

We may to some extent discover from the speeches what was the nature of the speakers, but not altogether, for we have no indication as to tone or manner of delivery.

However, from data of various kinds, we can form conceptions of many of the speakers.  Thus the defendant on a charge of receiving bribes (Or. xxi.) gives a long and prosy catalogue of his services to the State, with an account of the moneys that he has spent on liturgies (§§ 1-10) ; all this leads up to his conclusion that he, who desired little for himself and expended all his fortune for his country's good, had no inducement to take bribes to injure her.

From the *Mantitheus* we get quite a vivid and pleasing picture of a young Athenian of good birth and breeding, who ingenuously admits to having

---

[1] *For the Cripple*, § 7.

some fashionable affectations and owns to an overpowering ambition to distinguish himself as a speaker
in the ecclesia, as he has already done good service
in the field.

The speech throughout is frank and self-confident,
but not by any means boastful :

'From such records as these you ought to judge a man
who in his public life is guided by ambition combined with
moderation ; you ought not to detest a man because he
does his hair in the fashionable way : such habits hurt
nobody personally, and do no harm to the community ;
while all of you alike are benefited by those who willingly
face your enemies. So it is not fair either to love or to
hate any one on account of his looks ; you should judge
by his actions. Many people who talk little and dress
quietly have been the authors of great harm, while others
who do not affect such deportment have done you great
services. . . .

'I have observed, too, that some people are offended
with me because I have ventured to speak in public when
I am in their opinion too young : but in the first place I
have been forced to speak publicly about matters which
concern me, and besides, I think I am by nature somewhat
excessively ambitious.

'I reflect that my ancestors have never ceased to serve
the State, and—to be candid—I observe that you think
that such people alone deserve your notice.

'Seeing that such is your opinion, who would not be encouraged to act and speak on the State's behalf ? And
why should you be displeased with those who do so ? No
one else has a right to judge them ; it is for you alone.'[1]

A very different picture is that of the cripple (Oration xxiv.) who defends himself on a charge of
receiving a State pension under false pretences. He

[1] *For Mantitheus*, §§ 18-21.

seems to protest too much about his infirmity, his poverty, and his general helplessness, while he keeps a sneering tone throughout, and hardly troubles to conceal a malicious temper :

' I am almost grateful to the prosecutor for instituting this trial. Hitherto I have had no pretext for giving you an account of my life : now I have obtained one—through him. In my speech I shall attempt to show that he is a liar, and that up to the present day my life has been one that should win praise rather than be exposed to jealousy, for I cannot think that he has brought me to trial from any other motive than jealousy. But if a man feels jealousy towards one whom all others pity, what baseness will he not sink to, do you suppose ?

' It is not to gain money that he has laid this information, and he is not trying to punish an enemy ; he is a bad character, with whom I have had no dealings either friendly or hostile. So it is clear, Gentlemen, that he is jealous of me because, though thus afflicted, I am a better citizen than he is. For I think that one should compensate for bodily misfortunes by good habits of mind ; and if I show a disposition of mind to match my unfortunate body, and fashion my life accordingly, I shall be as bad as he is. . . .' [1]

' As to my riding, which he has had the audacity to mention, having no fear of fortune or respect for you, there is not much to say. I know that all who labour under any incapacity seek some such relief, and speculate how best they may alleviate their suffering. I am one of this class, and, being afflicted as you see, have found riding a great comfort for a journey of any length. . . .

' If I had the means, I would ride in comfort on a mule, instead of a borrowed horse ; but as I cannot afford a beast of my own, I am compelled often to use a borrowed horse. . . . I am surprised that he does not make it a ground for

---

[1] *For the Cripple*, §§ 1-3.

accusation that I walk with two sticks, while others use one—on the plea that only the affluent can afford two.'[1]

' Again, he says that I associate with numerous bad characters who have spent all their own money, and are plotting against those who want to keep what belongs to them. But reflect that this accusation does not hit me more than anybody else who practises a trade ; nor does it apply to my visitors more than those of the rest of the working-class. Every one of you pays visits to the perfumer, the barber, the shoemaker, or any tradesman, and most people go to the establishments nearest the market-place, and fewest to those farthest away. So if you condemn my visitors as scoundrels, it is clear that you must equally condemn those who spend their time in other people's shops ; and if they are guilty, all the inhabitants of Athens must be ; for you are all in the habit of paying visits and spending your time somewhere or other.'[2]

Another good example of this realism in depicting character is the speech *de Caede Eratosthenis*. Lysias seems to have given us just the kind of speech that is appropriate to a rather stupid man of the lower middle classes who, by his own showing, is no better than his neighbours, though no worse. Incidentally, the whole speech is an important contribution to our knowledge of domestic arrangements in an Athenian home :

' So things went on, till one day I returned unexpectedly from the country. After dinner the baby was crying and fidgeting—the servant had been teasing it on purpose, to make it cry, for Eratosthenes was in the house : I heard all about that afterwards.—I told my wife to go and feed the baby, to stop it crying. She refused at first, pretending to be glad to have me back after so long ; but when I grew annoyed and told her again to go, " Yes," said she," and

<hr>

[1] *For the Cripple*, parts of §§ 10-12.  [2] *Ibid.*, §§ 19-20,

leave you and the servant alone up here ; I know how you behaved one night when you were drunk." I laughed, but she got up and went away and shut the door, treating it as a joke, and drew the bolt outside. I thought nothing of it, and had no suspicion, and was glad to go to sleep after my day's work in the country. Early in the morning she came back and opened the door, and when I asked why the doors had banged in the night, she told me that the lamp beside the child's bed had gone out, and she had fetched a light from a neighbour. I made no remark, supposing that this was the truth. I had an idea that her face was powdered, although her brother had died less than a month ago ; but for all that I said nothing more about it, and left the house and went on my business without comment.' [1]

## § 6

Though Lysias shows dramatic instinct in the representation of character, he seldom employs theatrical effects for the purpose of overpowering the feelings of the court. He trusts more to logic than to the elements of pity and terror, and shows a moderation of language comparable to the self-restraint which characterizes his style in general. He avoids exaggeration of every kind ; even the story of his own arrest is told in a dispassionate, almost impersonal style.[2] There can be no doubt that Lysias thus gains greatly in dignity. The prison scene described by Andocides [3] may appeal more to our feelings, but certainly more impressive is the solemnity of a similar scene in Lysias :

' When they were condemned to death, and their end was near, they sent for various kinswomen—sister, mother, wife, as the case might be—to visit them in prison, in order

[1] *de Caede Eratosthenis,* §§ 11-14.
[2] *Supra,* p. 76.        [3] *Supra,* p. 62.

that they might, before they died, bid them a last farewell. Dionysodorus sent for my sister, who was his wife. Receiving the message, she came dressed in mourning as a fit tribute to her husband's condition.' [1]

The prisoner then disposed of his property, and 'solemnly warned his wife, if she should bear a son, to tell the child that Agoratus had killed his father, and bid him take vengeance on the murderer.'

There is no hint here of such weeping and wailing as Andocides describes ; nothing but the quiet pathos of the story itself to work upon the feelings. To a certain class of audience this style would appeal more truly than any extravagance of grief, and passages of this kind should be enough to refute the common charge against Lysias that he lacks pathos.

## § 7

Lysias was not without a sense of humour, and sometimes employed sarcasm which could be delicate and playful or bitter to the point of brutality according to circumstances ; thus in the *Epitaphios* he remarks how the Persians thought that their best chance of success would be to invade Greece 'while Greece was still quarrelling as to the best means of defence against invasion.' [2]

Other sentences may be found in the speech *For the Cripple*.[3] Sometimes a sarcastic reference is introduced by a play on words—as βουλεύειν— δουλεύειν in *Philo*, § 26—' He desires the position of a public servant ; that of a public slave is what he deserves.' Out of several instances in the *Nicomachus*

---

[1] *Agoratus*, §§ 39-40.
[2] *Vide infra*, p. 92, on the question of authenticity.
[3] *Supra*, pp. 83 *sqq.*

one may be quoted, in comparison with a rather similar passage in Andocides: ' He has now become a citizen instead of a slave, a rich man instead of a poor man, a legislator instead of an under-clerk.'

This is far less effective than the unexpected turn which Andocides gives to a similar passage.[1]

Finally, the fragment of the speech against Aeschines the Socratic contains a long humorous passage. Aeschines has a mania for borrowing money which he never repays. ' His neighbours are so badly treated by him that they all move as soon as they can and take houses at a distance. . . . The crowd of creditors round his doors at daybreak makes people think they are assembling for a funeral,' and so on, in a comic vein, till the speaker ends with a spiteful remark about Aeschines' mistress, that ' you could count her teeth more easily than the fingers of her hand.'

§ 8

Lysias composed an extraordinary number of speeches ; of the 425 attributed to him, Dionysius pronounced 233 to be genuine.[2] There are now extant thirty-four, either complete or, in some cases, with portions missing. A hundred and twenty-seven speeches are known by the preservation of their titles or of small fragments.

As we cannot trace with any certainty a chronological development in style, the most convenient classification of the speeches is according to their subject-matter.

---

[1] Lysias, *Nicomachus*, § 27 ; Andocides, *de Myst.*, § 93, quoted *infra*, p. 96.

[2] Ps.-Plut., *Lives of the Ten Orators* ; Dion., *de Lys.*, ch. 17, διακοσίων οὐκ ἐλάσσους δικανικοὺς γράψας λόγους.

### *Epideictic Speeches*

The fragment of the 'Olympiac' speech, which is undoubtedly genuine, is an interesting specimen of compositions of this class.

The Sophists had early realized the opportunities which the great assembly of all Greek States gave for an expression of national feeling, and though perhaps the speech-making was instituted chiefly for the display of oratory, the custom had grown up of making it an occasion for discussing broad political questions. Thus Gorgias had preached the necessity of union among Greeks, and in later time Isocrates in his *Panegyric* was to urge again the need of putting aside petty disputes among cities for the good of the Greek nation.

In 388 B.C. Dionysius of Syracuse had sent a magnificent embassy to the Olympic festival. Lysias, realizing that this despot of the West, who had reduced important cities of Sicily, had defeated Carthage, and was now threatening the towns of Magna Graecia, might become, especially if allied with Persia, a serious menace to the independence of the cities of Greece proper, urged them to sink their private animosities for the good of all, and as a foretaste of their enmity he called upon them to tear down the royal pavilion at Olympia and scatter its treasures.

In the extant fragment the speaker warns his hearers that much of the Greek world is in the hands of tyrants, and much under barbarian sway. This is owing to the weakness caused by internal discord. Empire depends on command of the seas, and Dionysius and Artaxerxes are both strong in ships.

'You ought therefore to lay aside your war with each other, and by harmonious action make a bid for safety; you should view the past with shame and the future with apprehension.'

He invites Sparta to take the lead. The substance of the end of the speech is known to us only from the 'argument,' but the fragment is long enough to be judged as a simple yet dignified composition.

The *Epitaphios* or Funeral Speech purports to relate to the Athenians who fell in the Corinthian war, *c.* 394 B.C., though it is impossible to determine the year precisely.

Such speeches were habitually delivered at Athens, a speaker of established reputation being generally chosen to perform the service. Now Lysias, not being a citizen, could not be so chosen, and, if the speech was really delivered, he can hardly have composed it; for a practised public speaker would probably not require the services of a professional logographos.[1]

An extract from the peroration will give a general idea of the style :

'And so we may deem these men most happy, in that they faced and met their end on behalf of all that is great and noble, not committing themselves to chance, nor awaiting the death that comes in nature's course, but choosing the noblest way of dying.

'For their memory is ageless, and their honour is envied of all men; we mourn for them as mortal in their nature, but we celebrate them as immortal for their valour. They are receiving a public funeral, and in their honour we institute displays of strength and wisdom and wealth, holding them who have died in battle worthy to be honoured

---

[1] However, Socrates, in Plato's *Menexenus*, 236 B, suggests that Pericles' famous Funeral Speech was composed for him by Apasia.

with the same honour as the immortals.  So I call them happy in their death, and envy them therefor, and think it should be said that life was worth the possessing only for those men who, endowed with mortal bodies, have left behind them through their valour a memorial that is immortal.  Still, we must follow ancient custom, and, obeying the law of our fathers, make lamentation for those whom we are burying to-day.' [1]

There is nothing striking or original in this peroration, which recalls the fragment of the funeral speech of Gorgias, especially in the forced and repeated contrasts between ' mortal ' and ' immortal.'  In manner and in substance it is infinitely inferior to the famous speech of Pericles, which, with all its extravagances of style, has a note of true feeling.  The *Epitaphios* of Lysias rings hollow ;  it is feeble in imagery, it contains very little reference to the dead, and holds out no hope of comfort to the living.  The allusions to the Persian war are part of the rhetorical paraphernalia such as stirred the bile of Aristophanes, while the historical references to the supposed circumstances of the speech are so vague as not to be appropriate to any particular occasion.

On internal evidence, therefore, we may well believe that it is not a real speech, but a declamatory exercise.

There is the further question, whether it was composed by Lysias or not.

The composer of a ' *declamatio* ' may allow himself liberties which he would not take in a real speech ; yet it is hard to believe that Lysias would have committed such faults of taste as to drag the wars of the Amazons into discussion or to indulge in the exaggerations of the opening sections : ' All time would not

[1] *Epit.*, §§ 79-81.

be enough for all men to prepare a speech adequate to such deeds!' and again, 'Everywhere and among all men do those who mourn for their own sorrows proclaim the valour of these dead!'

This is not appropriate to the Corinthian war nor to any war in the lifetime of Lysias, and Lysias did not elsewhere say things so inappropriate.[1]

The speech is probably an exercise composed by a writer who had before him the speech of Pericles and other such compositions. It is actually quoted by Aristotle, who, however, does not assign it to Lysias.[2] The general lack of restraint in tone is suspicious, and is, on the whole, the strongest argument against authenticity.

Only one fragment (Or. xxxiv.) remains of a speech composed for the ecclesia. According to its title, it was delivered in opposition to some proposals to abolish or limit the ancient constitution after the fall of the Thirty (403 B.C.). Dionysius doubts whether it was actually delivered, but considers it to be written in a style suitable for debate.[3] It is significant historically that the speaker dares to compare the position of Athens in relation to Sparta with that of Argos and Mantineia. The Athenians must have been broken in spirit to tolerate such a reference.

### *Public Causes*

These γραφαί fall under various heads; they deal with all offences against the State, directly comprising treason, sacrilege, embezzlement, unconstitutional

---

[1] The reference to the Amazons and the general vagueness of the historical setting are closely paralleled by the Funeral Speech in Plato's *Menexenus*, which is generally regarded as a parody.

[2] *Rhet.*, III. 10. 7.     [3] *de Lys.*, ch. 32.

procedure, evasion of military service, wrongful claims for admission to office ; or against the State in the person of an individual, *e.g.* charges of murder or attempted murder.

They range in importance from high treason (*e.g. Ergocles*) and deliberate murder (*e.g. Eratosthenes*) to the attempt of the Cripple (Or. xxiv.) to obtain an insignificant pension by alleged false pretences.

*For Polystratus* (Or. xx.), 411-405 B.C. This speech is entitled '*For Polystratus ; defence on a charge of attempting to subvert the democracy.*'

Polystratus had held office under the Four Hundred, and had even been a member of that body. The nature of the charge brought against him is uncertain, but as the penalty proposed was only a fine, it cannot have been so serious as the title implies. Modern critics decide that the speech is spurious, entirely on grounds of style and method. The arrangement is at times confused, the argument obscure, and the style weak.

This kind of argument against genuineness must always be a subjective one ; it is hard to prove the case. The speech *Against Theomnestus* (*see below*, p. 100) has faults unworthy of Lysias, and yet, according to the same critics, it is undoubtedly genuine.

It should be remembered that the present speech is earlier by some years (*c.* 407 B.C.) than any of the orations accepted as genuine, and perhaps in the case of an orator's earlier efforts we should look for less precision and finish.

Or. xxi., on a charge of taking bribes, is only the second half of the speech. The first part, dealing with specific charges, is lost. The defendant points to his distinguished public services as a proof that he is not the sort of man to be bribed to betray his country. The date is probably 402 B.C.

*Against Ergocles* (Or. xxviii.), *Against Epicrates* (Or. xxvii.), and *Against Philocrates* (Or. xxix.) may be taken together as speeches delivered by a public prosecutor, all in the year 389 B.C. ; they assume that the previous speakers have gone fully into the charges, so that they themselves need only recapitulate them. The speakers are vigorous and concise, but impersonal. There was no need in such formal orations for the kind of adaptation to the speaker's character which we find elsewhere. Ergocles was prosecuted and put to death for betraying Greek cities in Asia and enriching himself by embezzlement. Philocrates had been his subordinate and confederate. Epicrates was also accused of embezzling public money when in a position of trust.

*Against Nicomachus* (Or. xxx.), date probably 399 B.C.—The only charges against Nicomachus are that, having been appointed to revise certain laws, he was dilatory in his work and did not finish it within the appointed time, and has caused an excessive expenditure of public money—not, be it noted, for his own advantage. Though Nicomachus at the worst was unbusinesslike and indiscreet, the accuser thinks fit to shower abuse on him, chiefly in connection with his humble origin, for his father was a freedman.[1]

*Against the Corn-dealers* (Or. xxii.) is a plain, unpretentious speech arising out of the laws relating to the

[1] Cf. *supra*, p. 90.

corn supply ; the dealers were not allowed to make
a profit of more than one obol a bushel, and monopoly
was strictly guarded against. The date is uncertain ;
possibly about 390 B.C.

*On the Confiscation of the Property of the Brother of
Nicias* (Or. xviii.), about 396-385 B.C.—Nicias' brother
Eucrates was put to death by the Thirty in 404 B.C.,
and at some time later a decree was passed for the
confiscation of his estate. The sons and nephew of
Eucrates plead against the enforcement of this sentence. Of the fragment which remains the greater
part consists of an appeal to pity, which is very unusual in the speeches of Lysias.

*For the Soldier* (Or. ix.), 394-387 B.C. ; a defence of
Polyaenus, who is prosecuted for non-payment of a
fine, is of doubtful authenticity, though the arguments
concerning it are not conclusive.

*On the Property of Aristophanes* (Or. xix.), 387 B.C.,
is another case dealing with confiscation. The speech
is very carefully constructed to meet what was evidently
a difficult case.

*Against Evandrus* (Or. xxvi.), 382 B.C.—This is a
considerable fragment of a speech relating to a scrutiny
(δοκιμασία). Leodamas, the first man to be elected
as archon for the year 381 B.C., having been rejected
as unfit, the second choice, Evandrus, becomes archon
if he can pass the scrutiny ; but his enemies refer to
his actions in the time of the oligarchy, and, while
admitting that he has been blameless since the Restoration, refuse him all credit for this. The bitterness

G

and injustice of this speech are unusual in Lysias, but its genuineness is not suspected.

*For Mantitheus* (Or. xvi.),[1] about 392 B.C.; *Against Philo* (Or. xxxi.), 405-395 B.C.; and the wrongly entitled *Defence on a charge of subversion of the democracy* (Or. xxv.), 402-400 B.C., are all concerned with δοκιμασία. There is more bitterness in the κατὰ Φίλωνος than in the speech against Evandrus, but with more justification, for Philo, if the stories told of him are true, must have been a very objectionable scoundrel.

The speech *For the Cripple* (Or. xxiv.), about 400 B.C., is also concerned with a δοκιμασία, though of a different kind. A pension was given by the State to certain persons who could not, on account of bodily infirmity, support themselves, and had no other means of living. The defendant in this case is accused of claiming the pension, whereas he is comparatively well off.[2]

*Against Eratosthenes* (Or. xii.), 403 B.C.—This, the most famous of Lysias' speeches, has been to some extent dealt with already.[3] It is generally classed as a speech in a prosecution for murder, but it seems more probable that it was delivered on the occasion of the εὔθυνα of Eratosthenes; for the amnesty passed after the expulsion of the Thirty specially provided that any of them who chose to give an account of their actions should receive a fair trial.[4] Eratosthenes and Pheidon were the only two who embraced this opportunity.

The latter view finds some support in the fact that only the first part of the speech (§§ 1-37) deals with

---

[1] *Vide supra*, p. 85.  
[2] *Vide supra*, pp. 85-6.  
[3] *Supra*, pp. 76-7.  
[4] Andoc., *de Myst.*, § 90.

the murder of Polemarchus ;  the longer portion
(§§ 37-100) deals more generally with the character
of Eratosthenes and the crimes of the Thirty in general.

*Against Agoratus* (Or. xiii.), 400-398 B.C.—Agoratus,
an informer, is prosecuted for having caused the death
of the speaker's cousin, Dionysodorus.  There is much
historical matter in the speech, but the accuser keeps
definitely to the charge of murder, touching on political
matters only incidentally.

*On the Murder of Eratosthenes* (Or. i.), date uncertain,
is of interest chiefly as illustrating domestic life among
the middle class at Athens.[1]

*Defence against Simon* (Or. iii.), after 394 B.C. ;
and *On wounding with intent* (Or. iv.), date uncertain,
are both speeches in defence on the charge of wounding
with intent to kill ($\tau\rho\alpha\upsilon\mu\alpha\tau\sigma\varsigma$ $\dot{\epsilon}\kappa$ $\pi\rho\sigma\nu\sigma\acute{\iota}\alpha\varsigma$).  The defendant in the latter, wishing to prove that he was
formerly on good terms with the prosecutor, tells an
extraordinary story of corruption.  The prosecutor
was nominated by the defendant as judge at the
Dionysia, on the understanding that, if elected, he
should award the prize to the latter's tribe.  He left
a written note of this agreement ;  but unfortunately
he was not elected, so that the prize went to a chorus
which either sang better or organized its corrupt
practices with more skill.[2]

*For Callias* (Or. v.), date uncertain, is a defence,
apparently, on a charge of sacrilege.  The precise
charge is unknown.

*On the Sacred Olive* (Or. vii.), about 395 B.C., is in
defence of a man charged with uprooting the stump of

------

[1] *Vide supra*, p. 87.                    [2] § 3.

a sacred olive—a sacrilege punishable by banishment and confiscation of property.

*Against Alcibiades, I. and II.* (Or. xiv. and Or. xv.), about 395 B.C.—The first is on a charge of desertion, the second of avoiding military service—two different aspects of the same offence. The defendant, a son of the great Alcibiades, had presumed to serve in the cavalry when he was only entitled to be a hoplite. The young Alcibiades evidently paid for the sins of his father, to whom half of the present indictment is devoted. On this point we may compare the subject-matter of the speech of Isocrates in defence of Alcibiades,[1] and the speech against him which is attributed to Andocides, but is probably a later work.[2]

### Private Speeches

*Against Theomnestus* (Or. x.), 384-383 B.C., is a speech for the prosecution in an action for defamation. The speaker deals at quite disproportionate length with a verbal quibble by which the defendant has tried to escape justice. The argument is ingenious, but owing to the slightness of the subject-matter the speech has no interest except to students of method.[3]

*Against Diogiton* (Or. xxxii.), 400 B.C., is a truly excellent statement of the case against a dishonest guardian. In addition to the skilful handling of financial details, there is much dramatic skill in description and suggestion of character.

*On the Property of Eraton* (Or. xvii.), 397 B.C.—This speech occurred in a διαδικασία between an individual

---

[1] *Vide infra*, p. 150.    [2] *Vide supra*, p. 72.
[3] The second speech with the same title is only an epitome of the first.

and the State.  The speaker asserts a claim to the property of Eraton (which has been confiscated), for the repayment of a debt.

*Against Pancleon* (Or. xxiii.), date uncertain.—Pancleon, accused on some unknown charge, and supposed by the prosecutor to be a *metoecus*, has put in a plea that he is a Plataean citizen and therefore not amenable to the law under which he was indicted. He turns out after all to be a runaway slave.

These last two speeches consist almost entirely of narrative.

### Spurious or Doubtful Speeches

*Against Andocides* (Or. vi.), 399 B.C.—It is generally believed that this speech is not by Lysias, the most serious argument being that the writer of it is a blunderer.  As Jebb points out, he makes at least three damaging admissions calculated seriously to injure his own case.  It may, however, really be a speech delivered against Andocides.  It contains some statements which do not agree with Andocides' own admissions, but, as we have seen, it cannot be proved that Andocides was always veracious.  On the ground of general agreement with Andocides' statements we may believe that it was composed by some contemporary orator, and not, as has been sometimes asserted, by a late Sophist.  It may have been actually delivered at the trial of Andocides in 399 B.C.

*Eroticus.*—Phaedrus, in the dialogue of Plato which bears his name, reads aloud a speech of Lysias which Socrates criticizes.

If Plato could be taken literally, we should believe

that what is read was the authentic work of Lysias ; but Plato is if anything too emphatic in his attempts to produce this illusion, and most readers will probably be left with the impression that Plato is following his usual custom ; he tries to give his myths the solemnity of fact, and what he produces here is an imitation too close to be called a parody. We may compare Plato's reproduction of Aspasia's oration in the *Menexenus*.

The speech *To his Companions* (Or. viii.) cannot reasonably be attributed to Lysias, and indeed is so trivial that it can hardly be the work of any self-respecting forger. It is probably to be regarded as a declamatory exercise.

The speaker complains that his friends have slandered him by asserting that he forced his company on them ; they have sold him an unsound horse, and accused him of inducing others to slander them. He therefore abjures their friendship.

Extracts from six lost speeches are preserved by quotation in various writers :

*Against Cinesias* (Athenaeus, xiii. 551 D) ; *Against Tisis* (Dion., *de Demos.*, ch. xi.) ; *For Pherenicus* (Dion., *de Isaeo*, ch. vi.) ; *Against the Sons of Hippocrates* (*ibid.*) ; *Against Archebiades* (*ibid.*, ch. x.) ; *Against Aeschines* (Athenaeus, xiii., 611 E-612 C).[1]

The fragments of other speeches, in Suidas, Harpocration, and others, are negligible.

---

[1] Cf. *supra*, p. 90.

# CHAPTER V

## ISAEUS

### § 1

DIONYSIUS could find, in the authorities whom he consulted, no definite information about the life of Isaeus. The dates of his birth and death are unknown; we cannot, as Dionysius observes, say what were his political opinions, or even whether he had any at all.[1] We are even in doubt as to his birth-place; some authorities called him an Athenian, others a Chalcidian. The suggestion that he may have been the descendant of an Athenian who settled in Chalcis as a *cleruch* is plausible, but without any authority.[2] The inference, from the fact that he took no part in public life, that he was probably an alien, is not justifiable. The fact that, whether an Athenian or not, he never spoke at any of the great national assemblies, where rhetoricians from all Greek countries gave displays, seems to argue that he had no ambition for personal distinction as an orator, but was content to be a professional writer of speeches.

There is a legend that the young Demosthenes, impressed by the effectiveness of Isaeus' oratory, induced the latter to live in his house and train him thoroughly in all the arts of the forensic speech-writer; it is even said that the earliest speech of

---

[1]. Dion., *de Isaeo*, ch. 1.       [2] Jebb, vol. ii. p. 265.

Demosthenes, against Aphobus, was in reality composed by his master. The authority for these tales is quite insignificant, but the influence of Isaeus on Demosthenes was nevertheless considerable, whether or not they came much into personal contact.

Dionysius records, on the authority of Hermippus, that Isaeus 'was a pupil of Isocrates and a teacher of Demosthenes, and came into close contact with the best of the philosophers.' [1]

There is no evidence that he was ever a companion of Socrates, since his name is not anywhere mentioned by Plato.

His earliest speech (*On the Estate of Dicaeogenes*) is assigned with some probability to the year 390 B.C., and his latest (*On the Estate of Apollodorus*) to 353 B.C.

If the date 390 B.C. is correct, the period of his study under Isocrates may reasonably be placed during the period 393-390 B.C., when that orator was starting his school, and on this assumption we might place the birth of Isaeus approximately at 420 B.C. But the chronology rests entirely on internal evidence which in this case is ambiguous ; a later date for the speech is equally possible, and in that case the earliest speech is that *On the Estate of Aristarchus*, 377-371 B.C. Isaeus, then, need not have been born before 400 B.C. There is more certainty in the dating of the last extant speech about 353 B.C., but we have no means of knowing whether or not the orator lived long after its composition. He may have spent many years in retirement. Isocrates was writing up to the moment of his death, but he had great thoughts to express ; Isaeus, with no interest in politics, may, when he re-

---

[1] *de Isaeo*, ch. i.

tired from the monotonous task of writing speeches for others, have been glad to find no further necessity for composition. However, the approximate dates 420-350 B.C. will give a reasonable duration for such a life.

Isaeus is perhaps the only one of the orators for whom we cannot feel any enthusiasm. If we had, from external sources, the slightest clue to his real feelings, we might be able to collect from his speeches some hints that would help us to form an image of his personality. He is known to us only from speeches which he wrote for others, all of them, with the exception of one fragment, dealing with testamentary cases, which are not the most interesting province of law. He was not personally interested in any of these trials, unless we can believe the more than doubtful assertion of the Greek argument to the fourth oration, that he himself spoke in support of Hagnon and Hagnotheus, being their kinsman.

We may contrast his case with that of Antiphon, who similarly is known to us chiefly from speeches in one department of law—trials for homicide; but in Antiphon's case we are fortunate in having a short but illuminating notice of his life by Thucydides, which forms the outline of the picture; and in addition we have the tetralogies which to some extent help to fill in the details. Of Isaeus as a man we know less, almost, than we do of Homer. We gather only ·an impression of his wonderful efficiency in dealing with subjects of a particular class—his exhaustive knowledge of the intricacies of testamentary law, and his dexterity in applying that knowledge to the best purpose; a kind of efficiency which is admirable, but dull.

Isaeus is our chief authority for the Attic Laws of inheritance.[1] These laws were often arbitrary, and though they were to some extent simplified by the fact that a man who had sons could not legally will his property away from them, the intricacies of tables of consanguinity were so complex that only a specialist could be expected to have a complete mastery of them. There was no class of professional lawyers at Athens; the Attic Laws were very largely framed by amateurs, of which we have evidence in the number of recorded cases in which the proposers of laws were prosecuted for illegality, *i.e.* for enacting laws contrary to laws already established; and as the framing of them was a matter of haphazard improvisation, so their interpretation was often a question of the temper of the jury for the moment. No doubt some record of verdicts was kept, but the Athenians had no great respect for precedent, or at any rate could not make full use of it in the lack of professional judges who should be experts in such matters. Thus there were great opportunities for a man like Isaeus, who combined a minute knowledge of law and procedure with skill in applying his knowledge; who could quote at will either the law or precedent for departing from its letter, and, where the wording of the law left any room for ambiguous interpretation, could twist the meaning to one side or the other to suit his case.

The particular branch of law which Isaeus chose as his special province was important owing to the large number of cases dealing with inheritances which seem to have come before the Athenian Courts, and

---

[1] He is by far the most important; in some cases we can supplement him from Demosthenes, but other authorities are negligible.

these cases were often in themselves important owing to the religious significance of the fact of inheritance. An Athenian desired to leave behind him a male heir not only that his property might remain in the family, but that the family might have a representative who should carry on the private worship of the household gods, and in particular should duly perform the funeral rites of the testator and offer all the proper sacrifices at his grave. Heirship, therefore, carried with it certain definite religious duties, and a man who had no child living usually ensured the continuity of the family worship by adopting a son either in his lifetime or by will.

The skill of Isaeus in dealing with complicated cases is well shown by a consideration of the arguments of any of the remaining speeches ; for instance, Oration v. (*On the Estate of Dicaeogenes*) is concerned with the claims of a certain man's nephew as against his cousin, who inherited a third portion under a will subsequently proved to be false, and eventually succeeded to the whole under a second will which the claimants proved false. Two wills and the results of two previous trials have to be kept in mind, as well as the rather complicated relationship of the parties ; but Isaeus makes the case substantially clear. Again, in Oration xi. (*On the Estate of Hagnias*) twenty-three members of the family are referred to by name, and it is necessary to trace the family's ramifications through a large number of second cousins whose nearness of consanguinity is in some cases affected by the intermarriage of first cousins. The facts of the case are not easy to follow even on paper, and it appears that the judges on this occasion were puzzled into giving a wrong verdict.

The orator's methods may, however, be studied more conveniently in a simpler speech, *On the Estate of Ciron* (Or. viii.). The essential facts of the case are as follows :—Ciron by his first marriage had one daughter, the mother of the two claimants. Ciron married a second wife, the sister of Diocles. The son of Ciron's brother, instigated by Diocles, made a counter-claim on the grounds that (1) Ciron's daughter was illegitimate and consequently her sons were illegitimate ; (2) a brother's son in any case has a better claim than a daughter's son. The speaker, the elder of the claimants, first establishes his mother's legitimacy, proving that Ciron always treated her as his daughter and twice gave her a dowry, and regarded her sons as his natural heirs.

' Our grandfather Ciron died, not without issue, but leaving as issue my brother and myself, the sons of his legitimate daughter ; but the plaintiffs claim the inheritance on the assumption that they are the next of kin, and insult us by the insinuation that we are not sons of Ciron's daughter, and that he never had a daughter at all. This is due to the claimants' covetousness and the great amount of Ciron's estate, which they have seized, and now control. They have the impudence to say that he left nothing, and in the same breath to lay a claim to the inheritance.

' Now your judgment ought not, in my opinion, to have reference to the man who has urged the claim, but to Diocles of Phlya, known as Orestes, who has incited him to annoy us, endeavouring to withhold the property which Ciron left at his death, and to endanger our interests, so that he may not have to part with any of it, if you are misled by the assertions of the claimant. Since they are working for these ends it is right that you should be informed of all the facts, in order that no detail may escape you, and that you may have a full knowledge of all that has occurred, before you give your verdict. So I ask you to consult the interests of justice by giving to this case as serious consideration as you have given to any other case before. This is only just. Recall the numerous cases that have come before you, and you will find that no plaintiffs have ever made a more shameless or barefaced claim to property that does not belong to them than these two.

' Now it is a hard task, Gentlemen, for one entirely inexperienced in the procedure of the courts to hold his own in a trial for such an important issue against concerted speeches and witnesses who give false evidence ; but I have a confident hope that I shall obtain justice from you, and that my own speech will be satisfactory to the point, at least, of stating a just cause, unless I am thwarted by some obstacle of the kind which I apprehend. I therefore urge you, Gentlemen, to give me a courteous hearing, and if you consider that I have been wronged, to support the justice of my claim.

' First, I shall convince you that my mother was the legitimate daughter of Ciron. For events long past I shall rely on reported statements and evidence, for those within our memory I shall adduce witnesses who know the facts, as well as proofs which are stronger than depositions; and when I have laid this all before you I shall prove that I have a better right than the claimant to inherit the estate of Ciron.

' I shall start from the point at which my opponents began, and from thence onwards instruct you in the facts.

' My grandfather Ciron, Gentlemen, married my grandmother, who was his own first cousin, being the daughter of a sister of his own mother. After the marriage she in due course gave birth to my mother, and four years later she died.

' My grandfather, having only this one daughter, married his second wife, the sister of Diocles, who bore him two sons. He brought up my mother in the house with his wife and children, and during the lifetime of the latter, when his daughter was of marriageable age, he bestowed her on Nausimenes of Cholarge, giving her a dowry of clothing and gold ornaments, as well as twenty-five minae. Three or four years after this, Nausimenes fell ill and died, before my mother had borne him any children. My grandfather took her back to his house, but owing to the disorder of her husband's affairs he did not recover all the dowry he had given with her ; he then married her a second time to my father, with a dowry of 1000 drachmae.

'In face of the charges now brought by the plaintiffs, how can my statements be proved ? I sought and found the way.

'Ciron's domestic slaves, male and female, must know whether my mother was or was not his daughter ; whether she lived in his house ; whether he did or did not on two occasions give feasts in honour of her marriage ; what dowry each of her husbands received. Wishing to examine them under torture by way of supporting the evidence already in my hands, in order that you might put more confidence in their evidence when they had submitted to the examination than you would if they were only apprehending it, I requested the plaintiffs to surrender their slaves of both sexes to be examined on the above points and all others of which they have knowledge. But this man, who will shortly request you to believe his own witnesses, shrank from submitting to such an examination. But if I can prove that he refused, how can we avoid the presumption that his witnesses are now giving false evidence since he has shrunk from a test so searching ?

'To prove the truth of my assertion, take first this deposition and read it.[1]

*[The deposition.]*

'Now you hold the opinion, both personally and officially, that torture is the surest test ; and whenever slaves and

----

[1] §§ 1-11.

freemen come forward as witnesses and you have to arrive
at facts, you do not rely on the evidence of the freemen,
but torture the slaves and seek thus to discover the truth.
You are right in your preference; for you know that
whereas some witnesses have been suspected of giving
false evidence, no slaves have ever been proved to have
made untrue statements in consequence of the torture to
which they were submitted.[1]

' Who may be expected to know the early facts?  Obviously those who were acquainted with my grandfather,
and they have told us what they heard.  Who must know
about my mother's marriage?  The parties to the marriage
contracts, and their witnesses.  On this point the relations
of Nausimenes and of my father have given evidence.
And who knew that my mother was brought up in Ciron's
house, and was his legitimate daughter?  The present
claimants give clear evidence that this is true, by their
action in refusing the torture.  Surely, then, it would not
be reasonable for you to discredit my witnesses, while you
can hardly fail to disbelieve those of the other side.

' Besides these, we can bring other proofs by which you
shall know that we are sons of Ciron's daughter.  He
treated us as he naturally would treat his daughter's sons;
he never conducted a sacrifice without our presence, but
whether the sacrifice were small or great, we were always
there and joined in it.  Not only were we summoned for
such occasions, but he always used to take us to the rural
Dionysia, and we used to see the show with him, sitting
by his side; and we came to his house to keep every feast-
day.  And when he sacrificed to Zeus Ktesios, a sacrifice
to which he attached the utmost importance, never allowing slaves or even freemen, outside the family, to participate,
but doing everything by himself, we used to share in the
sacrifice; we helped him to handle the offerings, we helped

---

[1] § 12.  I have translated this section, though not relevant to the
matter under discussion, because it gives a good indication of
Athenian feeling on the subject of the torture of slaves.

him to place them on the altar, we helped him in everything, and, as our grandfather, he would pray the God
to give us health and wealth. But if he had not considered
us as his daughter's sons, and seen in us the only descendants left to him, he would never have done anything of the
kind, but would have kept by his side this man who now
claims to be his nephew. The truth of this is known best
of all by my grandfather's servants, whom the plaintiff
refused to surrender to torture ; but it is known accurately
enough by some of my grandfather's friends, whose evidence
I shall produce ' (§§ 14-17).

The speaker continues that he and his brother were
enrolled by Ciron in the *phratria*, and were allowed
to conduct the funeral by Diocles, who thus tacitly
admitted their claim.

He next proves by legal argument that direct descendants have a better claim than collateral relations.
By way of epilogue he gives an account of the property
and the machinations of Diocles, whose personal character he attacks, and at the end produces evidence that
Diocles has been proved guilty of adultery.

## § 2. *Literary Characteristics*

Isaeus studied under Isocrates, and it is therefore
reasonable to follow the chronological order and take
the master first ; but as the master survived the
pupil by several years, and was actively engaged in
literature down to the day of his death, ordinary
considerations of seniority do not apply in this case.
It is more satisfactory to study Isaeus in relation,
not to Isocrates, but to the earlier speech-writers,
Antiphon and Lysias. He is more closely connected
with them in his subject-matter, since he is, like them,

essentially a practical writer, and his businesslike style has more affinity to the terse condensation of Lysias than to the florid 'epideictic' diction of the author of the *Panegyric*.

In language there is not very much difference between Lysias and Isaeus; both use the current vocabulary, making a literary medium out of the popular speech of their day. A search through the latter's speeches re-discovers a certain number of words which, so far as our knowledge goes, have a poetical tinge; but practically all these may be found in other orators and prose-writers.[1]

Again, there are a few noteworthy metaphors, such as ἐκκόπτειν, to 'knock out' or 'knock on the head' —this is used again by Dinarchus—and καθιπποτροφεῖν, ' to race away one's money,' *i.e.* squander it on a stable. We know little of the idioms of the language spoken in the streets of Athens in the fourth century, but we do know that popular speech has always a tendency to the employment of rough metaphors, and where we come into contact with the spoken word we expect to find expressions of this kind.[2] A study of the private letters contained among the Oxyrhynchus Papyri will give many examples to the point.[3] Lastly, a few words recall the language of comedy.[4]

We may readily believe that, in admitting these few blemishes to the purity of his Atticism, the orator

---

[1] Jebb, *Attic Orators*, vol. ii. p. 277[3].
[2] Cleisthenes (*Herod.*, vi. 129), in a moment of extreme excitement, remarked to Hippoclides ἀπωρχήσαο τὸν γάμον—' You have danced away your chances of marriage.'
[3] Cf., too, the use of ὑπωπιάζω in the New Testament.
[4] *E.g.* γρῦξαι.

H

was indulging in a realism of which we find very few traces, as a rule, in literary prose.[1]

His grammar, according to strict Attic rule, is occasionally at fault,[2] and the MSS. exhibit a certain number of word-forms which are supposed to be un-Attic.[3]

Whether we should emend these passages to suit the supposed standard, or make the standard more liberal to admit such passages, is a matter for controversy. The MSS. of Thucydides exhibit a wealth of ingenious perversity in the way of grammar, and in that case, though many critics have spent their ingenuity on reducing the text to order and decency, an opposite school of criticism maintains that the historian may have chosen to write as he liked. The greatest artists are above the laws of their art, and Isaeus may have condescended to a level which he knew not to be the highest.

With regard, then, to the purity of language, Isaeus, though surpassed by Lysias and Isocrates, is not far behind them. He is on a level with Lysias also in clearness and accuracy of thought, and in what Dionysius calls ἐνάργεια, vividness of presentation. But in the structure of sentences some differences between these two must be noted. Lysias, as has already been stated, varied his structure considerably according to the subjects of his speeches, the succession of periods being broken by the introduction of

---

[1] It has been already remarked that the speech-writers are, as a rule, ridiculously unsuccessful in their attempt to make their clients speak in the way that is natural to them (*vide supra*, p. 37).

[2] *E.g.* Or. v. 23, ἡγούμενοι οὐκ ἂν αὐτὸν βεβαιώσειν, κ.τ.λ. Or. v. 31, ὡμολογήσαμεν ἐμμενεῖν οἷς ἂν γνοῖεν. Or. v. 43, δαπανηθείς (in middle sense).

[3] *E.g.* καθιστάνειν, ψηφίσεσθε, ἄξαντες.

a freer style; but at the same time he had a love of antithesis to which sacrifices had sometimes to be made.

Isaeus is free from this straining after antithesis, and is hardly bound at all by scholastic rules. We cannot truly say that his style is non-periodic, for formal periods are to be met with; but a marked characteristic of his style is his skill in the use of short sentences, often abrupt, nearly always vigorous. In argumentative passages especially, he uses the form of imaginary question and answer; in narrative he sometimes gives us a series of short sentences, connected in thought, but not formally bound together. He has the appearance of composing negligently, but from his effectiveness we conclude that the negligence was studied. The following passages illustrate these styles:

' Eupolis, Thrasyllus, and Mneson were brothers from the same two parents. Their father left them a considerable property, so that they were eligible for the performance of public services. This the three divided amongst them. Of these brothers, two died about the same time,' etc.[1]

The speech about Ciron's inheritance contains the best example of argument by question and answer:

' On what ground should a statement be believed? Should we not say, on the ground of the evidence? I fancy so. And on what ground should we believe witnesses? From the fact that they have been tortured? Naturally. And on what grounds should we disbelieve the statements of the plaintiffs? Because they shrink from this test? Most certainly.'[2]

[1] *The Estate of Apollodorus* (Or. vii.), § 5.
[2] *Ciron* (Or. viii.), § 28.

A third quotation gives a good example of the purely ornamental use of the rhetorical question ; it is precious as showing us that Isaeus was on occasion capable of applying a lighter touch.  He is so coldly logical as a rule that we turn with relief to any exhibition of ordinary feeling :

' Who was there who omitted to cut his hair short when the two talents arrived ?  Who was there who failed to wear black, hoping that his mourning would give him a claim to the inheritance ?   Or how many relatives and sons laid claim, by deed of gift, to the estate of Nicostratus ?  Demosthenes said he was his nephew, but when the present claimants disproved his statement, he retired.  Telephus said that Nicostratus had given him all his property.  He too soon ceased to be a claimant.  Ameiniades came before the archon and produced a son for Nicostratus—a child less than three years old, though Nicostratus had not been in Athens for eleven years past.  Pyrrhus of Lamptra said that the money had been dedicated by Nicostratus to Athena, but given by Nicostratus to himself.  Ctesias of Besaea and Cranaus first said that judgment had been given in their favour against Nicostratus for a talent, and when they could not prove it, asserted that he was their freedman.  They, like the rest, failed to establish their statement.

' These were the parties who in the first instance pounced at once upon the property of Nicostratus.  Chariades made no claim at the time.' [1]

Dionysius, a very keen critic on the literary side, misses in Isaeus the grace and charm of Lysias, but allows him more cleverness. [2]

This ' charm,' by which Dionysius could distinguish a genuine speech of Lysias, is incapable of definition and too elusive for our blunter wits to apprehend ;

---

[1] *Nicostratus* (Or. iv.), §§ 7-10.        [2] *de Isaeo*, ch. 3.

but we can form a general impression that the diction of Lysias has something in it more pleasing than that of Isaeus. Perhaps there is something in the illustration which the ancient critic applies, when he compares the speeches of the former to a clearly drawn picture of simple colour and design ; those of the latter to a more elaborate and ingenious composition, where there is more play of light and shade and the depth and brilliance of the colouring in some cases obscures the lines—with a suggestion that the drawing may be faulty.[1] This simile, however, applies more truly to the structure of the speeches than to the diction. Dionysius recurs to the style,[2] and quotes parallel extracts from the introductions to speeches by the two writers to demonstrate the simplicity of Lysias and the artificiality of Isaeus. The demonstration is not overpowering. The first specimen from Lysias is indeed simple and clear, but the extract from Isaeus, though the language is a little more elaborate, seems equally suitable for its purpose.

Lysias wrote as follows :

' I feel, Gentlemen, that I must tell you about my friendship with Pherenicus, so that none of you may be surprised that I, who have never before pleaded for any one else, am now pleading for him. I had a friend in his father Cephisodotus, and when our party was exiled to Thebes I stayed with him, as did any other Athenian who wished to.

' He did us many kind services, both officially and privately, before we were restored to our homes. So when his family met with the same misfortune, and came in exile to Athens, I felt that I owed them the greatest possible gratitude, and received them in such intimate fashion that nobody who came to the house, and did not know could tell which of

---

[1] *de Isaeo*, ch. 4.     [2] *Ibid.*, ch. 5.

us was the owner of it.   Now Pherenicus knows that there
are many who are cleverer speakers than I, and have more
experience of such business ; but he thinks that he can
rely absolutely on my friendship.   So I should think it
disgraceful, when he asks me and urges me to support his
claims, to allow him to lose Androclides' gift, if I can do
anything to prevent it.'[1]

The following is the parallel extract from Isaeus :

'Before now I have been of service to Eumathes, as
indeed he has deserved ; and now, so far as in me lies, I
shall try to help you to save him.   Now listen to me for
a short time, lest any of you suppose that I through recklessness or any other unjust motive have approached the
case of Eumathes.

'When I was a trierarch in the archonship of Cephisodorus, and a report was carried to my relatives that I had
been killed in the sea-fight, whereas I had some moneys
deposited with Eumathes, Eumathes sent for my relative
and friends, and declared the amount of the money which
was in his hands, and justly and honestly made payment
in full.

'In consequence of this I, when I got home in safety,
treated him as a still closer friend, and when he was starting
business as a banker I provided him with money.   After
this, when Dionysius claimed him as a slave, I vindicated
his liberty, knowing that he had been manumitted by
Epigenes before the court.   But I shall say no more on
this subject.'[2]

Dionysius thus criticizes them :

'What is the difference between these proëmia ?   In
Lysias the introduction of the subject is pleasing for this
one reason, that it is stated naturally and simply.

'"I feel, Gentlemen, that I must begin by telling you
about my friendship with Pherenicus"'—

---

[1] Lysias, fr. 46.          [2] Isaeus, fr. 15.

What follows has no appearance of premeditation, but is put just as an amateur might express it :

'" so that none of you may be surprised that I, who have never before pleaded for any one else, am now pleading for him." But in Isaeus what seems so simple is really premeditated, and we see at once that it is rhetorical: " Before now I have been of service to Eumathes, as indeed he has deserved ; and now, so far as in me lies, I shall try to help you in saving him." This is more exalted and less simple than the other ; still more is this true of the next sentence : " Now listen to me for a short time, lest any of you suppose that I through recklessness or any other unjust motive have approached the case of Eumathes." '

Dionysius finds that the expressions here used, προπέτεια, ἀδικία, πρὸς τὰ Εὐμαθοῦς πράγματα προσῆλθον, sound to him artificial rather than spontaneous. In this he may be right; but we feel him to be hypercritical when he blames the next sentence for lack of simplicity, and tries, by a few verbal alterations, to show how it might have been improved. He would re-write the sentence thus :— ' When I was trierarch, and it was reported at home that I had been killed, Eumathes, having some money of mine on deposit,' etc. Here he has certainly succeeded in omitting once the name Eumathes, which occurs twice in Isaeus ; but the other changes consist purely in the substitution of two temporal clauses introduced by ὅτε (when) for two participial clauses in the genitive absolute—a construction which is, surely, common enough in all Greek writers to escape the censure of being ' rhetorical.'

## § 3. *Structure of Speeches*

The exceptional power of Isaeus does not, then, depend upon any charm of language or any oratorical gift; it lies in his exhaustive legal knowledge and his remarkable skill in argument. He has an almost unique gift for circumstantial statement and proof of the facts bearing on his case. This is the cleverness (δεινότης) to which Dionysius so often refers with grudging admiration.

His speeches are not arranged according to a single plan, but, on the contrary, exhibit great variety of structure. Lysias keeps practically to one form— exordium, narrative, proof, epilogue. Isaeus, when the narrative is too long or complicated to be grasped all at once, does not set it out as a whole, but breaks it up into sections, each of which is accompanied by its evidence and argument.[1] ' The orator is afraid,' thinks Dionysius, ' that the argument may be hard to follow, on account of the number of its sections, and that the proofs of the various points, if all collected together, being so numerous as they must be, dealing with matters so numerous, may be detrimental to clearness.' The critic is referring particularly to the speech *For Euphiletus* (Or. xii.), a large fragment of which his quotations have preserved for us; but an analysis of any of the extant speeches will show that they are constructed skilfully on varying plans, un- hampered by technical rule, with an art that adapts its material according to the requirements of the case. This skill, which aims at success rather than literary finish, shows that Isaeus was above all a competent

[1] Cf. *de Isaeo*, ch. 14.

tactician—such a master of argument that, 'whereas we should be ready to believe Lysias even when he tells a lie, we can hardly regard Isaeus without suspicion even when he tells the truth.' [1]

Dionysius is no doubt led rather far away by his desire for a contrast ; he has given Isaeus a bad name and is seeking means to justify his condemnation of the man who ' takes a mean advantage of his adversary and outmanœuvres the judges.' [2]

This Greek of a late Hellenistic age thoroughly grasped the Athenian spirit, which demanded artistic composition and was yet suspicious of any man who was too obviously clever, a spirit against which we find Antiphon, the earliest of the orators, contending, when he makes his characters protest their own inexperience and insinuate that their opponents seem strong only because they have that same discreditable skill to make the worse cause appear the better.[3]

Isaeus sometimes reiterates his arguments ; he will even quote the same document twice. This is inartistic, but it pays. A notable advance on his predecessors is found in the form of some of his epilogues. The earlier orators were generally content, after stating the case, to finish with a general appeal to justice or pity. Isaeus on occasion makes a more practical use of his closing periods ; he recapitulates the case, pointing out that he has proved what he set out to prove ;[4] or gives a short summary of the narrative which he regards as now established, or of the claims urged by himself and his opponent. In one speech [5] he has actually reached the end and

<hr>

[1] *de Isaeo*, ch. 16.    [2] *Ibid.*, ch. 3.    [3] Cf. *supra*, p. 38.
[4] *E.g.* Orr. 2, 3, 7, 8, 9.    [5] Or. 8 (*Ciron*), § 46.

summarized his results, when the very last words surprise us by an unexpected attack on his adversary's character :

'I do not know that there is any need for me to say more, for I think there is no point on which you have not full knowledge ; but I will ask the clerk to take the last remaining deposition, showing how the claimant was convicted of adultery, and read it to the court.'

Some of the earlier speech-writers made an attempt at character-drawing, and tried to suit their speeches to the character ($\mathring{\eta}\theta os$) of their clients. In Isaeus this illusion is not maintained ; his style varies somewhat according to the subject, but every speech bears, as Dionysius observes, the stamp of the professional writer, which must have betrayed it to the acute perceptions of an Athenian jury.[1] Probably the accumulated experience of the orators had proved that such attempts at deception were on the whole useless ; for a certain class of client it would be necessary either to write a bad speech or let it be evident that the speaker was only a mouthpiece for an advocate cleverer than himself, and as success in the case was of more importance than artistic illusion, the proper choice was obvious. The *ethos* in Isaeus consists not in making the characters speak as they naturally would have spoken, but in putting their arguments for them in the way most likely to appeal to the reason and the feelings of the judges. Experience had further shown that though, from the lips of a real orator, appeals to sentiment and passion may have a great effect, such appeals by themselves, unsupported by

---

[1] *de Isaeo*, ch. 16.

argument, or made at an inauspicious moment, may do more harm than good. An appeal to the reason is always stronger, provided only that the speaker must avoid giving offence by a too presumptuous bearing.

When the court is already convinced by an argued demonstration of the justice of the case, an appeal to pity or indignation may be overpowering; without such preparation it is nothing but a last resort of weakness.

Isaeus, though he uses such appeals, as indeed he wields every weapon of the orator's armoury, uses them with moderation and discernment, showing in this, as in all his tactics, a sound knowledge of practical utility.

## § 4. *Speeches*

The 'Life' by the Pseudo-Plutarch tells us that sixty-four speeches were attributed to Isaeus, of which fifty were considered genuine. He also composed an *Art of Rhetoric*. We now possess eleven and a considerable fragment of a twelfth, and know the titles of forty-two others. The eleven speeches which are extant all deal directly or indirectly with inheritances. Six of these are connected with διαδικάσιαι—trials to decide who is the righteous claimant—and their titles are as follows :—*On the Estate of Cleonymus* (Or. i.), date 360-353 B.C. ; *On the Estate of Nicostratus* (Or. iv.), the date is uncertain—the author of the 'argument' asserts, with no plausibility, that Isaeus delivered the speech in his own person ; *On the Estate of Apollodorus* (Or. vii.), about 353 B.C. ; *On the Estate of Ciron* (Or. viii.) (*see above*, pp. 108-10), date uncertain, perhaps *circa* 375 B.C. ; *On the Estate of Astyphilus* (Or. ix.), date perhaps about 369 B.C. ; *On the Estate of Aristarchus*, date probably between 377 and 371 B.C.

Three speeches deal with prosecutions for false witness in connection with testamentary cases, viz. *On the Estate of Menecles* (Or. ii.), date about 354 B.C. ; *On the Estate of Pyrrhus* (Or. iii.), of uncertain date ; *On the Estate of Philoctemon* (Or. vi.),—the date of this speech can be fixed with certainty at 364-363 B.C., as we learn from § 14 that it is now fifty-two years since the Athenian expedition sailed to Sicily.

Oration v., *On the Estate of Dicaeogenes*, is in an ἐγγύης δίκη, an action to compel Leochares, who was surety for Dicaeogenes in an agreement connected with the will of the latter's cousin, also named Dicaeogenes, to carry out the contract, since Dicaeogenes, the principal, is a defaulter. The date can only be fixed by the references to the death of the testator, who was killed in battle at Cnidos. There are two engagements which might be referred to, the first in 412 B.C., the second in 394 B.C. Twenty-two years have elapsed between that event and the present trial, so the date is either 390 B.C.—many years earlier than that of any other speech of Isaeus—or 372 B.C.

*On the Estate of Hagnias* (Or. xi.) is in a prosecution of a guardian for ill-treatment of his ward under a will.

*For Euphiletus* (Or. xii.), a considerable fragment preserved by Dionysius, is the only specimen that we possess of a speech not connected with a will-case. It refers to an appeal by Euphiletus to a law-court against the decision of his fellow demes-men, who have struck him off the roll.

The remaining fragments are hardly important

except in so far as they provide us with the names of several lost speeches.   One of them (frag. 23) contains several sentences repeated verbally from Or. viii. (*Ciron*), § 28.

The fragment of the speech *For Eumathes*, preserved by Dionysius, has been referred to above (p. 118).

# CHAPTER VI

## ISOCRATES

### § 1. *Life*

ISOCRATES was born in 436 B.C., and lived to
the remarkable age of ninety-seven in full possession of his faculties. His childhood and youth were
passed amid the horrors of the Peloponnesian War;
he was already of age when the failure of the Sicilian
expedition turned the scale against Athens. In
mature manhood he saw the ruin of his city by the
capitulation to Lysander. He lived through the
Spartan supremacy, saw the foundation of the new
Athenian League in 378 B.C., and the rise and fall of
the power of Thebes. At the time when Philip obtained
the throne of Macedon he was already, by ordinary
reckoning, an old man, but the laws of mortality were
suspended in the case of this Athenian Nestor. Some
of his most important works were composed after his
eightieth year; the *Philippus*, which he wrote at the
age of ninety, shows no diminution of his powers;
he produced one of his longest works, the *Panathenaicus*,
in his ninety-seventh year, and lived to congratulate
Philip on his victory at Chaeronea in 338 B.C.

In a life of such extent and such remarkable variety
of experience we should expect to find many changes
of outlook and modifications, from time to time, of
earlier views. But Isocrates was a man of singularly

fixed ideas. With regard to education, he formulated in the discourse against the Sophists (391 B.C.) views which are practically identical with what he expressed nearly forty years later in the *Antidosis*, views which he maintains in his last work of all, the *Panathenaicus* (339 B.C.). With regard to Greek politics, he held till the close of his life the opinions propounded in the *Panegyricus* of 380 B.C. His aims were unchanged, though of necessity he modified the means by which he hoped to carry them out.

We have little information about the orator's early life. He tells us himself that his patrimony was dissipated by the Peloponnesian War,[1] so that he was forced to adopt a profession to make a living.

The story contained in the 'Life,' that he endeavoured to save Theramenes when condemned by the Thirty, has no other authority but the Pseudo-Plutarch. It appears from Plato's *Phaedrus*[2] that he was intimate with Socrates, that Socrates had a high opinion of him, and considered that the young man might distinguish himself either in oratory or in philosophy. Tradition names the Sophists Prodicus, Protagoras, and Gorgias among his early teachers. He is believed to have visited Gorgias in Thessaly.

Plutarch asserts that Isocrates at one time opened a school of rhetoric, with nine pupils, in Chios; and that while there he interfered in politics and helped to institute a democracy.[3] The story may be accepted with reservations. Isocrates himself never refers to

[1] *Antid.*, § 161.
[2] *Phaedr.*, pp. 278-9.
[3] καὶ ἀρχὰς δὲ [και] (τὰς?) περὶ τὴν Χίον κατέστησε καὶ τὴν αὐτὴν τῇ πατρίδι πολίτειαν. Ps.-Plut., 837 B.

it, and in *Ep.* vi. § 2 (to the children of Jason) excuses himself from visiting Thessaly on the ground that people would comment unfavourably on a man who had ' kept quiet ' all his life if he began travelling in his old age.[1] Jebb assumes a short stay in Chios in 404-403 B.C.

Between 403 and 393 B.C. Isocrates composed a certain number of speeches for the law-courts, in which, however, he never appeared as a pleader, for natural disabilities—lack of voice and nervousness, to which he refers with regret—made him unfitted for such work.

About 392 B.C. he opened a school at Athens, and in 391 B.C. published, in the discourse *Against the Sophists*, his views on education. His pupils were mostly Athenians, many of them afterwards being men of distinction.[2]

It was probably between 378 and 376 B.C. that Isocrates went on several voyages with Conon's son, Timotheus, who was engaged in organizing the new maritime league. From this time down to 351 B.C. he had many distinguished pupils from far countries— Sicily and Pontus as well as all parts of Greece—and amassed, as he tells us, a reasonable competence, though not a large fortune.

In the year 351 B.C., when a great contest of eloquence was held by Artemisia, widow of Mausolus of Caria, in honour of her husband, it is reported that all the competitors were pupils of Isocrates.

In the last period of his life, 351-338 B.C., Isocrates

---

[1] However, if we pressed this passage, we must regard the journey with Timotheus as unhistorical. All the evidence is to be found in Blass, *Att. Ber.*, vol. ii. pp. 16-17.

[2] *Antid.*, §§ 159 *sqq.*

still continued to teach, and was also busily occupied in writing. He published the *Philippus*, which is one of his most important works, and one of the greatest in historical interest, in 346 B.C. ; in 342 B.C. he began the lengthy *Panathenaicus*, which he had half finished when he was attacked by an illness, which made the work drag on for three years. It was finished in 339 B.C. In the following year, a few days after the battle of Chaeronea, he died. A report was current in antiquity that he committed suicide, by starving himself, in consequence of the news of this downfall of Greek liberty ; the story is quite incredible when we consider that the result of the battle gave a possibility of the fulfilment of the hopes which Isocrates had been cherishing for half his life, the end to which he had been labouring for over forty years—the concentration of all power into the hands of one man, who might redeem Greece by giving her union and leading her to conquest in the East.

His last letter, in fact, written after the battle of Chaeronea, congratulates Philip on his victory; and even if this letter is spurious, the probability, to judge from the tone of his earlier works, is that he would have hailed the Macedonian success as a victory for his imperial ideas.

## § 2. *Style*

Though Isocrates composed, in his youth, a few forensic speeches, it is not by such compositions that he must be judged ; indeed he himself, far from claiming credit for his activity in that direction, in later life adopted an apologetic tone when speaking of his earlier work. As a teacher of rhetoric he won great

I

renown, numbering, as he boasts, even kings among his pupils ; and he had a complete mastery of all the technique of the rhetorical art.

He was also a master of style, having theories of composition which he exemplified in practice with such skill that he must occupy a prominent place in any treatise on the development of Greek prose.

But his highest claim to consideration is as a political thinker. His bold and startling theories of Greek politics were expressed indeed in finished prose, and in rhetorical shape ; but the artistic form is only an added ornament ; if Isocrates had written in the baldest style he must have made a name by his treatises on political science, and by the fact that he took a broader and more liberal view of Hellenism than any Athenian before or after. Thus he, who perhaps never delivered a public speech, is of more importance than any of the other orators ; and though no politician in the narrow sense, he exerted a wider influence than any, not excepting Demosthenes, who devoted their lives to political activity, for he originated and promulgated ideas which completely changed the course of Greek civilization. It was probably he who was the first to instigate Philip to attempt the conquest of Asia, as he had before urged Dionysius and others to make the attempt—all for the sake of the union of Greek States and the spread of Hellenism ; certainly he encouraged the Macedonian in his project, and perhaps it may be said to be due to him that on Philip's death Alexander found the way prepared.

Isocrates could not fully foresee the results of Alexander's conquests ; Alexander himself modified and expanded his ambitions as he advanced ; but

undoubtedly Isocrates urged the general desirability
of the undertaking and saw clearly, up to a certain
point, the lines on which it ought to be carried out.
The petty law-suits which occupied Lysias and Andocides seem trivial and unimportant, even the patriotic
utterances of Demosthenes seem of secondary weight,
compared with these literary harangues of Isocrates,
in cases where civilization and barbarism, unity and
discord, are the litigants, and the court is the world.

Isocrates is named by Dionysius as an example of
the smooth (or florid) style of composition, which
resembles closely woven stuffs, or pictures in which
the lights melt insensibly into the shadows.[1]

It is clear that to aim consciously at producing such
effects as these is to exalt mere expression to supreme
heights, and to risk the loss of clearness and emphasis.
We may gather the opinions of Isocrates on the
structure of prose partly from his own statements,
partly from the criticisms of Dionysius, and partly
from a study of his compositions. The subject has
been very fully and carefully dealt with by Blass, and
in the present work only a summary of the chief
results can be attempted.

The most noticeable feature of the style is the care
taken to avoid hiatus. This is particularly remarked
by Dionysius, who, after quoting from the *Areopagiticus*
a long passage which he particularly admires, notes,
' You cannot find any dissonance of vowels, at any
rate in the passage which I have quoted, nor any,
I think, in the whole speech, unless some instance
has escaped my observation.'[2]

---

[1] *de Comp. Verb.*, ch. xxiii.
[2] *de Comp. Verb.*, ch. xxiii. He quotes *Areop.*, §§ 1-5.

We should expect to find that, to produce this effect, it was necessary to depart frequently from natural forms of expression, either by changing the usual order, or by inserting unnecessary words. It is probable that Isocrates resorted to both these devices; but such is the skill with which he handles his materials that careful reading is necessary to detect the distortions.[1]

Dionysius further notes that dissonance or clashing of consonants is rare, and herein Isocrates seems to have been at pains to follow the rules of euphony laid down in his own Τέχνη. In a fragment preserved by Hermogenes he tells his readers to avoid the repetition of the same syllable in consecutive words—as ἡλικὰ καλά, ἔνθα Θαλῆς.[2] The ingenuity of Blass has discovered passages in which the natural form of a phrase has been altered to avoid such juxtaposition of similar syllables.[3] Certain combinations of consonants, too, are hard to pronounce, and must therefore be avoided. There is, in truth, much justice in the remark of Dionysius that in reading Isocrates it is not the separate words but the sentence as a whole that we must take into account.

The third characteristic of Isocrates' style is his attention to rhythm.

The extravagance of Gorgias had hindered the development of the language by introducing into prose the rhythms and language of poetry; Thrasymachus,

---

[1] Isocrates allows elisions of certain short vowels, but he is more sparing than most poets in the use of it. In the epideictic speeches the commonest elision is of enclitics or semi-enclitics (τε, δέ, etc.) and of personal pronouns. Crasis, except of καὶ ἄν, is rare. In the forensic speeches (his early work) elision is much less restricted.

[2] Maxim. Planud. *ad Hermog.*, v. 469.     [3] Vol. ii. p. 144.

as we know from Aristotle's *Rhetoric*, had studied the effect of the foot ' *paeonius* ' (— $\cup\cup\cup$ or $\cup\cup\cup$ —) at the beginning and end of periods.[1] Isocrates, while deprecating the use of poetical metres in any strict sense, asserted that oratorical prose should have rhythms of its own, and favoured combinations of the trochee and the iambus. In this he differed from Aristotle, who disapproved of the iambic rhythm as being too similar to the natural course of ordinary speech, and of the trochaic, as being too light and tripping—in contrast to the hexameter, which he classed as too solemn for spoken language.[2]

The periods of Isocrates are remarkable for their elaboration. The analyses of Blass show us a complication of structure in some of the longer sentences which may almost be compared to that of a Pindaric ode. Never, perhaps, has there been a writer who attained such luxuriant complexity in his composition of sentences. But Isocrates is too much the slave of his own virtues ; his periods are so long, so complete, so uniformly artistic, that their everlasting procession is monotonous. Lysias, less perfect in form, has in consequence more variety ; Demosthenes, who could compose long periods, did not confine himself to them, but enlivened his style by contrast.

The structure of the period lends itself naturally to antithetical forms of expression. We observed in Antiphon the frequency of verbal antitheses of various kinds—the λόγῳ and ἔργῳ, the μὲν and δέ, and others. Isocrates, having before him the examples of his predecessors and the precepts of rhetoricians, and having theories of his own on sentence-construc-

---

[1] *Rhet.*, Book III. 8. 4.    [2] *Ibid.*

tion, developed very fully a scheme of parallelism in word, sense, and sound.

Thus a period will consist, as we have seen, of a succession of κῶλα or limbs, each one corresponding to another in size, and pairs of corresponding κῶλα will contain pairs of words parallel in sense, form or sound. So the whole period is bound closely together.

### *Vocabulary. Schemata*

His vocabulary avoids excess ; he is, in the judgment of Dionysius, the purest of Atticists, with the exception of Lysias. But if we compare the two we find much more tendency to fine writing in Isocrates. Using ordinary words he can produce notable effects, and he is always consciously striving after a certain pomposity of diction. This is most noticeable in the exhibition-writings, such as the *Helen* and *Busiris*, where grandiloquent compound words are not infrequent, and metaphors are commoner and more striking than in the speeches on real subjects.

One of his affectations, copied by nearly all subsequent orators, is the unnecessary piling up of words almost synonymous to express one idea.[1] On the other hand we sometimes find synonyms apparently contrasted in different parts of the sentence ; such contrast is only verbal, and is made for the purpose of rounding the period ; in either case we must note that the writer departs from simplicity in order to improve the sound of his words, but does not add much to the sense.[2]

---

[1] θαυμάζειν καὶ ζηλοῦν, ἐπαινεῖν καὶ τιμᾶν, etc.

[2] *E.g. Paneg.*, § 5, ὅταν ἢ τὰ πράγματα λάβῃ τέλος . . . ἢ τὸν λόγον ἴδῃ τις ἔχοντα πέρας, where τέλος and πέρας, two words for end or

Another characteristic is the use of the plural of abstract nouns, in much the same sense as the singular.[1] All these details—the partiality for compounds, for the accumulation of synonyms and for the use of the plural instead of the singular, may be classed together under the head of exaggerations of expression, and recorded as characteristics of the *epideictic* style.

In general, the tone is heightened, and Isocrates tends to appear florid when compared with Lysias ; if, on the other hand, we take Gorgias as a standard, we see how far Isocrates, who undoubtedly imitated the Sicilian style, has surpassed his model in the direction of refinement.


## § 3.  *On Education*

Prevented by natural disabilities from exercising his talents in public, but urged on by the necessity of earning a living, since the Peloponnesian War had dissipated his fortune, Isocrates turned to a profession for which he was well fitted, that of an educator.  During many years he was, like Gorgias, a teacher of rhetoric, and like Gorgias he may be classed as a Sophist.  This title is misleading.  In itself it means nothing more than an educator, or teacher of wisdom, and early writers use it in a laudatory sense ; Herodotus applies it to the Seven Sages.  In the fourth century it was debased, partly by the comic poets, as representing the

completion, are not really distinguishable, or, at any rate, the distinction is very slight.  So in *Evagoras*, § 11, εὐλογεῖν and ἐγκωμιάζειν are used antithetically (to praise—to eulogise).

[1] *E.g. Evagoras*, § 10, αὐταῖς ταῖς εὐρυθμίαις καὶ ταῖς συμμετρίαις ψυχαγωγοῦσι τοὺς ἀκούοντας.  Elsewhere we find μετριότητες, λαμπρότητες, αὐθάδειαι, ἀργίαι, etc.

popular habit of sneering at anything which the mob cannot understand, but more honestly and systematically by Plato, who, though he admitted that some of the Sophists, such as Protagoras, were men worthy of the highest respect, took many opportunities of disparaging Sophists as a class, and Sophistry as a profession.

There can be no doubt that he was quite sincere, for he takes great pains to bring out the distinction between the educators and his own master Socrates, whom Aristophanes had already marked as one of the crowd.[1]

To us it seems that the marked distinction cannot be maintained ; apart from Socrates' peculiarity of refusing to take fees from his pupils, he is distinguished only by possessing a higher moral tone than the rest of the Sophists.  Like them he was a sceptic as far as philosophy was concerned, and like them he was an educator.

We have, however, accepted the word at the value which Plato chose to put upon it ; but we must not suppose that this was the value at which it was usually current.  This is clear from the fact that Isocrates can use the word without any idea of disparagement.

Though he wrote a speech *Against the Sophists*, it is directed not against the profession as a whole, but against certain classes, whom he calls the ἀγέλαιοι σοφισταί—' Sophists of the baser sort.'

Isocrates' earliest work on education, the speech or tract *Against the Sophists* (Or. xiii.), dates from the beginning of his professional career, perhaps about the year 390 B.C.  We possess only part, perhaps less than half, of the speech.  What remains is purely destruc-

---

[1] Aristoph., *Clouds, passim.*

tive criticism which, as is clear from the concluding words, was meant to lead up to an exposition of the writer's own principles and theory. The loss is to be regretted, but is not irreparable, since the speech *On the Antidosis*, composed thirty-five years later, supplements it by a full constructive statement.

The introduction on the Sophists is sweeping in its severity :[1]

' If all our professional educators would be content to tell the truth and not promise more than they ever intend to perform, they would not have a bad reputation among laymen. As it is, their reckless effrontery has encouraged the opinion that a life of incurious idleness is better than one devoted to philosophy.'

He proceeds to criticize various classes :

' We cannot help hating and despising the professors of contentious argument (eristic), who, while claiming to seek for Truth, introduce falsehood at the very beginning of their pretensions. They profess in a way to read the future, a power which Homer denied even to the gods ; for they prophesy for their pupils a full knowledge of right conduct, and promise them happiness in consequence. This invaluable commodity they offer for sale at the ridiculous price of three or four minae. They affect, indeed, to despise money—mere dross of silver or gold as they call it— yet, for the sake of this small profit they will raise their pupils almost to a level with the immortals. They profess to teach all virtue ; but it is notable that pupils, before they are admitted to the course, have to give security for the payment of their fees.'

The general tone of this censure recalls the attacks of the Platonic Socrates on the ' eristic ' Sophists ; but

---

[1] Cf. Isocrates' reference to this passage in *Antid.*, § 193.

it is certain that the 'eristics,' whom Isocrates here attacks, are some of the lesser Socratics. This is made obvious by the reference in § 3 to the knowledge (ἐπιστήμη) which, according to these teachers, will lead to right conduct or virtue, and so to happiness. The Socratic view that knowledge is the basis of virtue, and virtue of happiness, is well known. Socrates himself did not profess to teach virtue for a fee; but the Megarians, the followers of his pupil Euclides, did, and at them the sarcasm of Isocrates seems to be directed. Elsewhere, indeed, Isocrates refers definitely to the Platonic school as belonging to the eristic class.[1]

The teachers of 'Political Discourse' fall next under ban, that is, the teachers of practical rhetoric, whether forensic or deliberative.[2] 'They care nothing for truth'—whereas the eristics, at any rate, professed to seek it—'they consider that their profession is to attract as many pupils as possible by the smallness of their fees and the greatness of their promises. They are so dull, and think others so dull, that though the speeches which they write are worse than many non-professionals can improvise, they undertake to make of their pupils orators equal to any emergency. They say that they can teach oratory as easily as the alphabet, which is a subject fixed by unchangeable rules, whereas the conditions for a speaker are never quite the same on two occasions. A speech, to be successful, must be appropriate to the subject, to the occasion, and to the speaker; and in some degree original. Instruction can give us technical skill; but cannot call

---

[1] *Hel.* (Or. x.), § 1, οἱ δὲ διεξιόντες ὡς ἀνδρία καὶ σοφία καὶ δικαιοσύνη ταὐτόν ἐστι.

[2] §§ 9 *sqq.*

into existence the oratorical faculty, which a good speaker must have innate in him.'

No doubt Isocrates himself professed to give a practical training for public life ; but he states here what he repeats with more emphasis in a later writing : [1] ' For distinction either in speech or in action, or in any other work, there are three requisites : natural aptitude, theoretical training, and practical experience. . . . Of these the first is indispensable, and by far the most important.'    The Sophists claimed to dispense with the first, and this is the ground of the philosopher's quarrel with them.

The third section of the speech, following naturally on the second, deals with writers of technical guides to rhetoric (τέχναι).

' They profess to teach litigation, choosing for themselves this offensive title which would be more appropriate in the mouths of their detractors.   They are worse than those who wallow in the mire of " eristic," for they at least pretend to be concerned with virtue and moderation, while those whom we are considering now undertake only to teach men to be busy-bodies from motives of base covetousness.' [2]

Here again Isocrates, who himself composed an ' Art ' of rhetoric, does not condemn all who may try to teach the subject ; his complaint is that the majority of such teachers have confined themselves to the ignoble branch of the profession.   This criticism is obviously a valid one, and is echoed by Aristotle, who declares that speaking before a public assembly is less knavish (κακοῦργον) than speaking in a law-court.[3]

The speech entitled *On the Antidosis* is really Isocrates' defence of his life and profession.   In

[1] *Antid.*, §§ 187-189.          [2] §§ 19 *sqq.*          [3] *Rhet.*, i. 1. 10.

355 B.C. he was challenged by one Megacleides to undertake the trierarchy, or else to accept an *antidosis*, or exchange of properties. The matter was the subject of a trial, in consequence of which Isocrates performed the trierarchy. Some time—perhaps two years—later, he wrote this speech, which is of no historical importance, since even the name of the plaintiff, Lysimachus, is fictitious. The introduction (§§ 1-13) makes it clear that the law-suit is only introduced for the sake of local colour. The speech itself begins with a semblance of forensic form in § 14, but the pretence is very soon dropped. The cloak is resumed in the Epilogue (§§ 320-323) ; but the greatest part of the speech has nothing to do with any trial, real or imaginary.

The treatise, as we may call it, falls into two parts : in §§ 14-166 the writer defends his own character ; in §§ 167-319 he defends his system of education.

The indictment against which he pleads is that he is in the habit of corrupting the younger generation by teaching them habits of litigation. He has little difficulty in showing that his chief work has lain in a far nobler field than that of forensic rhetoric. While others have been engaged in the paltry contentions of the law-courts he has composed speeches bearing upon the politics of all Greece. This he proves by reciting long extracts from his most famous works : the *Panegyric* (§ 59) ; *On the Peace* (§ 66) ; *Nicocles* (§ 72).

The second half of the speech contains, as has been noted, a statement and defence of Isocrates' theory.

' Philosophy,' he says, ' is for the soul what Gymnastic is for the body.'

This analogy he elaborates.

'The gymnastic trainer teaches his pupils first to perform the separate movements, then to combine them. The educator follows the same order, and both insist on long and diligent practice ; but the trainer of the body cannot always make a man an athlete, nor can the trainer of the mind make everybody an orator. There are three essentials requisite for success—natural aptitude, proper teaching, and long practice ; and moreover there must be a will on the part of both teacher and pupil to persevere. The natural ability is by far the most important element. Training, however complete, may break down utterly if the speaker lacks nerve.[1]

'Some people expect a marked improvement after a few days of study with a Sophist, and demand a complete training in a year. This is ridiculous ; no class of education could produce such results ; and there is no need to disparage us as a class because we cannot do more than we profess. We cannot make all men orators, but we can give them culture.

'Others assert that our philosophy has an immoral tendency. I shall not defend all who claim to be educators, but only those who have a right to the name. We have nothing to gain by making men immoral ; on the contrary the greatest satisfaction for a Sophist is that his pupils should become wise and honourable men, respected by their fellows. Our pupils come from Sicily, from Pontus, and from other distant regions ; do they come so far to be instructed in wickedness ? Surely not ; they could find plenty of teaching at home. They incur the trouble and expense because they think that Athens can give them the best education in the world.

'Again, power in debate is not in itself a demoralizing thing. The greatest statesmen of this and earlier generations studied and practised oratory—Solon, who was called one of the Seven Sophists, Themistocles, Pericles. You blame the Thebans for lacking culture ; why blame us who

---

[1] τὸ τολμᾶν, § 192.

try to impart it ?   Athens honours with a yearly sacrifice the Goddess Persuasion ; our enemies attack us for seeking the faculty which this goddess personifies.

' We are even attacked by the " Eristics " : [1] far from retorting, I am ready to admit that there is good to be got even from eristic disputation, from astronomy,[2] and from geometry : they are useful as a preliminary to higher studies.

' My own view of philosophy is a simple one.   It is impossible to attain absolute knowledge of what we ought or ought not to do ; but the wise man is he who can make a successful guess as a general rule, and philosophers are those who study to attain this practical wisdom.   There is not, and never has been, a science which could impart justice and virtue to those who are not by nature inclined towards these qualities ; but a man who is desirous of speaking or writing well, and of persuading others, will incidentally become more just and virtuous, for it is character that tells more than anything.

' Thoughtful speaking leads to careful action.   Your superior culture raises you above the rest of Greece, just as mankind is superior to the lower animals and Greeks to barbarians : do not, then, punish those who would give you this culture.' [3]

These two treatises taken together, and supplemented by a few passages from other speeches, give us a fair idea of Isocrates' system.   His ' Philosophy ' is to be distinguished from all merely theoretical speculation, such as the physical theories of the Ionians, or the logic of Parmenides ; from ' eristic '—the art of arguing for argument's sake—from geometry and astronomy ; from literary work which has no practical use ; from the rhetoric of the law-courts.   Boys at school may

---

[1] *Vide supra*, p. 137.     [2] *Or* astrology ?
[3] *Antid.*, Summary of §§ 181-303.

profitably study grammar and poetry ; at a later age the applied mathematics, and even ' eristic,' are good mental training ; but it must be recognized that they are only a preparation for the Isocratean ' philosophy,' which is for the soul what gymnastic is for the body.

As the gymnastic-master teaches first the various thrusts and parries, so to speak, the teacher of philosophy makes his pupils learn first all the styles of prose composition.[1] He then makes them combine (συνείρειν) the things which they have learnt. The subjects for such exercises must be properly chosen—they must be practical and must deal with wide interests.

Practice on these lines will prepare a man, as far as his nature allows, for speaking and acting in a public capacity ; so that what Isocrates calls his ' philosophy ' is really a science of practical politics.

Isocrates seems to have been thorough in all things ; himself a hard worker who took extraordinary care over his compositions, he expected his pupils to work hard. He was not content, like some Sophists, with making them learn his own ' fair copies ' by heart ; they must do the work for themselves. He scoffs at those teachers who claim to ' finish ' their pupils in a year ; his pretensions are more modest, but even so he requires a course of three or four years. He believed in individual attention rather than class-teaching, if we may regard an anecdote of the Pseudo-Plutarch, who recounts that three pupils once came to him together, but he admitted only two, telling the third to come next day. He endeavoured to impart to his students something of that broadness of view, so prominent in his own speeches, which enabled him to look beyond

---

[1] *Antid.*, § 11, ιδέαι.

the trials of the law-courts, beyond the interests of party or even of individual state, and lift his eyes to a conception of national unity ; and something of that loftiness of spirit which, in an age of selfish and scurrilous orators, enabled him to pursue his course towards the truth, unbiased by personal considerations, and never descending to invective or abuse.

### § 4. *Patriotism*

Isocrates was no less a patriot than Demosthenes, though he differed very widely in his political views from the later orator. What these views were may be gathered from a series of speeches on national subjects extending over a period of more than forty years.

The *Panegyricus*, the first of these, was probably composed for publication at one of the great national assemblies, perhaps the Olympic festival, about 380 B.C. This was certainly a time when the long-continued dissensions of the city-states had brought the affairs of Greece to a crisis. There seemed to Isocrates to be no solution of the difficulties, no chance of established peace or contentment, unless some enterprise could be found which should unite the sympathies of the rival cities, induce them to put their own quarrels aside, and throw them whole-heartedly into a cause which concerned Hellas as a nation.

The only motive which had ever been able to unite the Greeks, even temporarily, was hatred of the barbarians, and Isocrates works upon this feeling. He draws a vivid picture of the miserable state tc which the Greek world has been reduced by civil war, and shows how the influence of Persia, besides keeping this war alive, has in other ways worked towards the ruin of Greece. Having discussed with outspoken candour the claims of Sparta and Athens to leadership, he suggests that they should agree by a compromise, and urges that they and all other States should unite in a racial war against the Persians.

This speech had no practical effect. The rise of Thebes shortly after this date changed the balance of power, and on the whole did not improve conditions. Despairing of originating any joint action within Greece itself, Isocrates looked farther for a leader, and in or about 368 B.C. we find him writing to Dionysius of Syracuse, who at the time held an empire far more powerful than that of any State of Greece proper, and suggesting that he should come forward as the champion of the Greek national spirit.[1]

In 356 B.C. Isocrates turned again towards Sparta, this time writing to Archidamus, who had recently succeeded his father Agesilaus in the kingship, and urging him to take steps which will ' put an end to civil war in Greece, curb the insolence of the barbarians, and deprive them of part of their ill-gotten gains.' Archidamus, if he could be as vigorous as his father and more unselfish, might well seem to be a suitable leader for the crusade on which Isocrates had set his heart.

At this time Philip of Macedon, though he was beginning to attain notoriety, was probably regarded by the majority of Greeks as a pauper prince, sitting insecurely on a throne which he had usurped, and from which he might at any time be removed by rebellion or assassination. But in this year he obtained possession of the gold mines of Pangaeum, and it was soon

---

[1] *Ep.* I, § 87. This letter is referred to in *Philippus*, § 81 ; the text of the letter remaining to us is incomplete.

K

realized that Macedon was to play a leading part in Greek politics.

In 346 B.C. Isocrates addressed Philip as one capable of taking the lead, first in combining the Greek States into a union, and secondly, in leading them to conquer the barbarian.[1]   The ten years of desultory hostilities between Philip and Athens had now been ended by the peace of Philocrates, and Isocrates, thinking that Amphipolis, for which they had been fighting, was an undesirable possession for either party, imagined and hoped that the peace might be made permanent.

Though the *Panegyric* and the addresses to Dionysius and Archidamus had failed, Isocrates hoped that an appeal to Philip might be more successful.

' I decided,' he writes, ' to broach the subject to you, not as a special compliment, though I should be glad if my words could find favour with you, but from the following motive.   I saw that all other men of distinction have to obey their cities and their laws, and may do nothing beyond what they are told ;  and moreover none of them are capable of dealing with the matter I now intend to discuss.

' You alone have had given you by fortune a full authority to send embassies to whom you will, and receive them from where you choose, and to say whatever you think expedient.   Besides, you possess wealth and power beyond any other Greek—the two things which are the most potent either to persuade or to compel :  and you will find persuasion useful for the Greeks and compulsion for the barbarians.' [2]

A summary of a few extracts will indicate the tenor of the speech.

' It is your duty to try to reconcile the four great cities

---

[1] *Philippus*, 346 B.C.                    [2] *Ibid.* (Or. v.), §§ 14-17.

—Argos, Sparta, Thebes, and Athens ;  bring these four to
their right mind, and you will have no difficulty with the
rest, which all depend on them (§§ 30-31).  Your ancestors are Argive by descent, and these cities should never
have been at enmity with you or each other.  All must
make allowances, as all have been at fault (§§ 33-38).
If Athens or Sparta were now, as once, predominant,
nothing could be done ;  but all the great cities are now
practically on a level.  No enmities are so deep-seated
that they cannot be overcome : Athens has at different
times been allied with both Thebes and Sparta.  Sparta,
Argos, and Thebes all desire peace ; Athens has come to
her senses before the others, and already made peace.
She will be ready to give you her active sympathy '
(§§ 39-56).

'History provides many instances of men who, with
few advantages, even with disabilities, have achieved great
tasks :  you, with all your resources, should find the present
task easy ' (§§ 57-67).

'Success in such a cause would be magnificent ;  even
failure would be noble :  your slanderers impute to you the
design of subjugating Greece ;  you will convince them of
their error ' (§§ 68-80).

'So much for your duty to Greece ;  now turn to the
conquest of Asia.  Agesilaus failed because he stirred up
political animosities.

'The Greeks under Cyrus defeated the Persian army,
and though left leaderless they made good their retreat.
All conditions are favourable for you.  The Greeks of Asia
were hostile to Cyrus, but will welcome you.  The present
King of Persia is less of a man than his predecessor, against
whom Cyrus fought ;  and Persia is divided against itself.
Cyprus, Cilicia, and Phoenicia, which provided the king
with ships, will do so no longer ' (§§ 83-104).

'You may aim at conquering the whole Persian Empire ;
failing of that you might win all that is west of a line drawn
from Cilicia to Sinope.  Even this would be an enormous

advantage.   You could found cities for the hordes of mercenaries who are driven by destitution to wander and prey upon the settled inhabitants—a growing menace to Greeks and Persians alike.   You would thus render these nomads a great service, and at the same time establish them as a permanent guard of your own frontiers.   If this proved too much for you, at the very least you could free the Greek cities of Asia.   However great or little is your success, you will at least win great renown for having led a united expedition from all Greece ' (§§ 119-126).

' No other state or individual will undertake the task ; you are free from restrictions, as all Hellas is your native land.   You will fight, I know, not for power or wealth, but for glory.   Your mission, then, is this :—To be the bene-factor of Greece, the king of Macedon, the governor of Asia ' (§§ 127-155).

It may be said that Isocrates overrated the purity of Philip's motives.   On the other hand, it may be con-ceived that Philip would have greatly preferred to march to Asia as the general of a Greek force willingly united.   He, whom Isocrates reckons as a Greek of royal or semi-divine descent, whom Demosthenes stigmatized as a barbarian of the lowest type, had much more of the Greek than the barbarian in his nature. To Athens at least he always showed extraordinary clemency, treating her with a respect far beyond her merits, and honouring her for her ancient greatness. He did all that was possible to conciliate her, and this policy he handed on to his son.   But he could not start for the East, leaving so many irreconcilable enemies behind him ; and the refusal of the States to accept his hegemony made Chaeronea inevitable.

Those who read, not this short summary, but the essay as a whole, must be struck by the firm grasp which the writer has on contemporary history, and by his insight into the forces at work. He under-estimated the conservatism of the city-states, wrongly imagining that the majority could be as broad-minded as himself.

The chapters on Asia show considerable knowledge both of the conditions and the requirements. His advice about the founding of cities was followed literally by Alexander, who, immediately after his first victory, initiated this policy for securing his conquests.

In 342 B.C. Isocrates wrote again to Philip, reproaching him for his recklessness in exposing his own life in battle. He repeated some of the arguments of the first essay, and summarized his advice as follows : ' It is far nobler to capture a city's good-will than its walls.' After Chaeronea, in the year 338 B.C., he wrote once more, recalling his former advice, and reflecting with satisfaction that the dreams of his youth were some of them already fulfilled, and others on the point of fulfilment.

## § 5. *Remaining Works*

The general contents of the *Panegyricus* have already been discussed, but only a careful study of the speech will reveal the skill with which one topic is made to lead up to another, the nice proportion of the parts, and the adroitness displayed in gathering and binding together the various threads of the argument. Numerous paragraphs which seem at first to be almost digressions are found, when we take the speech as a whole, to be essential to its unity, and though in its course a large number of topics is handled, the main subject is never left out of view. The level of style is high throughout, and no extracts can properly represent it.

A short analysis may, however, serve to indicate the coherence of the arguments : [1]

' I am here to offer advice about the necessity of war with Persia and unity among the Greeks.   Others have handled the same theme, but the fact of their failure renders any excuse for a fresh attempt superfluous, and the subject admits of being treated better than it has been ' (§§ 1-14).

' My predecessors have missed an important point ;  that nothing can be done until the leaders—Athens and Sparta —are reconciled, and persuaded to share the leadership.

' Sparta has accepted a false tradition, that leadership is hers by ancestral right.   I shall try to prove that the leadership really belongs to Athens ;  Sparta then should consent to a joint command ' (§§ 15-20).

' Athens first possessed maritime empire, and her civilization is the oldest in Greece (§§ 21-25).   Her claims to hegemony are as follows :—

' A. (*a*) Tradition, which has never been refuted, records that Athens first provided the necessities of life.   Demeter taught in Attica the cultivation of corn and instituted the Mysteries.

' (*b*) Athens undoubtedly led the way in colonization, thus enlarging the boundaries of Greek land, and driving back the barbarians (§§ 28-37).

' (*c*) Athens had the earliest laws, and the earliest constitution.   She established the Piraeus, the centre of Greek trade.   She provides in herself a perpetual festival, at which the arts are encouraged.   Practical philosophy and oratory are so highly honoured at Athens that the name '' Greek '' is applied properly not by claim of blood but by virtue of the possession of Athenian culture (§§ 38-50).

' B. (*a*) From heroic times downwards Athens has shown herself the helper of the oppressed.   Even Sparta grew great through her support (§§ 57-65).

---

[1] Isocrates is said to have spent ten years over the composition of the *Panegyricus* ;  it was probably published in 380 B.C.

' (*b*) Athens in the earliest times and in the Persian Wars distinguished herself against the barbarians (§§ 66-74).

' In old days the rivalries between opposite political parties and between Athens and Sparta were noble ones, and the honourable competition of the two cities shamed the other Greeks into taking arms against Xerxes.  Athens, however, furnished more ships than all the rest put together.  Her claim to leadership, up to the end of the Persian War, is therefore established ' (§§ 75-79).

' It is true that Athens treated her revolted allies—Melos and Scione—severely : rebels must expect punishment.  On the other hand, our loyal subjects enjoyed for seventy years freedom from tyranny, immunity from barbarian attacks, settled government, and peace with all the world ' (§§ 100-106).

' Sparta and her partisans inflicted more harm in a few months than Athens in the whole duration of her empire ' (§§ 110-114).

' Our rule was preferable to the so-called " peace and independence " which Sparta has given the cities.  The seas are overrun by pirates, and more cities are raided now than before the peace was made.  Tyrants and harmosts make life in the cities intolerable.  The Great King, whom Athens confined within stated limits, has raided the Peloponnese (§§ 115-119) ; Sparta has abandoned the Ionians to slavery, and herself caused devastation in Greece, and burdened the islanders with taxation.  It is monstrous that we Greeks, owing to our petty quarrels, should devastate our own country, when we might reap a golden harvest from Asia ' §§ (120-132).

' We have allowed the Great King to attain unheard of power—simply through our quarrels, for he is not really strong.

' Numerous instances from history betray the inferiority of the Persian leaders and organization.  They have often been defeated on the coast of Asia ; when they invaded Greece we made an example of them ; finally, they cut a ridiculous figure before the walls of their own palaces '[1] (§§ 133-149).

' This is what we might expect from their manner of life ; the mass of the people are more fit to be slaves than soldiers ; the nobles are by turns insolent and servile, and being permanently corrupted by luxury they are weak and treacherous. They deserve our hatred, and, in fact, our enmity can never be reconciled. One of the reasons even of Homer's popularity is that he tells of a great war against Asia ' (§§ 150-159).

' The time is favourable for attack ; Phoenicia and Syria are devastated ; Tyre is captured ; Cilicia is mostly in our favour ; Egypt and Cyprus are in revolt. The Greeks are ready to rise ; we must make haste, and not let the history of the Ionic revolt repeat itself. The present suffering in Greece passes all records, and for this the present generation deserves some recompense—another reason for haste. The leading men in the cities are callously indifferent, so we who stand outside politics must take the lead, as I am doing ' (§§ 160-174).

' The treaty of Antalcidas need not stand in our way ; it has been broken already in spirit. We only observe the provisions which are to our own shame, *i.e.* those by which our allies are given over to the Persians. It was never a fair covenant—we submitted to terms dictated by the king.

' Honour and expediency alike demand that we should combine to undertake this war, whose fame will be greater than that of the Trojan war ' (§§ 175-189).

We may now consider the group of speeches which deals with the internal affairs of Greece.

*Plataicus* (Or. xiv.). Plataea, destroyed in 427 B.C., was restored by Sparta in 386 B.C. as a menace to Thebes, but was forced into the Boeotian Confederacy in 376 B.C. In 373 B.C. it was surprised by a Theban army and again destroyed. The inhabitants escaped

---

[1] *I.e.* the victory of the 10,000 at Cunaxa.

to Athens, and their case was discussed in the ecclesia, and also at the congress of allies.  The present speech is professedly delivered by a Plataean before the Athenian ecclesia.  It consists chiefly of an appeal to sentiment through history ;  the speaker recalls the ancient relations of Plataea and Athens, and thence infers the present duty of Athens.  The speech is in a form suitable for delivery before the assembly, and may have been so delivered.

*On the Peace* (Or. viii.), on the other hand, is a political treatise.  It dates from 355 B.C., when the Social War was near its end.  The main theme of the speech is the necessity of peace between Athens and all the world, but the urging of this policy naturally brings in a criticism of the war-party, and a severe indictment not only of present politics but of the conditions of the old empire of Athens.  The speech is remarkable from the fact that for once Isocrates abandons his even and temperate language, and allows indignation and even bitterness to give colour to his criticisms.

' The acquisition of empire,' he says, ' over unwilling subjects, is both unjust and impolitic.  Ambition is like the bait which entices a wild beast into a trap.  Our administration is rotten ;  our citizens have lost faith in personal effort, and we employ mercenaries to fight our battles. Our politicians are our worst citizens, and we appoint as generals incompetent men who are not fitted for any position of trust.  We hold our own, but only because our rivals are as weak as we are.  The follies of our assembly win allies for Thebes ;  their follies in turn are our salvation. It would pay either State to bribe the assembly of the other to meet more often.

' Our hope lies in abandoning our empire ;  it is unjust, and moreover, we could not maintain it when we were rich,

and now we are poor. The statesmen of imperial Athens
did all that they could to make their city's policy unpopular. They displayed the tribute extorted from the
allies, thus reminding all the world of their tyranny ; and
paraded the children of those who had fallen in wars in
various parts of the world—the victims of national covetousness. Far different was the position of Athens under
Themistocles and Aristides. National life is demoralized
by Empire. The history of Sparta's supremacy is another
case to the point. Pericles was a demagogue, and led the
city on a disastrous career, but he at least enriched the
treasury, not himself. Our modern demagogues are merely
self-seeking, and their covetousness reduces not only the
state but the citizens to penury.

' Peace, at the price I have indicated, is the only remedy.
We must deliver Greece, not despoil her. Athens should
hold among Greek States the position that the kings
occupy in Sparta ; they are not tyrants ; they have a
higher standard of conduct than any private person, and are
held in such respect that any man who would not throw
away his life for them in the field is reckoned meaner than
a deserter.'

There is much truth in the invectives aimed at the
old empire ; Isocrates could see behind the glowing
colours in which the glories of the Periclean age are
sometimes painted, and equally with Demosthenes he
realized, and did not shrink from noticing, the weakness
of Athens in his own days. But his advice, though
noble, is unpractical. He failed, in spite of his knowledge of history, to fathom the depth of Greek selfish-
ness. No State that relied solely or chiefly on moral
worth could have a voice in the council of Greece, far
less dominiate its policy.

The *Areopagiticus* (Or. vii.), perhaps composed in
the same year, in many points supplements the *de Pace*.

It is chiefly devoted to a contrast between the old days
of dignified government under the constitutions of
Solon and Cleisthenes, and the unsatisfactory conditions of life in the orator's time.  The description of
the old constitution is, perhaps, a fancy picture, but
the contrast serves to bring out the evils at which
Isocrates is aiming in the modern State.  The speech
deals with the inner life of Athens rather than with her
foreign policy, and the chief credit for good government and good life in the old days is given to the
Council of the Areopagus, that majestic  body which
even now ' has so strong an influence that the worst
men of modern times, if promoted to membership of it,
are pervaded by its spirit, and, losing the meanness of
their own hearts, think and act in accordance with the
Council's high traditions.'

The *Archidamus* (Or. vi.) is put into the mouth of
the Spartan king of that name, for whom, as we know
from a letter, Isocrates had a deep respect.  It professes
to be part of a debate in 366 B.C., on the proposal of the
Thebans to grant peace on condition that Sparta recognized the independence of Messenia.  It probably
contains a fair representation of the feelings of the
Spartans at the time when it was proposed to make
an independent and permanently hostile state of the
Messenians, whom for generations they had regarded
as their slaves.

There still remain works of three classes—the ' horta-
tory letters,' the ' displays,' and forensic speeches.

### *Hortatory Letters*

*To Demonicus* (Or. i.), 372 B.C. (?).  This letter, addressed to a young monarch, of whom nothing else is
known, is destined to be a ' storehouse ' ($\tau\alpha\mu\iota\epsilon\hat{\iota}o\nu$)

of moral maxims, comprising duty to the gods, duty to men, and duty to oneself. It contains a vast number of maxims, mostly of a practical or semi-practical nature—'We test gold by fire, friends by misfortune.' 'Never swear by the gods where money is concerned; some will think you a perjurer, others a covetous man.' Occasionally the moral tone is higher—'If you do wrong, never hope to be undiscovered; if others discover you not, your own conscience will discover you to yourself.'

*To Nicocles* (Or. ii.), 374 B.C., addressed to Nicocles, who became king of Salamis in Cyprus in 374 B.C., deals with the duties and responsibilities of a king. 'Remember your high position, and be careful that you never do anything unworthy of it.'

*Nicocles, or the Cyprians* (Or. iii.), 372 B.C., is a complement to Or. ii. In it the king himself is represented as discoursing on the duties of subjects towards their king. 'Do to your king as you would wish your own subjects to do to you.'

### Epideictic Speeches

Many of the Sophists wrote imaginary speeches on legendary themes, and Isocrates, though this art was outside his province, strayed into it as a critic. The *Busiris* (Or. xi.), 391 B.C., addressed to a Sophist Polycrates, contains first a criticism of a speech composed by Polycrates on that subject, and secondly an exposition of how Isocrates himself would treat such a theme. Incidentally, Isocrates accepts the early legends as true on the whole, while rejecting certain parts of them as unbecoming.

The *Encomium of Helen* (Or. x.), 370 B.C., begins with criticism of a certain encomium which is generally believed to be the extant one attributed to Gorgias. The previous writer has written not an encomium but an apology; Isocrates himself will write a real encomium, omitting all the topics which have been used by others.

The *Evagoras* (Or. ix.), 365 B.C. (?), was composed for a festival celebrated by Nicocles in memory of his father, Evagoras of Salamis, who died 374 B.C. It contains a laudatory account of the king's career, and an encouragement to the son to emulate his father's virtues.

The *Panathenaicus* was begun when Isocrates was 94 years old, *i.e.* in 342 B.C. Owing to an illness, he was not able to finish it for three years. It contains much of the material which had already been used in the *Areopagiticus*. Its main topic is the greatness of Athens, considered historically, and not with reference to contemporary politics. But it contains long digressions—a defence of his own system against the attacks of certain baser Sophists (§§ 5-34); a discourse on Agamemnon (§§ 62-73); a personal explanation (§§ 99 *sqq.*), in which the author explains that the speech would naturally end at this point, and details the conversations and discussions which led him to continue it. He was blamed for being too harsh against Sparta, and though he silenced his critics, he had some misgivings. The result is to increase the length of the speech by one third, and completely to spoil the balance and destroy whatever unity it possessed.

### Forensic Speeches

Six forensic speeches have come down to us; they belong to the early days of Isocrates, who in later years regretted that he had ever been concerned with such an art ; they may be dismissed in a few words :

*Against Lochites* (Or. xx.), 394 B.C., is an action for assault ; *Aegineticus* (Or. xix.), 394 B.C., a claim to an inheritance ; *Against Euthynus* (Or. xxi.), 403 B.C., an action to recover a deposit ; *Trapeziticus* (Or. xvii.), 394 B.C., a similar action, against the famous banker Pasion ; περὶ τοῦ ζεύγους (Or. xvi.), 397 B.C., spoken by the younger Alcibiades against a man Tisias, who asserts that the elder Alcibiades, father of the speaker, robbed him of a team of four horses.   This is an action for damages amounting to five talents.   *Against Callimachus*, 399 B.C., a παραγραφή or special plea entered by the defendant, who contends that an action for damages brought against him cannot be  maintained.

### *Letters*

Reference has already been made to certain letters, to Dionysius, 368 B.C., Archidamus, 365 B.C., Philip and Alexander, 342 B.C.   Others extant are addressed to the children of Jason (*Ep.* vi.), 359 B.C.—*i.e.* Thebe and her half-brothers, children of the tyrant of Pherae, who was murdered in 370 B.C. ;  to Timotheus (*Ep.* vii.), 345 B.C.—a king of Heraclea on the Euxine ;  to the Rulers of Mitylene (*Ep.* viii.), 350 B.C.—the oligarchs who had recently overthrown the democracy ;  to Antipater (*Ep.* iv.), 340 B.C., at the time, apparently, regent of Macedonia during Philip's absence in Thrace.   This list of the correspondents of Isocrates, with some of whom at least he is on terms of familiarity, may serve to indicate his importance in the Greek world.

Isocrates is also credited with the composition of a
τέχνη or treatise on the art of rhetoric, now lost, except
for a single quotation ; and the editions of the text
contain a number of apophthegms attributed to him.
None are important.

CHAPTER VII

MINOR RHETORICIANS

THE contemporaries of Isocrates are over-shadowed by his genius ; nevertheless there were in his time other speakers and teachers of ability. The only one of them who deserves serious consideration is Alcidamas, a pupil of Gorgias or of his school, who, though a rival of Isocrates, had come under the influence of the latter's style. We possess under his name a sophistical exercise, the *Accusation of Palamedes by Odysseus*, which is of no importance, and may be spurious, and a declamation *On the Sophists*, which is probably genuine ; at least we may say that it is the work of an able critic and a graceful writer. His other works included two rhetorical exercises, the *Praise of Death* and the *Praise of Nais*, and a *Messenian Oration*, which was apparently a counterblast to the *Archidamus* of Isocrates.

*The Sophists* is really an attack on the methods of Isocrates, and is directed against the practice of labori-ously composing written speeches, which are no real help to a man who wishes to be an orator, whether in the assembly or the law-courts. Certain so-called Sophists, he contends, who, while quite incapable of speaking, have practised writing, pride themselves on this accomplishment, and though they can call only one small department of rhetoric their own, claim to be masters of the complete science. He would not disparage the art of writing, but he considers it of secondary importance, while other accomplishments deserve far more attention. Any man of ability, given the time, can learn to write moderately well ; but in order to speak well you must apply a careful training to the development of certain special gifts. To be able to speak extemporaneously is a very important gift ; a man who possesses it can adapt himself to the mood of his audience, while one who relies on prepared orations must often miss a great opportunity, for it is beyond human powers to learn by heart enough speeches to be ready at a moment's notice to speak on any subject and to any kind of audience. A man accustomed to the use of written speeches, when forced to speak *ex tempore*, will not maintain his proper level of performance.[1] Many arguments, of more or less value, are adduced ; in all of them there is a certain cleverness.

Dionysius thought the style of Alcidamas coarse and trivial ;[2] Aristotle says that he used his epithets ' not as seasoning but as meat.'[3] These strictures do not apply to the one surviving work. He seems to have been raised above the dead level of rhetoricians by possessing ideas ; in the speech advocating the freedom of the Messenians occurred the sentence, ' God has made all men free ; nature has made no man a slave ' ; and his description of the *Odyssey* as ' a noble mirror of human life,' is a fine expression in itself, though Aristotle objects that such ornaments detract

---

[1] The truth of this maxim is illustrated by our records of the *impromptu* performances of Demosthenes, *vide infra*, p. 190.

[2] *de Isaeo*, ch. xix., παχύτερον ὄντα τὴν λέξιν καὶ κοινότερον.

[3] *Rhet.*, iii. 3. 3.

L

from the value of a speech, as giving the impression of over-preparation.[1]

Polycrates, a rhetorician of the same period, is known to have composed a fictitious *Accusation of Socrates*, to which Isocrates refers.[2] His *Encomium of Busiris*, the cannibal king of Egypt, stirred Isocrates to write his own *Busiris*, in order to show how such a theme ought to be treated. Dionysius found his style inane, frigid, and vulgar.[3] Lycophron, an imitator of Gorgias, is quoted several times by Aristotle ; and Cephisodorus, the best known rhetorician of the school of Isocrates, wrote an admirable defence of his master against the attacks of Aristotle.[4]

These minor teachers, who are mentioned only as offshoots from the prominent schools, had no permanent influence on the growth either of rhetoric or of oratory.

[1] Arist., *Rhet.*, iii. 3. 4.

[2] *Busiris*, §§ 5-6. He endeavoured to make Socrates responsible for the misdeeds of Alcibiades.

[3] *de Isaeo*, ch. xx.

[4] Dion., *de Isocrate*, ch. xviii. : τὴν ἀπολογίαν τὴν πάνυ θαυμαστὴν ἐν ταῖς πρὸς Ἀριστοτέλη ἀντιγραφαῖς ἐποιήσατο.

# CHAPTER VIII

## AESCHINES

### § 1. *Life*

ESCHINES was for twenty years a bitter enemy of Demosthenes. This enmity was perhaps the chief interest in his life; at any rate it is the dominant motive of his extant speeches. Demosthenes on his side could not afford to despise an enemy whose biting wit and real gift of eloquence assured him an attentive hearing, whether in the courts or before the ecclesia, and thus gave him an influence which the vagueness of his political views and the instability of his personal character could never entirely dissipate. Aeschines had no constructive policy, but he had just the talents which are requisite for the leader of a captious and malicious opposition. To the fact of the long-maintained hostility between these two men we owe a good deal of first-hand information about each of them, both as regards public and private life. It is true that we cannot accept without reservation the statements and criticisms made by either speaker about his rival; but in many cases they agree about facts, though they put different interpretations on them, and so, with care, we may arrive at a substratum of truth.

Aeschines was born about 390 B.C.[1] His father Atrometus, an Athenian citizen of pure descent,[2] was exiled by the Thirty, and fled to Corinth, with his wife. He served for some time as a mercenary soldier in Asia, and finally returned to Athens, where he kept a school. His wife, Glaucothea, filled some minor religious office, initiating the neophytes in certain mysteries, apparently connected with Orphism. Aeschines seems to have helped both his parents in their work, if we may suppose that there is a grain of truth mixed with the malice of Demosthenes :

' You used to fill the ink-pots, sponge the benches, and sweep the schoolroom, like a slave, not like a gentleman's son. When you grew up you helped your mother in her initiations, reciting the formulas, and making yourself generally useful. All night long you were wrapping the celebrants in fawn-skins, preparing their drink-offerings, smearing them with clay and bran,' etc.[3]

The whole of the description from which the foregoing passage is taken is an obvious caricature, and its chief value is to show that Demosthenes, if circumstances had not made him a statesman, might have been a successful writer of mediocre comedy ; but it seems to point to the fact that Aeschines' parents were in humble circumstances, that he himself had a hard life as a boy, and did not enjoy the usual opportunities of obtaining the kind of education desirable for a states-

---

[1] See *Timarchus*, § 49, where Aeschines states, in 346 B.C., that he is rather over forty-five years old.

[2] Aesch., *de Leg.*, § 147.   Dem. (*de Cor.*, 129 *sqq.*) asserts that he was originally a slave named Tromes (*Coward*), but changed his name to Atrometus (*Dauntless*).

[3] Dem., *de Cor.*, §§ 258-259.   See further *infra*, p. 249.

man.[1]  After this, at an age when other aspirants to
public life would have been studying under teachers
of rhetoric, he was forced to earn his living.  He was
first clerk to some minor officials, then an actor—
according to Demosthenes he played small parts in an
inferior company, and lived chiefly on the figs and
olives with which the spectators pelted him.[2]  He also
served as a hoplite, and, by his own account, distinguished himself at Mantinea and Tamynae.  In 357
B.C. he obtained political employment, first under
Aristophon of Azenia, then under Eubulus, and later
we find him acting as clerk of the ecclesia.

He married into a respectable family about 350 B.C.,
and in 348 B.C. he first appears in a position of public
trust, being appointed a member of the embassy to
Megalopolis in Arcadia.  On this occasion he went out
admittedly as an opponent of Philip, but came back a
partisan of peace.  The reasons for this change of view
will be discussed later.  His own explanation, that he
realized war to be impracticable, is reasonable in itself.[3]
Two years later he was associated with Demosthenes
in the famous embassies to Philip, which, after serious
delays, resulted in the unsatisfactory peace of Philocrates.  The peace was pronounced by Demosthenes
to be unworthy of Athens,[4] though he urged that, good
or bad, it must be upheld ; and besides uttering insinuations against the conduct of Aeschines as an ambassador, he prepared to prosecute him for betraying

[1] However, his elder brother, Philocrates, was elected general
three times in succession, and his younger brother, Aphobetus, was
sent as an ambassador to the Great King.—Aesch., *de Leg.*, § 149.
[2] *de Cor.*, § 262, *vide infra*, p. 249.
[3] *de Leg.*, § 79 ; *vide infra*, p. 168.
[4] See *de Pace* (*passim*) delivered in the same year.

his trust by taking bribes from Philip.  He associated with himself as a prosecutor one Timarchus.  Aeschines prepared a counter-stroke.  He prosecuted Timarchus on the ground that he was a person of notorious immorality, and, as such, debarred from speaking in public.  Timarchus appears to have been found guilty. In 343 B.C. Demosthenes brought the action in which his speech *de Falsa Legatione* and that of Aeschines bearing the same title were delivered, and Aeschines was acquitted by the rather small majority of thirty votes. In the next year Aeschines prepared for reprisals, but when on the point of impeaching Demosthenes he in his turn was thwarted by a counter-move on his rival's part.[1]

In 339 B.C. Aeschines was a *pylagorus* at the Amphictyonic Council, and an inflammatory speech which he made there led to the outbreak of the Sacred War.

In 337 B.C., the year after the battle of Chaeronea, the proposal of Ctesiphon to confer a crown on Demosthenes for his services to Athens gave Aeschines a new weapon with which to strike at his enemy.  He impeached Ctesiphon for illegality.  The case was not actually tried till 330 B.C., when Aeschines, failing to obtain a fifth of the votes, was fined a thousand drachmae, and, being unable or unwilling to pay, went into exile.  He retired to Asia Minor, and lived either in Ephesus or Rhodes.  He is said by Plutarch to have spent the rest of his life as a professional Sophist, that is to say, no doubt, as a teacher of rhetoric ;[2] but we have no further information about his life or the manner or date of his death.

---

[1] Aesch., *Ctes.*, §§ 222-225.

[2] *Dem.*, ch. 24, περὶ ῾Ρόδον καὶ Ἰωνίαν σοφιστεύων κατεβίωσεν.

## § 2.  *Public Character*

Aeschines cannot be considered as a statesman, since he had no definite policy.  He was, as he admitted himself, an opportunist.  ' Both individual and state,' he says, ' must shift their ground according to change of circumstances, and aim at what is best for the time ' ;[1] and though he claims to be ' the adviser of the greatest of all cities,' [2] he never had in public matters any higher principle than this following of the line of least resistance.

It is necessary, however, to consider whether he was actually the corrupt politician that Demosthenes makes him out to be.

Athenian opinion with regard to corrupt practices was less strict than ours ;  Hyperides admits that there are various degrees of guiltiness in the matter of receiving bribes ;  the worst offence is to receive bribes from improper quarters, *i.e.* from an enemy of the State, and to the detriment of the State.[3]

This principle implies a corollary that to receive bribes for doing one's duty and acting in the best interests of one's country is a venial offence, if indeed it is an offence at all ;  in which case a man's guilt or innocence may be a matter for his individual conscience to determine.

Demosthenes definitely accused Aeschines of changing his policy in consequence of bribes received from Philip.  It is known that at the beginning of his public life he was an opponent of Macedon, and we have his

---

[1] *de Leg.*, § 16, τοῖς γὰρ καιροῖς ἀνάγκη συμ.περιφέρεσθαι πρὸς τὸ κράτιστον καὶ τὸν ἄνδρα καὶ τὴν πόλιν.
[2] *Ibid.*, § 157, ὁ τῆς μεγίστης σύμβουλος πόλεως.
[3] Hyper., *adv. Dem.*, xxiv.

own account of his conversion on the occasion of the embassy to Megalopolis :

'You reproach me for the speech which I made, as an envoy, before ten thousand people in Arcadia ; you say that I have changed sides, you abject creature, who were nearly branded as a deserter. The truth is that during the war I tried to the best of my ability to unite the Arcadians and the rest of the Greeks against Philip ; but when I found that nobody would give help to Athens, but some were waiting to see what happened and others were marching against us, and the orators in the city were using the war as a means of meeting their daily expenses, I admit that I advised the people to come to terms with Philip, and make the peace which you, who have never drawn a sword, now say is disgraceful, though I say that it is far more honourable than the war.'[1]

After the conclusion of the peace of Philocrates the accusations were more definite. Demosthenes asserts that Aeschines had private interviews with Philip when on the second embassy, and that for his services he received certain lands in Boeotia ;[2] he recurs to this charge in the *de Corona*, many years later. Aeschines does not deny or even mention this charge either in the speech *On the Embassy* or in the accusation of Ctesiphon. Demosthenes, having, apparently, little direct evidence, tries to establish his case by emphasizing the relations of Aeschines with the traitor Philocrates ; but this is a weak argument, for though Aeschines at one time boasted of these relations, on a later occasion he repudiated them, and even ventured to rank Demosthenes himself with Philocrates.[3] Per-

---

[1] *de Leg.*, § 79.
[2] Dem., *de Falsa Leg.*, §§ 145, 166-177 ; *de Cor.*, § 41.
[3] *Timarchus*, § 174 ; *Ctes.*, § 58.

haps we should attach more importance to the other fact urged by Demosthenes, that Aeschines from time to time urged the city to accept Philip's vague promises of goodwill; but before we condemn him on this ground we must recollect that Isocrates, a man of far greater intelligence than Aeschines, and of undoubted honesty, had come so completely under the spell of Philip's personality as to place a thorough belief in the sincerity of his professions.[1]  Aeschines may have been duped in the same manner.

But the most severe condemnation of Aeschines' policy is contained in his own speeches.

During a visit to the Macedonian army in Phocis he was guilty of a gross piece of bad taste by joining with Philip in dancing the paean to celebrate the defeat of Phocis.  He admits the charge, and maintains that it was even a proper thing to do.[2]  His conduct at the Amphictyonic Council was far more serious.[3]  He was invited to make a speech, and as he began, was rudely interrupted by a Locrian of Amphissa.  In revenge it ' occurred to him ' [4] to recall the impiety of the Amphissians in occupying the Cirrhaean plain.  He caused to be read aloud the curse pronounced after the first Sacred War, and by recalling the forgotten events of past generations worked up his audience to such a pitch of excitement that on the following morning—for it was too late to take action that night—the whole population of Delphi marched down to Cirrha, destroyed the harbour buildings, and set fire to the town.  Though this

---

[1] *Supra*, p. 148.        [2] *de Leg.*, § 163.
[3] *Vide supra*, p. 166.
[4] ἐπῆλθέ μοι, Aesch., *Ctes.*, § 118, where A. complacently relates the whole incident.

action undoubtedly plunged Greece into an Amphictyonic War, Aeschines, quite regardless of the awful consequences, can only dwell upon the remarkable effects of his own oratory.

### § 3. *Personality*

Something of the personal characteristics of Aeschines may be gathered from his own writings and those of Demosthenes. He must have been a man of dignified presence, for even if he only played minor parts, as Demosthenes so frequently asserts, he acted, on occasion,. in good company, as his enemy, in an unguarded moment, admitted. The conditions under which Greek tragedy was performed required a majestic bearing even in a tritagonist, and the taunt of Demosthenes, who calls him ' a noble statue,' makes it certain that Aeschines did not fall short of these requirements.[1] The words of Demosthenes probably imply that the dignity was overdone, that the statuesque pose of the ex-actor appeared pompous and exaggerated in a lawcourt. Aeschines himself condemned the use of excited gestures by orators. He urged the necessity of restraint, and often insisted that an orator should, while speaking, hold his hand within his robe.[2] This declared prejudice on his part gave Demosthenes his opportunity for a neat retort—' You should keep your hand there, not when you are speaking, but when you go on an embassy.'[3] On this occasion Demosthenes scored a point, but where wit and repartee were in question, the honours generally rested with Aeschines.

[1] *de Cor.*, §§ 129, 262, etc. Further, *de Falsa Leg.*, § 246. A tritagonist would ordinarily have to play the parts of kings and tyrants, who must as a rule be majestic characters (cf. ὁ Κρέων Αἰσχίνης, *de Falsa Leg.*, § 247).

[2] *Timarch.*, § 25.  [3] Dem., *de Falsa Leg.*, § 252.

Another striking characteristic of Aeschines was his magnificent voice, which he used with practised skill ; Demosthenes, who had serious natural disabilities as a speaker, envied him bitterly, and in consequence was always trying to ridicule his delivery.[1]  Conscious, no doubt, of his natural advantages, to which Demosthenes had once paid a more or less sincere tribute,[2] Aeschines was apparently unmoved by these taunts ; but he seems to have been deeply injured when Demosthenes compared him to the Sirens, whose voices charm men to their destruction.  His indignation can find no repartee ; he can only expostulate that the charge is indecent, and even if it were true, Demosthenes is not a fit man to bring it ; only a man of deeds would be a worthy accuser ; his rival is nothing but a bundle of words.  Here, recovering himself a little, he delivers himself of the idea that Demosthenes is as empty as a flute—no good for anything if you take away the mouthpiece.[3]

In the case of other orators I have laid but little stress on personal characteristics, because as a rule the orator must be judged apart from his qualities as a man.  In considering Isaeus, for instance—an extreme case, certainly—personal qualities and peculiarities are of no importance at all.  But so many personal traits appear in the writings of Aeschines that we cannot afford to neglect them ; they form important data for our estimate of him, both as a speaker and a public character.  There is some excuse, then, for dealing at

---

[1] Dem., *de Falsa Leg.*, § 255, σεμνολογεῖ . . . φωνασκήσας, etc. ; *de Cor.*, § 133, σεμνολόγου ; and numerous references to τριταγωνίστης.

[2] Aesch., *de Leg.*, § 41, τὴν φύσιν μου μακαρίζων, etc. (of the behaviour of Demosthenes during the first embassy).

[3] *Ctes.*, §§ 228-229, ἐξ ὀνομάτων συγκείμενος, etc.

greater length with his personality than with that of any other of the Attic orators. The question of his public morality has already to some extent been discussed ; [1] an examination of his more private qualities may possibly throw further light on the question of his culpability.

He was, as we saw, to some extent a self-made man ; he had at least risen far above the station in which he was born. All through his speeches we find traces of his pride in the position and the culture which he has attained—his *vanité de parvenu*, as M. Croiset styles it. He is proud of his education, and boasts of it to excess, not realizing that he thus lays himself open to the charge of having missed the best that education can give. Demosthenes is just, though on the side of severity :

' What right have you,' he asks, ' to speak of education ? No man who really had received a liberal education would ever talk about himself in such a tone as you do ; he would have the modesty to blush if any one else said such things about him ; but people who have missed a proper education, as you have, and are stupid enough to pretend that they possess it, only succeed in offending their hearers when they talk about it, and fail completely to produce the desired impression.' [2]

Aeschines considered ἀπαιδευσία, want of education, almost as a cardinal sin, and could never conceive that he himself was guilty of it.[3]   He displays his learning by quotations from the poets, which are sometimes, it must be admitted, very appropriate to his argument,

---

[1] *Supra*, pp. 167-170.          [2] Dem., *de Cor.*, § 128.
[3] References to himself as πεπαιδευμένος, to his adversaries as ἀπαίδευτοι, to their ἀπαιδευσία, τὸ ἀμαθές, etc., are very common in the speeches against Timarchus and on the embassy.

and by references to mythology and legend, which are sometimes frigid. His use of history betrays a rather superficial knowledge of the subject ; it is hardly probable that he had studied Thucydides, for instance. Still, he possessed a fair portion of learning ; what leads him astray is really his lack of taste. He is at his best in the use of quotation when he adduces the lines of Hesiod on the man whose guilt involves a whole city in his own ruin—the passage will be quoted later.[1] The verses give a real sting to his denunciations, and the opinion which he expresses on the educational influence of poetry is both solemn and sincere. But he cannot keep to this level. His much boasted education results generally in an affectation of a sort of artificial propriety in action and language, and a profession of prudery which is really foreign to his nature. He professes an admiration for the self-restraint of public speakers in Solon's time, and during the greatness of the republic, and speaks with disgust of Timarchus, who ' threw off his cloak and performed a *pancration* naked in the assembly.'[2] In the opening of the same speech he makes a strong claim to the merit of ' moderation ' ; in the prosecution of Timarchus his moderation consists in hinting at certain abominable practices, which he does not describe by name.

' I pray you, Gentlemen, to forgive me if, when forced to speak of certain practices which are not honourable by

---

[1] *Infra*, pp. 184, 187.

[2] *Timarch.*, § 26. Aeschines adds a characteristically Greek touch—' his body was so horribly out of condition through his drunkenness and other excesses that decent people covered their eyes.' It was the neglect of the body, rather than the exposure of the arms and legs, which is exaggerated into ' nakedness,' that really shocked the spectators, in addition to the ' rough-and-tumble ' gestures of the orator.

nature, but are the established habits of the defendant, I am led away into using any expression which resembles the actions of Timarchus. . . . The blame should rest on him rather than on me. It will be impossible to avoid all use of such expressions, . . . but I shall try to avoid it as far as possible.'[1]

Notice again the hypocritical reticence or ' omission ' (*paraleipsis*)—a rhetorical device familiar to readers of Cicero—which insinuates what it cannot prove :

' Mark, men of Athens, how moderate I intend to be in my attack on Timarchus. I omit all the abuses of which he was guilty as a boy. So far as I am concerned they may be no more valid than, say, the actions of the Thirty, the events before the archonship of Euclides, or any other limitation which may ever have been established.'[2]

' I hear that this creature ' (an associate of Timarchus) ' has committed certain abominable offences, which, I swear by Zeus of Olympus, I should never dare to mention in your presence ; he was not ashamed of doing these things, but I could not bear to live if I had even named them to you explicitly.'[3]

In spite of the prosecutor's modesty, particular references to the offences of Timarchus are frequent enough throughout the speech ; the reticence is assumed for the purpose of insinuating that only a tithe of the offences are really named. The whole tone of the speech, therefore, is disingenuous and dishonest.

---

[1] *Timarch.*, §§ 37-38.

[2] *Timarch.*, § 39. Ἄκυρος is used in a double sense ; the early actions of Timarchus are unratified in the sense of not proved ; the actions of the Thirty are not ratified by the succeeding governments. It is a looseness of expression which does not spoil the general sense, and there is, perhaps, an implied reference to the *Amnesty*, declared after the expulsion of the Thirty. Similarly Aeschines declares an *amnesty* for all the offences of Timarchus before a certain date.

[3] *Ibid.*, § 55. In § 70 there is a further apology. Cf. also § 76.

On the other hand, the orator's tribute to the judges' respectability is at times overdrawn. They are informed that 'Timarchus used to spend his days in a gambling-house, where there is a pit in which cock-fights are held, and games of chance are played—I imagine there are some of you who have seen the things I refer to, or if not, have heard of them.'[1] No large assembly could ever take quite seriously such a compliment to its innocence, and it must have been meant as a lighter touch to relieve the dark hues around it. Such playful sallies are not infrequent, and, like this one, are often quite inoffensive.[2]

A far more serious arraignment of the character of Aeschines is brought by Blass, who, having made a very careful study of the speech against Timarchus, finds a strong presumption, on chronological grounds, that the majority of the charges are false. It is certainly remarkable that the charges of immorality rest almost entirely on the statements of the prosecutor. He expresses an apprehension that Misgolas, a most important witness, will either refuse to give evidence altogether, or will not tell the truth. To meet trouble half-way like this is a very serious confession of weakness, which is confirmed by the orator's further comment on the state of the case. He has, he says, other witnesses, but 'if the defendant and his supporters persuade them also to refuse to give evidence—I think they will not persuade them ; at any rate not all of them—there is one thing which they never can do, and that is to abolish the truth and the reputation which Timarchus bears in the city, a reputation which I have not secured for him ; he has earned it for himself. For

<hr>

[1] *Timarch.*, § 53.          [2] Cf. *infra*, p. 191.

the life of a respectable man should be so spotless as not to admit even the suspicion of offence.' [1]

Blass considers that the minor charges, directed against the reckless extravagance with which Timarchus had dissipated his inherited property, are better substantiated; but these alone would have been hardly enough to secure his condemnation.

Against Blass' theories we must set the little that we know about the facts. Timarchus was certainly condemned and disfranchised.[2] Now an Athenian jury was not infallible, and whether in an ordinary court of justice or, as for this case, in the high court of the ecclesia, political convictions might triumph over partiality; nevertheless, a man who was innocent of the charge specifically brought against him, especially if he had not only committed no real political offence, but had played no part in political affairs—a man, moreover, who had the powerful influence of Demosthenes behind him—might reasonably expect to have a fair chance of being acquitted. Aeschines himself was acquitted a few years later on a political charge, though his political conduct required a good deal of explanation, and he had all the weight of Demosthenes not for him, but against him.

Aeschines might well feel a legitimate pride at the high position to which he had climbed from a comparatively humble starting-point; but to reiterate the reasons for this pride is a display of vanity. He likes to talk of himself as ' the counsellor of this the greatest of cities,' as the friend of Alexander and Philip. ' Demosthenes,' he says, ' brings up against me the fact

<hr>

[1] *Timarch.*, § 48.
[2] **Dem.**, *de Falsa Leg.*, §§ 2, 257.

of my friendship with Alexander.'[1] Demosthenes retorts that he has done nothing of the sort. 'I reproach you, you say, with Alexander's friendship ? How in the world could you have gained it or deserved it ? I should never be so mad as to call you the friend of either Philip or Alexander, unless we are to say that our harvesters and hirelings of other sorts are " friends " and " guests " of those who have hired their services.'[2]

And again—'On what just or reasonable grounds could Aeschines, the son of Glaucothea, the tambourine-player, have as his host, or his friend, or his acquaintance, Philip ?'[3] Demosthenes' estimate of the position is probably the truer one ; Aeschines, with all his cleverness, was not the man, as Isocrates was, to meet princes on terms of equality.

His vanity about his speeches and the effect which they produced is attested by the various occasions on which he quotes them, or refers to them. He gives a summary of a speech which he made as an envoy to Philip ;[4] a speech delivered before the ecclesia is epitomized ;[5] a speech made before ' thousands and thousands of Arcadians ' is mentioned.[6] The notorious speech delivered to the Amphictyons is quoted at some length,[7] and its disastrous effect described, the speaker's delight in his own powers blinding him completely to the serious and far-reaching consequences of his criminal indiscretion.

His private life, in spite of some damaging admissions in the *Timarchus*, seems to have been satisfactory

---

[1] ξενία, expressing the mutual relations of host and guest, cannot be adequately translated into English.

[2] *de Cor.*, § 51.

[3] *Ibid.*, § 284.

[4] Aesch., *de Leg.*, §§ 25-33.

[5] *Ibid.*, §§ 75-78.

[6] *Ibid.*, § 79.

[7] *Ctes.*, §§ 119-121.

M

according to Athenian standards. Demosthenes accused him of offering a gross insult to an Olynthian lady. Whether or not the statement was an entire fiction, we are not in a position to judge. Aeschines indignantly denies the charge, and asserts that the Athenian people, when it was made, refused to listen to it, in view of their confirmed respect for his own character :

' Only consider the folly, the vulgarity of the man, who has invented so monstrous a lie against me as the one about the Olynthian woman. You hissed him down in the middle of the story, for the slander was quite out of keeping with my character, and you knew me well.' [1]

Whatever his origin may have been, he was not ashamed of it. He more than once refers with affectionate respect to his father.[2] His love for his wife and children is on one occasion ingeniously introduced in an eloquent passage to influence the feelings of his hearers. This use of ' pathos ' was familiar enough to Greek audiences, but Aeschines shows his originality by the form in which he puts the appeal—aiming directly at the feelings of individual hearers for their own families, rather than asking the assembly collectively to pity the victims of misfortune :

' I have by my wife, the daughter of Philodemus and sister of Philon and Echecrates, three children, a daughter and two sons. I have brought them here with the rest of my family in order that I may put one question and prove one point to my judges ; and this I shall now proceed to do. I ask you, men of Athens, whether you think it likely that,

---

[1] Aesch., *de Leg.*, § 153.

[2] *E.g.*, *de Leg.*, § 147. His esteem for his mother is expressed, *ibid.*, § 148.

in addition to sacrificing my country and the companion-
ship of my friends and my right to a share in the worship
and the burial-place of my fathers, I could betray to Philip
these whom I love more than anything in the world, and
value his friendship higher than their safety ?   Have I ever
become so far the slave of base pleasures ?   Have I ever
yet done anything so base for the sake of money ?   No ;
it is not Macedon that makes a man good or bad, but
nature ;  and when we return from an embassy we are the
same men that we were when you sent us out.' [1]

Lastly, he could speak of himself with dignity, as in
the passage, quoted above,[2] where he rebuts a charge
against his private character, and in the following :

'My silence, Demosthenes, is due to the moderation of
my life ;  I am content with a little ;  I have no base desire
for greatness ;  and so my silence or my speech is due to
careful deliberation, not to necessity imposed by habits
of extravagance.  You, I imagine, are habitually silent
when you have got what you want ;  when you have spent
it, you raise your voice.' [3]

## § 4.  *Style*

The vocabulary of Aeschines consists mostly of words
in ordinary use which require no comment.   Though he
was a great admirer of poetry, his ordinary writing
does not display more poetical or unusual words than
that of any other orator.

The difference between his style and that of a writer
such as Lysias is, essentially, a difference not of vocabulary but of tone ;  the tones of Aeschines are raised.
He tends to use words which are stronger than they
need be, to be ' angry ' when only surprise is called for ;
to be ' excessively indignant ' when a moderate resent-

<hr>

[1] *de Leg.*, § 152.          [2] p. 178.          [3] *Ctes.*, § 218.

ment would meet the case, to ' detest ' when to dislike would be enough.[1]  He makes unnecessary appeals to the gods more frequently than any other orator except Demosthenes.  Exaggeration is part of the secret of his *splendor verborum*, as the Roman critic described it ; but by far the greatest part is his instinct for using quite ordinary words in the most effective combinations.  His best passages, if analysed, contain hardly any words which are at all out of the common, and yet their vigour and dignity are unquestionable.[2]  The ancients, however, denied purity of diction to Aeschines, perhaps on account of the characteristics just described.

He is, as Blass observes, occasionally obscure ; that is, it is possible to find sentences which are not quite easy to understand ; but on the whole these are very rare.  No writer, even a Lysias, can be at all times perfectly lucid.[3]  As a rule Aeschines is as simple in the construction of his sentences as he is in the arrangement of his speeches, and he is much easier to understand than, for instance, Demosthenes.

He has not the consummate grace and terseness which critics admire as the chief beauties of Lysias ; sometimes unnecessary repetitions of a word are to be found, sometimes two synonyms are used where one word would suffice ; but such repetitions often give us lucidity, though at the expense of strict form, and the accumulation of synonyms increases the emphasis.[4] Only the great artist, who is perfectly confident that

---

[1] Cf. the frequent use of δεινός and δεινῶς—δεινὴ ἀπαιδευσία, ἀναισχυντία ; δεινῶς σχετλιάζειν, ἀσχημονεῖν, ἀγνοεῖν, etc., and compounds such as ὑπεραγανακτῶ, ὑπεραισχύνομαι.

[2] *E.g.* the fine passage about Thebes, *infra*, p. 186.

[3] The speech of Lysias against Eratosthenes, for instance, contains many complicated sentences which are unnecessarily obscure.

[4] ὁρώντων φρονούντων βλεπόντων ὑμῶν.  *Ctes.*, § 94.

he has found the right word to express adequately his whole meaning in exactly the right way, can afford to do without all superfluous strokes. Aeschines is not a perfect artist in language; he aims not at artistic beauty but effect, to which style is nothing but a subordinate aid. The composition of artistic prose is, for him, far from being an end in itself.

His speeches were designed not to be read by literary experts, but to be delivered from the platform, and he aimed, not at pleasing the critics' taste but at working on the passions of the ordinary citizen. Some of his most important orations were not written at all, though he probably preserved notes of them,[1] and the three which he did write out in full were preserved not for their literary beauty but for their subject-matter. The time for the rhetoric of culture was past; the course of events required the kind of oratory that would stir men to action. As to the effectiveness of his speeches, there can be no doubt. We know—on his own authority, certainly; but it has never been disputed—how his harangue moved the Amphictyons; and we know that, without any conspicuous moral qualities, with no advantages from family influence and no definite political principles, he became a power in Athens solely by virtue of his eloquence.

Aeschines varies the length of his sentences very considerably; some of them are long, and consist of strings of participial and relative clauses. These, however, occur mostly in narrative passages, where such discursive style is excusable: for instance, the long sentences in the *de Legatione*, §§ 26-27, §§ 75-77, and § 115, contain reports of Aeschines' own earlier speeches.

---

[1] Cf. his frequent references to his speeches, *supra*, p. 177.

The first of these (§§ 26-27) is monotonous owing to the series of genitives absolute which compose an inordinately long protasis, the main verb not occurring till near the end of the sentence, and then being followed by another genitive clause.

A long sentence early in the *Ctesiphon* gives a *résumé* of the circumstances by which the orator is impelled to speak ; the clauses are mostly connected by καί, though all depend on a relative at the beginning. No skill is displayed in the structure of such sentences, and their possible length is limited only by the amount of water in the *clepsydra*. Up to a certain length, they are forcible, but if the limit is exceeded, the effect is lost, for the point which the orator wishes to make is too long deferred, since the main clause, containing the statement which the preceding relative clauses illustrate or explain, is not reached until the heavy accumulation of relative clauses has wearied the perception.

In general, however, Aeschines is moderate in length ; his sentences, on the average, are shorter than those of Isocrates, and he tacitly adheres to the rule that a period should not be so long that it cannot be uttered in one breath.

Though not pedantic, he was far from being without a taste for composition. In all the speeches we find examples of the deliberate avoidance of hiatus, and in the *de Legatione* he bestowed some care on the matter.

The avoidance may generally, though not always, be traced in an unusual order of words.[1]  Examples of harsh hiatus are rare, though there are many unim-

---

[1] *E.g. de Leg.*, § 183, τοὺς εἰς τὸν μέλλοντ' αὐτῷ χρόνον ἀντεροῦντας. Blass, vol. iii. pt. 2, p. 232, notes that there is more consistent care on this point in the *de Legatione* than in the other two speeches.

portant instances.  Quite apart from theoretical rules, a good orator will instinctively avoid awkward combinations of letters, for euphony is necessary for fluent speaking.  Aeschines, secure in the possession of a perfect delivery, might admit sounds which Isocrates and other theorists considered harsh ; it was with practical declamation that he was concerned.

The use of the rhetorical ' figures ' is a prominent characteristic of Aeschines.  The verbal contrasts which Gorgias and the Sophists affected, many of which seem to us so frigid and tedious, have too much honour from Aeschines ; for instance, the purely formal antithesis—' He mentions the names of those whose bodies he has never seen,' [1] where the sound of the jingle—ὀνόματα, σώματα—is more important than the sense.  The effect of such ' like endings ' (*homoeoteleute*) cannot as a rule be reproduced, though sometimes a play upon words will indicate it : *e.g. οὐ τὸν τρόπον ἀλλὰ τὸν τόπον μόνον μετήλλαξεν*—' he has changed, not his habits, but only his habitation.' [2]  In such assonance there is an undoubted aiming at comic effect.  A forcible repetition of words is found in such sentences as the following : ' What I saw, I reported to you as I saw it ; what I heard, as I heard it ; now what was it that I saw and heard about Cersobleptes ? I saw . . .' etc.[3]  Repetitions of this and similar kinds seem to break at times from the speaker's control, and pass all measure.[4]

---

[1] *Ctes.*, § 99.          [2] *Ibid.*, § 78.          [3] *de Leg.*, § 81.

[4] Cf. *Ctes.*, § 198, ὅστις μὲν οὖν ἐν τῇ τιμήσει τὴν ψῆφον αἰτεῖ, τὴν ὀργὴν τὴν ὑμετέραν παραιτεῖται, ὅστις δ' ἐν τῷ πρώτῳ λόγῳ τὴν ψῆφον αἰτεῖ ὅρκον αἰτεῖ, νόμον αἰτεῖ, δημοκρατίαν αἰτεῖ, ὧν οὔτε αἰτῆσαι οὐδὲν ὅσιον οὔτ' αἰτηθέντα ἑτέρῳ δοῦναι.

Aeschines does not seem to have paid any attention to rhythmical writing ; his style is too free to be bound by unnecessary restrictions ; verses and metrical passages occur sporadically, but they are rare.   He seems to have fallen into them by accident, since they occur in positions where no special point is marked by an unusual rhythm.[1]

Direct quotations of poetry, for which he had a great liking, are, on the other hand, very frequent. No other orator, except Lycurgus, is comparable to him in this respect,  and Lycurgus uses his power of quotation with much less force than Aeschines, who often employs it aptly.   He gives us the impression that serious religious conviction is at the back of his quotation from Hesiod :

> ‘ Often the whole of a city must suffer for one man’s
>     sin.’ [2]

In other cases the quotations are excessively long and, like those of Lycurgus, have hardly any bearing on the point.

His metaphors are sometimes vivid and well chosen —ἀμπελουργεῖν τὴν πόλιν—‘ to strip the city like a vineyard ’; ἔναυλον ἦν πᾶσιν—‘ it was dinned into everybody’s ears.’   Some of the most forcible occur in passages which purport to be quotations or paraphrases of Demosthenes : e.g. ἐπιστομίσαι, ‘ to bridle ’ the war-party ; ἀπορράψειν τὸ Φιλίππου στόμα, ‘ to

---

[1] E.g. iambics, *Ctes.*, § 239, ἃ σωφρονῶν ὁ δῆμος οὐκ ἐδέξατο ; and *de Leg.*, § 66, μίαν δὲ νύκτα διαλιπὼν συνηγόρουν, etc. ; anapaestic effect, *ibid.*, 223, ἀεὶ τὸ παρὸν λυμαινόμενος, τὸ δὲ μέλλον κατεπαγγελλόμενος ; and a curious combination, *ibid.*, 91, ἀπάντων μετασχὼν τῶν πόνων τῇ πόλει, (∪ − − | ∪ − − | − ∪ − | − ∪ −).

[2] *Ctes.*, § 135.           [3] *de Leg.*, §§ 110, 21.

sew up Philip's mouth.'[1]   These are probably caricatures of Demosthenes' daring phrases.

Turning now from the consideration of the materials
to the finished product, we find that Aeschines can
attain a high level of style.   His denunciation of the
sharp practices prevailing in the course of his day is
impressive ;  we know that he is speaking the truth,
and he does not make the mistake of exaggerating.
The seriousness is relieved, but not impaired, by the
light thread of sarcasm which runs through the whole
fabric :

' The hearing of such cases, as my father used to tell me,
was conducted in a way very different from ours.   The
judges were much more severe with those who proposed
illegal measures than the prosecutor was, and they would
often interrupt the clerk and ask him to read over again the
laws and the decree ;  and the proposers of illegal measures
were found guilty not if they had ridden over all the laws,
but if they had subverted one single clause.   The present
procedure is ridiculous beyond words ;  the clerk reads the
illegal decree, and the judges, as if they were listening to
an incantation or something that did not concern them,
keep their minds fixed on something else.   And already,
through the devices of Demosthenes, you are admitting a
disgraceful practice ;  you have allowed the course of justice
to be changed, for the prosecutor is on his defence, and the
defendant conducts his prosecution ;  and the judges sometimes forget the matter of which they are called on to be
arbiters, and are compelled to vote on questions which
they ought not to be judging.   The defendant, if he ever
refers to the facts at all, tells you, not that his proposal was
legal, but that somebody else has proposed similar measures
before his time, and has been acquitted.'[1]

<hr>

[1] *Ctes.*, §§ 192-193.

The following passage has been many times pointed out, and justly, as a fine example of the higher style of Aeschines' rhetoric. Taken apart from its context, and without any consideration of the truth of the insinuations which it makes, it is a notable piece of ' pathetic ' pleading. The Romans, with a fondness for epigrammatic contrast, attributed to Aeschines more of sound and less of strength than to Demosthenes. This is true if we regard their works as a whole ; but in isolated passages like this, Aeschines finds his level with the best of Attic orators :

' Thebes, our neighbour Thebes, in the course of a single day has been torn from the midst of Greece ; justly, perhaps, for in general she followed a mistaken policy ; yet it was not human judgment but divine ordinance that led her into error. And the poor Lacedaemonians, who only interfered in this matter originally in connection with the seizure of the sanctuary, they who once could claim to be the leaders of the Greeks, must now be sent up to Alexander to offer themselves as hostages and advertise their disaster ; they and their country must submit to any treatment on which he decides, and be judged by the clemency of the conqueror who was the injured party. And our city, the common asylum of all Greeks, to whom formerly embassies used to come from Greece to obtain their safety from us, city by city, is struggling now not for the leadership of the Greeks but for the very soil of her fatherland. And this has befallen us since Demosthenes took the direction of our policy. A passage in Hesiod contains a solemn warning appropriate to such a case. He speaks, I believe, with the intention of educating the people, and advising the cities not to take to themselves evil leaders.

' I shall quote the lines, for I conceive that we learn by heart the maxims of the poets in childhood, so that in manhood we may apply them :—

‘ " Often the whole of a city must suffer for one man's sin,
Who plotteth infatuate counsel, and walketh in evil ways,
On such God sendeth destruction, by famine and wasting
     plague,
And razeth their walls and armies, and shatters their
     ships at sea." ' [1]

We know that Aeschines took education very
seriously—more seriously, in fact, than anything else—
and his reference here to the educative influence of the
poets gives proof of his earnestness, which may have
been a transient emotion, but was, for the moment, a
strong one.

Setting apart a few such serious passages, Aeschines
is at his best when he is directly accusing Demosthenes. His attacks are nearly always characterized
by a humorous manner which does not make them
any the less forcible, and they generally contain just
enough truth to make their malice effective. The fact
that Aeschines himself had too deep a respect for the
truth to be prodigal in the use of it does not diminish
the virulence of his attack on his rival's veracity, while
any question as to the exactitude of his statements
would be drowned in the laugh that followed the
concluding paragraph :

‘ The fellow has one characteristic peculiarly his own
when other impostors tell a lie, they try to speak vaguely
and indefinitely, for fear of being convicted of falsehood ;
but when Demosthenes seeks to impose upon you, he first
of all enforces his lie with an oath, invoking eternal ruin
on himself ; secondly, though he knows that a thing never
can happen at all, he dares to speak with a nice calculation
of the day when it is going to happen ; he utters the names

<hr>

[1] *Ctes.*, §§ 133-136.

of people whose faces he has never seen, thus cheating you into hearing him, and assuming an air of truthfulness ; and so he thoroughly merits your detestation, since, being such a scoundrel as he is, he discredits the usual proofs of honesty.

' After talking in this way he gives the clerk a decree to read—something longer than the *Iliad*, and more empty than the speeches he makes or the life he has led ; full of hopes that can never be realized, and armies that will never be mustered.' [1]

The pleasing custom followed by the orators of antiquity, whether Greek or Roman, of defiling the graves of the ancestors of their political opponents, and defaming their private lives, can be as well exemplified from Aeschines as from his rival. Aeschines shows no great originality in particular terms of abuse—Dinarchus has a greater variety of offensive words—but the following extract from his circumstantial fictions about Demosthenes is more effective, because more moderate in tone, than the incredible insults with which the latter described the family circumstances and the career of Aeschines : [2]

' So, on his grandfather's account, he must be an enemy of the people, for you condemned his ancestors to death ; but through his mother's family he is a Scythian, a barbarian, though he speaks Greek ; so that even his wickedness is not of native growth. And what of his daily life ? Once a trierarch, he appeared again as a speech-writer, having in some ridiculous fashion thrown away his patrimony ; but as in this profession he came under suspicion of disclosing the speeches to the other side, he bounded up on to the tribunal ; and though he took great sums of money from his administration, he saved very little

---

[1] *Ctes.*, §§ 99-100.      [2] Dem., *de Cor.*, §§ 129, 259.

for himself. Now, however, the king's treasure has drowned his extravagance—but even that will not be enough ; for no conceivable wealth can survive evil habits.

' Worst of all, he makes a living not out of his private sources of income, but out of your danger.' [1]

But he is really at his best where some slight slip on the part of his opponent gives him the opportunity of magnifying a trivial incident into importance. In the following caricature the indecision of Demosthenes is better expressed by the vacillating language thrust into his mouth than it could have been by the most eloquent description in the third person :

' While I was in the middle of this speech, Demosthenes shouted out at the top of his voice—all our fellow-envoys can support my statement—for in addition to his other vices he is a partisan of Boeotia. What he said was something to this purpose :—" This fellow is full of a spirit of turbulence and recklessness ; I admit that I am made of softer stuff, and fear dangers afar off. However, I would forbid him to raise disturbances between the States, for I think that the right course is for us ambassadors not to meddle with anything. Philip is marching to Thermopylae ; I cover my face. No man will judge me because Philip takes up arms ; I shall be judged for any unnecessary word that I utter, or for any action in which I exceed my instructions." ' [2]

The failure of Demosthenes to rise to the occasion when he had the opportunity of delivering an impressive speech before Philip, during the first embassy, forms the groundwork for excellent comedy on the part of Aeschines. Demosthenes, by his rival's account, was usually so intolerable as a companion that

---

[1] *Ctes.*, §§ 172-173.      [2] *de Leg.*, §§ 106-107.

his colleagues refused to stay in the same lodging with him whenever another was obtainable ; but he had found opportunity to impress them with his own sense of his importance as an orator. These professions are well indicated in a few words. The account of his failure, of Philip's patronizing encouragement, of the fiasco in which the whole proceedings terminated, are sketched with a delicate malice that must have made any defence or explanation impossible ; indeed Demosthenes seems to have attempted no reply :

' When these and other speeches had been made, it was Demosthenes' turn to play his part in the embassy, and everybody was most attentive, expecting to hear a speech of exceptional power ; for, as we gathered later, even Philip and his companions had heard the report of his ambitious promises. When everybody was thus prepared to listen to him, the brute gave utterance to some sort of obscure exordium, half-dead with nervousness, and having made a little progress over the surface of the subject he suddenly halted and hesitated, and at last completely lost his way. Philip, seeing the state he was in, urged him to take courage, and not to think he had failed because, like an actor, he had forgotten his part ; but to try quietly and little by little to recollect himself and make the speech as he intended it. But he, having once been flurried, and lost the thread of his written speech, could not recover himself again ; he tried once more, and failed in the same way. A silence followed, after which the herald dismissed the embassy.' [1]

Aeschines not only excelled in this class of circumstantial caricature, but he could win a laugh by a single phrase. It is well known that Midias, after various discreditable quarrels, put the final touch to his insolence by a public assault on Demosthenes,

[1] *de Leg.*, §§ 34-35.

whose face he slapped in the theatre. Demosthenes
on many occasions made capital out of this assault;
which fact inspires the remark of Aeschines, 'His face
is his fortune.'[1] Of his dexterity in repartee a single
instance may be quoted: Demosthenes, in an outburst of indignation, had suggested that the court
should refuse to be impressed by the oratory of a man
who was notoriously corrupt, but should rather be
prejudiced by it against him.[2] Aeschines, catching at
the words, rather than the spirit, retorted, 'Though
you, gentlemen, have taken a solemn oath to give an
impartial hearing to both parties, he has dared to urge
you not to listen to the voice of the defendant.'[3]

### § 5. *Treatment of subjects : general estimate*

During his tenure of the office of γραμματεύς—
clerk to the ecclesia—Aeschines must have gained a
thorough knowledge of the procedure of that assembly,
and of law. This comes out in his general treatment
of his subjects, and particularly in his legal arguments,
which are clear and convincing. In the speech against
Ctesiphon, where the irregularities of the proceedings
about Demosthenes' crown gave him a good subject for
argument, he makes out a very strong case.

In the structure of his speeches he follows a chronological order. He realized well that the style of his
eloquence lent itself naturally to bright and attractive
narrative. His versatility saves him from becoming
tedious ; at one time he can speak with a noble solem-

---

[1] *Ctes.*, § 212, οὐ κεφαλὴν ἀλλὰ πρόσοδον κέκτηται. The play upon
words is not easy to reproduce: κεφαλή, of course, suggests κεφ-
άλαιον, ' principal,' or ' capital,' while πρόσοδος is ' income ' or
' revenue.'

[2] *de Falsa Leg.*, § 339.          [3] Aesch., *de Leg.*, § 1.

nity which reminds M. Croiset of the eloquence of the pulpit,[1] at another, the lightness of his touch almost conceals the bitterness of his sentiments and the seriousness of his purpose.[2]  He can speak of himself with dignity, of his family with true feeling ; careful argument succeeds to lucid narrative ; crisp interrogation, reinforced by powerful sarcasm, to masterly exposition. He can awaken his hearers' interest by an indication of the course which he intends to follow, and this interest is sustained by all the resources of an eloquence which, though at times sophistical, and though disfigured by occasional blemishes, has more of naturalness and shows less traces of scholastic elaboration, than that of any other great orator.  He is abler than Andocides, more varied than Lysias, more alive than Isaeus.

His natural gifts place him above Lycurgus, though our insight into the latter's high character gives him a powerful claim to our consideration.  Blass ranks him below Hyperides, but a study of the lighter passages in Aeschines leads us to believe that, had he turned his attention to private cases, he might have equalled or surpassed that polished orator on his own chosen ground.  The unanimous judgment of ancient and modern times places him far below Demosthenes, who stands apart without a rival ; but in one quality, at least, he surpasses the paragon.  Demosthenes, according to the opinion of Longinus, is apt to make his hearers laugh not with him but at him ;[3] Aeschines never turns the laugh against himself.

[1] *La Litt. Grecque,* iv. 643, with reference particularly to *Ctes.,* § 133 (quoted above, p. 186) and §§ 152 *sqq.*
[2] *E.g.* on Demosthenes, quoted *supra,* pp. 187-188.
[3] *de Sublim.,* ch. xxiv., οὐ γέλωτα κινεῖ μᾶλλον ἢ καταγελᾶται.

Aeschines is perhaps less read than he deserves ; he
has suffered from historical bias, and the prevalent
contempt for his qualities as a statesman has led to an
undue disregard of his virtues as an orator. There is
nothing unfamiliar in this judgment ; other orators
have suffered in the same way at the hands of prejudiced historians.[1]

It is interesting to read the account of Aeschines in
Blass' *Attische Beredsamkeit* ; the gifted scholar apparently starts with a strong prejudice against his author,
and is almost too ready to insist on his faults ; but time
after time he is obliged to admit the existence of positive
merits, and in the end he seems, almost against his will,
to have been forced to modify his judgment ; while
the care and impartiality with which he has detailed
all points, good and bad alike, provides material for a
more favourable estimate such as that of Croiset.

### § 6.  *Contents of Speeches*

A short account of the subject-matter of the three
speeches may conclude this chapter.

1. *Against Timarchus.*

The speech begins (§§ 1-2) with a statement of the
prosecutor's motives ; § 3 states the position which he
intends to assume—that Timarchus, by breaking the
laws, has made the bringing of this action inevitable.
Laws relating to the matter are read and fully discussed (§§ 4-36).

---

[1] Mommsen (Book v., ch. xii. pp. 609-610, Eng. ed. of 1887)
could write of Cicero : ' Cicero had no conviction and no passion ;
he was nothing but an advocate, and not a good one.' . . . ' If
there is anything wonderful in the case, it is in truth not the orations
but the admiration which they excited.'

This preliminary legal statement, apart from the particular case, puts the prosecution on a sounder footing than if the speech had begun at once with the narrative.

§§ 37-76. *The first charge* (immorality). Narrative of the private life of Timarchus, interspersed with evidence and argument as to his political disabilities.

§§ 77-93. Examples of disability imposed on other grounds. Precedents for a verdict in accordance with general knowledge even when the evidence is defective.

§§ 94-105. *The second charge.* Timarchus is a spendthrift. Narrative and evidence about his prodigality.

§§ 106-115. *The third charge.* His corruptness in public life.

§ 116, recapitulation. §§ 117-176, anticipation of the defence.

§§ 177-195. Epilogue, announced beforehand (§ 117) as an ' exhortation to a virtuous life.' § 196, a short conclusion—' I have instructed you in the laws, I have examined the life of the defendant ; I now retire, leaving the matter in your hands.'

2. *On the Embassy.*

Demosthenes had accused Aeschines of treason ; his speech, it is to be noted, dealt really with the second embassy only, and the events in Athens subsequent to it, though he makes some reference to the third embassy, and implies that Aeschines was corrupt even before the second. He follows no chronological order, so that his story is hard to follow. Aeschines, on the other hand, has a great appearance of lucidity, treating all events in chronological order; but this is misleading, for, in order to divert attention from the period in which his conduct was questionable, he spends a disproportionate time in describing the first embassy, in connection with which no accusation is made by Demosthenes.

The exordium (§§ 1-11) contains a strong appeal for an impartial hearing. The events of the first embassy to Philip are the subject of an amusing narrative at the expense of Demosthenes (§§ 12-39); the return of the envoys and their reports, etc., occupy §§ 40-55. The same clearness does not appear in the rest of the speech. Aeschines has to make a defence on various charges brought against himself, so a plain narrative is not enough. The chief charges were that Aeschines was in the pay of Philip, and that he deceived the people as to Philip's intentions, thus leading them into actions which proved disastrous. The former charge could not be proved by Demosthenes, however strong his suspicions were; the facts relating to the peace of Philocrates and the delay in the ratification of the agreement with Philip were matters of common knowledge; it was only a question of intention. The defence of Aeschines is that he deceived the people because he was himself deceived—a confession of credulity and incompetence. The narrative is not continuous; details about the embassy to Philip, the embassy to the Arcadians, and the fate of Cersobleptes, are to some extent mixed together. Reference is also made to some specific charges, *e.g.* the case of the Olynthian woman, the speech before the Amphictyons, the singing of the paean, etc. In the two latter cases there is no defence, but an attempt at justification

(§§ 55-170).   The epilogue begins with an historical survey of Athenian affairs, which is stolen either from Andocides or from some popular commonplace book, and contains the usual appeal to the judges to save the speaker from his adversaries' malice.

He ends by calling on Eubulus and Phocion to speak for him.   (§§ 171-178.)

Stress has been laid in these pages on the somewhat disjointed character of the sections dealing with the principal charges, and it cannot be denied that the defence is sometimes vague ;  that Aeschines seems to aim not at refuting but eluding the accusations.   These imperfections come out on an analysis ;  but the speech taken as a whole is a very fine piece of advocacy, and makes the acquittal of the speaker quite intelligible.

### 3. *Against Ctesiphon.*

The speech opens with an elaboration of a trite commonplace, modelled on the style of Andocides, about the vicious cleverness of the speaker's opponents and his own simple trust in the laws.   Aeschines proposes to prove that the procedure of Ctesiphon was illegal, his statements false, and his action harmful. (§§ 1-8.)

*First charge*—' The proposal to grant a crown to Demosthenes was illegal, because Demosthenes was at the time liable to εὔθυνα (§§ 9-12).   All statements to the contrary notwithstanding, a consideration of the laws proves conclusively that Demosthenes was so liable.'   (§§ 13-31.)

*Second charge*—' It was illegal for the proclamation of the crown to be made in the theatre.'   (§§ 32-48.)

*Third charge*—' The statements on which the pro-

posal was made, viz. that the public counsel and public
actions of Demosthenes are for the best interests of the
people, are false.'   (§ 49.)

The first two charges are dealt with by means of legal
argument, in which Aeschines, as usual, displays considerable ability.   The third and longest section of the
speech (§§ 49-176) is less satisfactory.   The orator
proposes to set aside the private life of his enemy,
though he hints that many incidents might be adduced
to prove its general worthlessness (§§ 51-53), and to
deal only with his public policy.   This he does, in
chronological order and at great length.   Numerous
occasions are described on which the policy of Demosthenes was detrimental to Athens.   The arguments
with which the narrative is interspersed are often of
a trivial nature, consisting sometimes of appeals to
superstition, as when he tells us that troops were sent to
Chaeronea, although the proper sacrifices had not been
performed ;  and attempts to show that Demosthenes
is an ἀλιτήριος, for whose sin the whole city must suffer.
Taken in detail, some of these passages are impressive ;
but the weakness of the whole is that Aeschines himself does not declare any serious or systematic policy.
This section contains incidentally digressions, in the
taste of the day, about the family and character of
Demosthenes.[1]

§§ 177-190 contain some references to heroes of antiquity, by way of invidious comparison; §§ 191-202, the
deterioration of procedure in the courts.[2]

§§ 203-205, recapitulation ;  §§ 206-212, further in-
crimination of Demosthenes, and §§ 213-214, of Ctesi-

---

[1] *E.g.*, in particular, §§ 171-176, partly quoted *supra*, p. 188.
[2] Quoted *supra*, p. 185.

phon.  §§ 215-229, chiefly refutation of charges against Aeschines.  §§ 230-259, further general discussion of the illegality of the measure and the unworthiness of Demosthenes.  The final appeal to the past—' Think you not that Themistocles and the heroes who fell at Marathon and Plataea, and the very graves of our ancestors, will groan aloud if a crown is to be granted to one who concerts with the barbarians for the ruin of Greece ? ' ends abruptly and grotesquely with an invocation to ' Earth and Sun and Virtue and Intelligence and Education, through which we distinguish between the noble and the base.'

It reminds us strangely of the invocations put into the mouth of Euripides by Aristophanes.[1]

[1] *Frogs*, 892, αἰθήρ, ἐμὸν βόσκημα, καὶ γλώττης στροφίγξ, καὶ ξύνεσι, etc.

# CHAPTER IX

## DEMOSTHENES

### § 1. *Introduction*

THE art of rhetoric could go no further after Isocrates, who, in addition to possessing a style which was as perfect as technical dexterity could make it, had imparted to his numerous disciples the art of composing sonorous phrases and linking them together in elaborate periods. Any young aspirant to literary fame might now learn from him to write fluent easy prose, which would have been impossible to Thucydides or Antiphon. If the style seems on some occasions to have been so over-elaborated that the subject-matter takes a secondary place, that was the fault not so much of the artist as of the man. Isocrates never wrote at fever-heat ; his greatest works come from the study ; he is too reflective and dispassionate to be a really vital force.

With Demosthenes and his contemporaries it is otherwise ; they are men actively engaged in politics, actuated by strong party-feeling, and swayed by personal passion. This was the outcome of the political situation : just as feeling was strong in the generation immediately succeeding the reign of the oligarchical Thirty at Athens, so now, when Athens and the whole of Greece were fighting not against oligarchy but the empire of a sovereign ruler, the depths were stirred.

A new feature in this period is the publication of political speeches. From the time of the earliest orator—Antiphon—the professional *logographoi* had preserved their speeches in writing. The majority of these were delivered in minor cases of only personal importance, though some orations by Lysias and others have reference indirectly to political questions.

Another class of speeches which were usually preserved is the *epideictic*—orations prepared for delivery at some great gathering, such as a religious festival or a public funeral. Isocrates was an innovator to the extent of writing in the form of speeches what were really political treatises ; but these were only composed for the reader, and were never intended to be delivered.

Among the contemporaries of Demosthenes we find some diversity of practice. Some orators, such as Demades and Phocion, never published any speeches, and seem, indeed, hardly to have prepared them before delivery. They relied upon their skill at improvisation.

Others, for instance Aeschines, Lycurgus, and Dinarchus, revised and published their judicial speeches, especially those which had a political bearing. Hyperides and Demosthenes, in addition to this, in some cases gave to the world an amended version of their public harangues. Demosthenes did not always publish such speeches ; there are considerable periods of his political life which are not represented by any written work ; but he seems to have wished to make a permanent record of certain utterances containing an explanation of his policy, in order that those who had not heard him speak, or not fully grasped his import, might have an opportunity for further study of his views after the ephemeral effect of his eloquence had passed away.   It is probable that most of the speeches so published belong to times when his party was not predominant in the State, and the opposition had to reinforce its speech by writing.   The result is of importance in two ways, for the speeches are a serious contribution to literature, of great value for the study of the development of Greek prose ;  and they are of still greater historical value ;  for, though untrustworthy in some details, they provide excellent material for the understanding of the political situation, and the aims and principles of the anti-Macedonian party.

## § 2.   *Life, etc.*

Demosthenes the orator was born at Athens in 384 B.C.   His father, Demosthenes, of the deme of Paeania, was a rich manufacturer of swords ;  his mother was a daughter of an Athenian named Gylon, who had left Athens, owing to a charge of treason, at the end of the Peloponnesian War, settled in the neighbourhood of the Cimmerian Bosporus (Crimea),[1] and married a rich woman who was a native of that district. We know nothing more of her except that Aeschines describes her as a Scythian.   She may have been of Hellenic descent ;  even Plutarch doubts the assertion of Aeschines that she was a barbarian ;  the suspicion, however, was enough for Aeschines, who is able to call his enemy a Greek-speaking Scythian.

Demosthenes the elder died, leaving his son seven years old and a daughter aged five.   By his will two nephews, Aphobos and Demophon, and a friend

---

[1] Aesch. (*Ctes.*, § 171) says only ἀφικνεῖται εἰς Βόσπορον, which is ambiguous, as there were several Βόσποροι.  The fact that he calls the woman Σκυθίς seems to prove that he meant the Crimea.

Therippides, were appointed trustees. The two former, as nearest of kin, were, according to Attic custom, to marry the widow and her daughter, but these provisions were not carried out. During the years of Demosthenes' minority his guardians ruined the sword business by their mismanagement, and squandered the accumulated profits.

At the age of eighteen Demosthenes, who had been brought up by his mother, laid claim to his father's estate. The guardians by various devices attempted to frustrate him, and three years were spent in attempts at compromise and examinations before the arbitrators. During this time Demosthenes was studying rhetoric and judicial procedure under Isaeus, to whose methods his early speeches are so deeply indebted that a contemporary remarked ' he had swallowed Isaeus whole.' [1]  At last, when he was twenty-one years old, he succeeded in bringing his wrongs before a court ; thanks to the training of Isaeus he was able to plead his own case, and he won it. The ingenuity of his adversaries enabled them to involve him in further legal proceedings which lasted perhaps two years more. In the end he was victorious, but by the time he recovered his patrimony there was very little of it left.

Being forced to find a means of living he adopted the profession of a speech-writer, which he followed through the greater part of his life.[2]  He made speeches

---

[1] Pytheas, quoted by Dionysius.

[2] The last private speeches of which the genuineness is undoubted are dated about 346 and 345 B.C., but others, *e.g. Against Phormio*, of which the authenticity was not questioned in ancient times, go down to 326 B.C. or even later. The genuineness of the *Phormio* is at least probable.

for others to use, as his father had made swords, and he was as good a craftsman as his father.   He succeeded by this new trade in repairing his damaged fortunes.

In addition to forging such weapons for the use of others, he instructed pupils in the art of rhetoric. This practice he seems to have abandoned soon after the year 345 B.C., when public affairs began to have the chief claim on his energies.[1]   From that time forward he wielded with distinction a sword of his own manufacture.

It is said that as a youth barely of age he made an attempt to speak in the ecclesia, and failed.   His voice was too weak, his delivery imperfect, and his style unsuitable.   The failure only inspired him to practise that he might overcome his natural defects.   We are familiar with the legends of his declaiming with pebbles in his mouth and reciting speeches when running up hill, of his studies in a cave by the sea-shore, where he tried to make his voice heard above the thunder of the waves.

The training to which he subjected himself enabled him to overcome to a great extent whatever disabilities he may have suffered from, but he never had the advantage of a voice and delivery such as those of Aeschines.   Legends current in the time of Plutarch represent him as engrossed in the study of the best prose-writers.   He copied out the history of Thucydides eight times, according to one tradition.   This we need not accept, but it may be taken as certain that he studied the author's style carefully.   He may not

---

[1] Aesch. (in 345 B.C.) in the *Timarchus*, §§ 117, 170-175, refers to him as a teacher.   In the *Embassy* (343 B.C.) there is no reference to this profession.

have been a pupil of Isocrates or Plato, but from the former he must have learnt much in the way of prose-construction and rhythm, and the latter's works, though he dissented from the great principle of Plato that the wise man avoids the *agora* and the law-courts, may well have inspired him with many of the generous ideas which are the foundation of his policy. From the study of such passages as the Melian controversy and others in which the historian bases Justice upon the right of the stronger, he may have turned with relief to the nobler discussion of Justice in the Republic, and indeed, in his view of what is right and good, Demosthenes approaches much nearer to the philosopher than to the historian.

A professional speech-writer at Athens might make a speciality of some particular kind of cases, and by thus restricting his field become a real expert in one department, as Isaeus, for instance, did in the probate court ; or, on the other hand, he might engage in quite general practice. A farmer might have a dispute with his neighbours about his boundaries, or damage caused by the overflow of surface water ; [1] a quiet citizen might seek redress from the law in a case of assault against which he was unable or unwilling to make retaliation in kind ; [2] an underwriter who had been defrauded in some shady marine transaction might wish to bring another knave to account. [3] But besides these private cases, whether they are purely civil, [4] or practically, if not technically, criminal actions, there is other work of more importance for a *logographos*.

---

[1] *Against Callicles.*    [2] *Against Conon.*
[3] The speeches *Against Zenothemis, Lacritus, Dionysodorus,* and *Phormio.*    [4] *E.g. Against Boeotus.*

The State may wish to prosecute an official who has abused its trust.   In times when honesty is rarer than cleverness it may find the necessity of appointing a prosecutor rather for his known integrity than for his ability in the law-courts.   Such a prosecutor will need professional assistance ;  and this need evoked some of the early political speeches of Demosthenes, *Against Androtion, Timocrates*, and *Aristocrates* (355-352 B.C.). It is noticeable that we have no trace of his work between the speeches delivered against his guardians and the first of this latter group.   Probably he spent these ten years partly in study and partly in the conduct of such cases as fell to the portion of a beginner. In this time he must gradually have built up a reputation, but he may not have wished to keep any record of his first essays which, when he had arrived at his maturity as a pleader, could not, perhaps, have seemed to him worthy of his reputation.

It is impossible to exaggerate the importance of these varied activities to the career of Demosthenes. In the course of these early years he must have made himself familiar with many branches of the law ;  he was brought into intimate relations with individuals of all classes, and all shades of political opinion.   In order to be of use vicariously in political cases he must have made a careful study of politics.   Such studies were of great value in the education of a statesman, and by means of the semi-public cases in which he was engaged, though not on his own account, and perhaps not always in accordance with his convictions, his own political opinions must gradually have been formed.

In 354 B.C., the year after the trial of Androtion,

Demosthenes appeared in person before the dicastery on behalf of Ctesippus in an action against Leptines. This was a case of some political importance. A few months later he came forward in the assembly to deliver his speech *On the Symmories*, which was shortly followed by another public harangue *On behalf of the people of Megapolis* (353 B.C.). Two years later he came to the front not as a mere pleader, but a real counsellor of the people, and began the great series of *Philippics*.

His career from this point onward is divided naturally into three periods.

In the first, 351-340 B.C., he was in opposition to the party in power at Athens. The beginning of it is marked by some famous speeches, the *First Philippic* and the first three *Olynthiac* orations (351-349 B.C.). Till this time the Athenians had not realized the significance of the growth of the Macedonian power. It was only eight years since Philip, on his accession to the throne, had undertaken the great task of uniting the constituent parts of his kingdom which had long been torn by civil war, of fostering a national feeling, and creating an army. He had won incredible successes in a few years. By a combination of force and deceit he had made himself master of Amphipolis and Pydna in 357 B.C. In the following year he obtained possession of the gold mines of Mt. Pangaeus, which gave him a source of inexhaustible wealth, and enabled him to prepare more ambitious enterprises. This was an important crisis in his career : the bribery for which he was famous and in which he greatly trusted could now be practised on a large scale.

In the early speeches of Demosthenes there is little

reference to Philip ; he is certainly not regarded as a dangerous rival of Athens. There is a passing mention of him in the *Leptines* (384 B.C.) ; [1] in the *Aristocrates* he plays a larger part, but is treated almost contemptuously : 'You know, of course, whom I mean by this Philip of Macedon' (ἴστε δήπου Φίλιππον τουτονὶ τὸν Μακέδονα) is the form in which his name is introduced (§ 111). He is considered as an enemy, but only classed with other barbarian princes, such as Cersobleptes of Thrace.

But Philip was not content with annexing towns and districts in his own neighbourhood in whose integrity Athens was interested—Amphipolis, Pydna, Potidaea, Methone, and part of Thrace. He interfered in the affairs of Thessaly, which brought the trouble nearer home to Athens (353 B.C.). In 352 B.C. he proposed to pass through Thermopylae, and take part in the Sacred War against Phocis, but here Athens intervened for the first time and checked his progress.

After this one vigorous stroke the Athenians, in spite of Philip's renewed activities in Thrace and on the Propontis, relapsed into an apathetic indifference, from which Demosthenes in vain tried to rouse them.

The language of the *First Philippic* shows that Demosthenes fully recognized the seriousness of the situation, and the imminent danger to which the complacency of his countrymen was exposing them ; he wishes to make them feel that the case, though not yet desperate, is likely to become so if they persist in doing

---

[1] § 61. 'Pydna and Potidaea, which are subject to Philip and hostile to you.' Also § 63.

nothing, while a whole-hearted effort will bring them into safety again :

§ 2.   ' Now, first of all, Gentlemen, we must not despair about the present state of affairs, serious as it is ;  for our greatest weakness in the past will be our greatest strength in the future.   What do I mean ?   I mean that you are in difficulties simply because you have never exerted yourselves to do your duty.   If things were as they are in spite of serious effort on your part to act always as you should, there would be no hope of improvement.   Secondly, I would have you reflect on what some of you can remember and others have been told, of the great power possessed not long ago by Sparta ;  yet, in face of that power you acted honourably and nobly, you in no wise detracted from your country's dignity ;  you faced the war unflinchingly in a just cause. . . .'

§ 4.   ' If any of you thinks that Philip is invincible, considering how great is the force at his disposal, and how our city has lost all these places, he has grounds for his belief ;  but let him consider that *we* once possessed Pydna, Potidaea, and Methone, and the whole of that district ; and many of the tribes, now subject to him, were free and independent and better disposed to us than to Macedon. If Philip had felt as you do now, that it was a serious matter to fight against Athens because she possessed so many strongholds commanding his own country, while he was destitute of allies, he would never have won any of his present successes, or acquired the mighty power which now alarms you.   But he saw clearly that these places were the prizes of war offered in open competition ;  that the property of an absentee goes naturally to those who are on the spot to claim it, and those who are willing to work hard and take risks may supplant those who neglect their chances.'

§ 8.   ' Do not imagine that he is as a God, secure in eternal possession.   There are men who hate and fear and envy him, even among those who seem his closest associates. These feelings are for the present kept under, because through your slowness and your negligence they can find no opening.   These habits, I say, you must break with.'

§ 10.   ' When, I ask, when will you be roused to do your duty ?—When the time of need comes, you say.   What do you think of the present crisis ?   I hold that a free nation can never be in greater need than when their conduct is of a kind to shame them.   Tell me, do you want to parade the streets asking each other, " Is there any news to-day ? " What graver news can there be than that a Macedonian is crushing Athens and dictating the policy of Greece ? " Philip is dead," says one.   " Oh no, but he is ill," says another.   What difference does it make to you ?   Even if anything happens to him you will very soon call into existence a second Philip if you attend to your interests as carefully as you are doing now.   For it is not so much his own strength as your negligence that has raised him to power.'

The orator proceeds to give detailed advice for the conduct of the war ; he asks for no ' paper forces,' [1] such as the assembly is in the habit of voting, irrespective of whether they can be obtained or not—ten or twenty thousand of mercenaries or the like.   He requires a small but efficient expeditionary force, of which the backbone is to be a contingent of citizen-hoplites, one quarter of the whole ; a small but efficient fleet, and money to pay both army and navy—this was a matter often overlooked by the assembly—and an Athenian general in whom the host will have confidence.   The advice was moderate and sound in the extreme.   Demosthenes probably knew what he was talking about when he said that two thousand hoplites,

[1] ἐπιστολιμαίους δυνάμεις, § 19.

O

two hundred cavalry, and fifty triremes were enough for the present. A resolute attack on Philip by such a force would probably have put fresh heart into the many enemies whom he had not yet completely subdued.

There is a further point which marks the difference between the present advice and that of previous counsellors. The army is not to be enlisted for a particular expedition only ; it is to be maintained at its original strength as long as may be necessary.[1] Soldiers will serve for a certain limited time, and at the end of their term will be replaced by fresh troops.[2] The army which he suggests will not be enough to defeat Philip unaided, but enough to produce a strong impression. They might send a large force, but it would be unwieldy, and they could not maintain it.[3]

The *First Philippic* failed to produce the effect desired. The *Olynthiac* speeches which closely followed it were also ineffectual. In 349 B.C. Philip seized a pretext for making war on Olynthus, which appealed for help to Athens. The alliance, which had been sought in vain in 357 and 352 B.C., was now, apparently, granted with little opposition, and Chares with two thousand mercenaries sent to the help of the Olynthian league. Demosthenes tries to emphasize the importance of the situation ; the aid which has been voted is not enough ; they ought to act at once, sending two forces of citizens, not mercenaries ; the one to protect Olynthus, the other to harass Philip elsewhere. Large

---

[1] § 19, δύναμιν . . . ἢ συνεχῶς πολεμήσει. . . .

[2] § 21, χρόνον τακτὸν στρατευομένους, μὴ μακρὸν τοῦτον, ἀλλ' ὅσον ἂν δοκῇ καλῶς ἔχειν, ἐκ διαδοχῆς ἀλλήλοις.

[3] § 23, οὐ τοίνυν ὑπέρογκον αὐτήν (οὐ γὰρ ἔστι μισθὸς οὐδὲ τροφή), οὐδὲ παντελῶς ταπεινὴν εἶναι δεῖ.

supplies of money are necessary, and he hints that the Athenians have such supplies ready at hand. He refers to the Festival Fund ($\theta\epsilon\omega\rho\iota\kappa\acute{o}\nu$), but concerning this he is in a delicate position. The ministry of Eubulus was in power, and a law of Eubulus had pronounced any attempt to tamper with the $\theta\epsilon\omega\rho\iota\kappa\acute{o}\nu$ a criminal offence. Demosthenes, being one of a weak minority, could only move cautiously, suggesting that a change of administration was desirable, but not proposing a definite motion.

There is a marked difference in tone between the first two speeches and the third. In the former Demosthenes insists that everything is still to be done, but he points out that there are many weak points in Philip's armour, and a vigorous and united policy may still defeat him. In the third he makes it clear that the opportunity is past, and the lost ground can only be recovered by desperate measures. He openly advocates the conversion of the Festival Fund into a military chest, and this is the main theme of the oration, to which every argument in turn leads up.[1]

The efforts of Athens were dilatory and insufficient; Olynthus and the other cities of the Chalcidian League fell in the following year (349 B.C.); they were destroyed, and all the inhabitants made slaves. Attempts to unite the Peloponnesian States against the common enemy were futile, and negotiations were begun between Philip and Athens. They were conducted at first informally by private persons, but in 347 B.C., on

---

[1] I have assumed the traditional order of the Olynthiac speeches to be the correct one. The question is much disputed, and is lucidly discussed by M. Weil in his introductions to the speeches (*Les Harangues de Démosthène*).

the proposal of Philocrates, an embassy was sent to Philip. Philip's answer, received in 346 B.C., demanded that Phocis and Halus should be excluded from the proposed treaty. Demosthenes contested this point, but Aeschines carried it. A second embassy was sent, and the discreditable Peace of Philocrates was signed. The result was the ruin of Phocis. Although Demosthenes disapproved of the peace, later in the year, in his speech *On the Peace,* he urged Athens to keep its conditions, arguing that to break it would bring upon them even greater disaster.

In consequence of the peace, Philip had been able to convoke the Amphictyonic Council, and pass a vote for the condemnation of Phocis. Twenty-two towns were destroyed, and the Phocian votes in the Council transferred to Philip, who was also made president of the Pythian Games. Thus the barbarian of a few years ago had received the highest religious sanction for his claim to be the leader of Greece. Athens alone, whose precedence he had usurped, refused to recognize him, and Demosthenes saw that to persist in a hostile attitude might involve all the States in a new Amphictyonic war. It was better to surrender their scruples, and to regard the convention not, indeed, as a permanent peace, but a truce during which fresh preparations might be made. Six years of nominal peace ensued, during which Philip extended his influence diplomatically. Whether from principle or policy he treated Athens with marked courtesy, and, through his agents, made vague offers of the great services which he was prepared to render. Many of the citizens believed in his sincerity, notably Isocrates, who in 346 B.C. spoke of the baseless suspicions caused by the assertions of malicious

persons, that Philip wished to destroy Greek freedom.[1]
Demosthenes was never duped by these professions.
He was now a recognized leader, and was gathering to
his side a powerful body of patriotic orators such as
Lycurgus and Hyperides. Philip, after organizing
the government of Thessaly and allying himself with
Thebes, interfered in the Peloponnese by supporting
Messene, Arcadia, and Argos against Sparta.

An Athenian embassy, led by Demosthenes, was
sent to these states to advise them of the danger which
they incurred by their new alliance. Some impression
was produced, and apparently an embassy was sent by
some of the states to Athens. In reply to their re-
presentations, of which no trace is preserved, Demosthenes delivered the *Second Philippic*. In it he ex-
poses the king's duplicity. ' The means used by
Athens to counteract his manœuvres are quite inadequate ; we talk, but he acts. We speak to the
point, but do nothing to the point. Each side is
superior in the line which it follows, but his is the more
effective line (§§ 1-5). Philip's assurances of goodwill
are accepted too readily. He realized that Thebes, in
consideration of favours received, would further his
designs. He is now showing favour to Messene and
Argos from the same motive. He has paid Athens the
high compliment of not offering her a disgraceful
bargain (§§ 6-12). His past actions betray him ; as he
made the Boeotian cities subject to Thebes, he is not
likely to free the Peloponnesian States from Sparta.
He knows that he is really aiming at you, and that you
are aware of it ; that is why he is ever on the alert,
and supports against you Thebans and Peloponnesians,

---

[1] Isocr., *Philippus*, § 73-74.

who, he thinks, are greedy enough to swallow his present offers, and too stupid to foresee the consequences' (§§ 12-19).   The epilogue contains an indictment of those whose policy is to blame for the present troubles.   In accordance with Demosthenes' general practice Aeschines and Philocrates, at whom he aims the charge, are not mentioned by name.

The anti-Macedonian party grew in strength in 343 B.C.  Hyperides impeached Philocrates, who retired into exile and was condemned to death.   About the same time Demosthenes himself brought into court an action against Aeschines, which had been pending for three years, for traitorous conduct in connexion with the embassy to Philip.   The position was a difficult one for two reasons : his own policy in that matter could not be sharply distinguished from that of Aeschines ; the accusation depended largely on discrimination of motives, and he had practically no proof of the guilt of Aeschines.   Considering the technical weakness of the prosecutor's case it is not surprising that Aeschines escaped ; it is more remarkable that he was acquitted only by a small majority.

In 342 B.C. Philip, whose influence in the Peloponnese had slightly waned, began a fresh campaign in Thrace, and in 341 B.C. had reached the Chersonese. The possession of this district meant the control of the Dardanelles, and, as Athens still depended largely on the Black Sea trade for her corn supply, his progress was a menace to her existence. Diopeithes, an Athenian mercenary captain, had in 343 B.C. taken settlers to Cardia, a town in the Chersonese in nominal alliance with Macedon. Cardia was unwilling to receive them, and Philip sent help to the town.   Diopeithes, who, in accordance with the habit of the times, in order to support his fleet, exacted 'benevolences' from friends and foes impartially, happened to plunder some districts in Thrace which were subject to Macedon. Philip addressed a letter of remonstrance to Athens, and his adherents in the city demanded the recall of Diopeithes. Demosthenes in his speech *On the Chersonese* urged that the Chersonese should not be abandoned at such a crisis : a permanent force must be maintained there. He defends the actions of Diopeithes by an appeal to necessity. The Athenians were in the habit of voting armaments for foreign service without voting them supplies ; consequently the generals had to supply themselves.

' All the generals who have ever sailed from Athens take money from Chios, Erythrae, or from any other Asiatic city they can. Those who have one or two ships take less ; those with a larger force take more. Those who give, whether in large or small amounts, are not so mad as to give them for nothing ; they are purchasing protection for merchants sailing from their ports, immunity from ravages, safe convoy for their own ships and other such advantages. They will tell you that they give " Benevolences," which is the term applied to these extortions.

' Now in the present case, since Diopeithes has an army, it is obvious that all these people will give him money. Since he got nothing from you, and has no private means to pay his soldiers with, where else do you imagine he can get money to keep them ? Will it fall from the skies ? Unfortunately, no. He has to live from day to day on what he can collect and beg and borrow.' [1]

In addition to including a plan of campaign, the speech contains, as many of the orations do, a frank

---

[1] *Chers.*, §§ 24-26.

statement of the position of affairs, and the usual invectives against Athenian apathy. The concluding section, however, contains a more solemn warning than is usual, showing that Demosthenes almost despairs of success.

' If you grasp the situation as I have indicated, and cease to make light of everything, it may be, it may be that even now our affairs may take a favourable turn ; but if you continue to sit still and confine your enthusiasm to expressions of applause and votes of approval, but shirk the issue when any action is required of you, I cannot conceive of any eloquence which, without performance of your duty, can guide our State to safety.' [1]

The *Third Philippic* was delivered in the same year (341 B.C.). The situation is in all essentials the same. Demosthenes again demands that help should be sent to the Chersonese and the safety of Byzantium assured ; but he does not enlarge on these points, which have been treated by previous speakers.[2] ' We must help them, it is true, and take care that no harm befalls them ; but our deliberations must be about the great danger which now threatens the whole of Greece.' [3] It is this breadth of view which distinguishes the *Third Philippic*, and makes it the greatest of all the public harangues.

In the *Chersonese* Demosthenes had suggested the dispatch of numerous embassies ; he now enlarges on this topic ; the interests of Athens must be identified with those of all Greece, and all States must be made to realize this. Philip's designs are against Greek liberty as a whole ; Athens must arm and put herself at the head of a great league in the struggle for freedom.

[1] § 77.  [2] § 19.  [3] § 20.

'I pass over Olynthus, Methone, and Apollonia, and thirty-two cities in the Thracian district, all of which he has so brutally destroyed that it is hard for a visitor to say whether they were ever inhabited. I am silent about the destruction of a great nation, the Phocians. But how fares Thessaly? Has he not deprived the cities of their governments, and established tetrarchies, in order that they may be enslaved, not only city by city, but tribe by tribe? Are not the cities of Euboea now ruled by tyrants, though that island is close on the borders of Thebes and Athens? Does he not expressly state in his letters "I am at peace with those who will obey me"? And his actions corroborate his words. He has started for the Hellespont; before that he visited Ambracia; he holds in the Peloponnese the important city of Elis; only the other day he made plots against Megara. Neither Greece nor the countries beyond it can contain his ambition.'[1]

This short extract is a fair example of Demosthenes' vigorous use of historical argument, but it can give little idea of the speech as a whole. It abounds, indeed, in enumerations of recent events bearing on the case, and in contrasts between the present and the past.

This running appeal to example to a great extent takes the place of reasoned argument, but the effect of the whole, with its combined appeals to feeling and reason, is convincingly strong.

The orator himself must have attached great importance to this speech as an exposition of his policy, for he appears to have published two recensions of it. Both are preserved in different families of MSS. The shorter text contained in S (*Parisinus*) and L (*Laurentianus*) omits many phrases and even whole passages which occur in the other group. It is believed that the

---

[1] §§ 26-27.

shorter is the final form in which Demosthenes wished to preserve the speech.[1]

The *Fourth Philippic* contains the suggestion that Athens should make overtures to the Persian king for help against Philip. The speech is probably a forgery, but one of a peculiar kind. About a third of the text consists of passages taken directly from the speech *On the Chersonese*, and one division (§§ 35-45) is in favour of a distribution of the Theoric Fund, which is quite opposed to the policy of the *Olynthiacs* and the Chersonese speech. On the other hand, some passages are in a style and tone quite worthy of Demosthenes, and consistent with his views. There can be little doubt that we have here a compilation from actual speeches of Demosthenes, expanded by a certain amount of rhetorical invention. The 'answer to Philip's letter' and the speech περὶ συντάξεως are, on the other hand, simple forgeries. This concludes the list of the *Philippic* speeches.

Our record of Demosthenes' public speeches ceases with the *Third Philippic*, at the moment when his eloquence had reached its greatest height. The great speeches belong to the years of opposition ; now, after

---

[1] The subject is admirably discussed by M. Weil (*Les Harangues de Démosthène* (2me éd.), pp. 312-316). His arguments should be carefully read by those interested in the subject. I quote only his conclusions : ' Nous avons déjà vu que plusieurs passages, qui manquent dans S et L, ne pouvaient guère émaner que de Démosthène lui-même ' (p. 314). ' Le résultat de cet examen, c'est que nous nous trouvons en présence de deux textes également autorisés, et que les additions et les modifications qui distinguent l'un de l'autre doivent être attribuées à l'orateur lui-même . . .' (p. 315). These conclusions are adopted by Blass (*Att. Bered.*, 1893) and Sandys (1900), who, however, considers that the shorter version was the orator's first draft. Butcher (*Demosthenes*, 3rd ed., 1911) considers that the shorter text represents ' the maturer correction of the orator.'

eleven years of combat, he had established himself
as chief leader of the assembly.   He spoke, no doubt,
frequently and impressively, but, engaged in important administrative work, he had no leisure or need
for writing.

The years 340-338 B.C. were a time of vigorous revival for Athens.   For a short but brilliant period it
seemed that the city-state might emerge triumphant
from the struggle against monarchy.   Enthusiasm
inspired the patriotic party to noble efforts.   Euboea
was removed from Philip's influence, and Athens in-
augurated a new league, including Acarnania, Achaea,
Corcyra, Corinth, Euboea, and Megara.   Philip himself
suffered a check before Byzantium, which had appealed to Athens for help, and had not called in vain.

In internal affairs, a new trierarchic law not only
increased the efficiency of the fleet, but abolished a
great social grievance by making the burden of trierarchy fall on all classes in just proportion to their
means, whereas hitherto the poorer citizens had
suffered unduly.   A still greater reform was the execution of the project, so long cherished, for applying
the Theoric Fund to the expenses of war (339 B.C.).
In 338 B.C. Lycurgus was appointed to the Ministry of
Finance, an office which he was to fill with exceptional
efficiency for twelve years to come.

But Philip held many strings, and was most dangerous when he seemed to turn his back on his enemies.
Unsuccessful on the Hellespont, he withdrew his fleet
and undertook an expedition by land against a Scythian
prince who had offended him.   This journey had no
direct relation to his greater designs, and Athens was
pleased to think that he might be defeated or even

killed. He was, indeed, wounded, but he returned to Macedonia in 339 B.C., having accomplished what was probably his chief object, to restore the confidence of his soldiers after their reverses in recent encounters with the Greeks.

Meanwhile events in Greece, which perhaps were partly directed by his influence, pursued a course favourable to his plans.

In 340 B.C. two enemies of Demosthenes, Midias and Aeschines, represented Athens as *pylagorae* at the Amphictyonic Council. Aeschines describes how, apparently from no political motive but for the satisfaction of a personal grudge, he himself inflamed the passions of the Amphictyons to the point of declaring a sacred war against the Locrians of Amphissa. Any war between Greeks was to Philip's advantage. The Amphictyonic War was carried on in a dilatory way, and in the autumn of 339 B.C. the Council, still under the influence of Aeschines, nominated Philip to carry the affair to a conclusion. The king had recovered quickly from his wound, and eagerly embraced the sacred mission which allowed him to pass through Thessaly and Thermopylae unmolested. On reaching Elatea, once the principal town of Phocis, but now desolate, he halted and began to put the place in a state of defence. The news was received at Athens with great consternation, as Demosthenes vividly describes.[1] An assembly was hastily summoned, and Demosthenes explained the full import of this action. It was a threat to Athens and Thebes alike. All the masterly eloquence of the great statesman was exerted to the utmost of his powers to induce Athens to forget

---

[1] *de Cor.*, §§ 169-170.

long-standing enmities and offer to Thebes the help of her entire fighting force freely and unconditionally.   It was probably the greatest triumph of eloquence ever known that Demosthenes was successful in his plea. War was inevitable sooner or later, and it is greatly to his credit that he brought about the Theban alliance, though it ended disastrously for all the Greeks concerned in the battle of Chaeronea (338 B.C.).

Henceforward the influence of Athens on external affairs was strictly limited, though she retained her independence, for Philip was a generous foe.[1]   Demosthenes busied himself with internal matters ;  to him was committed the repair of the fortifications, to the expense of which he gave a contribution of 100 minae. For this act Ctesiphon proposed in 337 B.C. that he should be rewarded with a gold crown.  Aeschines indicted Ctesiphon for an illegal motion, and the famous case of *The Crown*, which produced great speeches from both the rivals, was the result.  The case, however, was not heard till six years later.

In 336 B.C. Philip was murdered.  Demosthenes set the example of rejoicing by appearing in public crowned with flowers, though he was in mourning for his daughter at the time.  The great hopes which the city-states had entertained were dashed to the ground by the energy of Alexander, who, though only twenty years old, proved himself an even greater general and statesman than his father.

Thebes was induced to revolt by Demosthenes, who was supported by Persian gold, but Alexander crushed

---

[1] Philip seems to have had a genuine admiration for Athens, and always treated her with extraordinary consideration.  For a full appreciation of this attitude see Hogarth, *Philip and Alexander*.

and destroyed Thebes before help could reach it, and sent an ultimatum to Athens. He demanded the surrender of Demosthenes, Lycurgus, and eight other orators of their party. They were saved, it appears, by the intervention of Demades.[1]

Alexander departed for Asia, and Athenian statesmen were left to quarrel about the politics of their city. It was now that the great case in which Demosthenes and Aeschines were concerned came up for trial. The matter nominally in dispute was only a pretext; it was really a question of reviewing and passing judgment on the political life of the two great antagonists for the last twenty years.

The charges of illegality brought against Ctesiphon were three : (1) That the decree, falsely asserting that Demosthenes had done good service to the State, involved the insertion of a lie into the public records. (2) That it was illegal to crown an official who, like Demosthenes, was still subject to audit. (3) That proclamation of the crowning in the theatre was illegal.

On (2) and (3), the technical points, the prosecutor had a strong case, but the first section was the only one of real importance, since the process was really aimed at Demosthenes. The main part of the speech of Aeschines against Ctesiphon is accordingly devoted to an indictment of the public life of Demosthenes. Four periods are taken : (1) From the war about Amphipolis to the peace of Philocrates (357-346 B.C.). (2) The years of peace (346-340 B.C.). (3) The ministry of Demosthenes (340-338 B.C.). (4) The years after Chaeronea (338-330 B.C.).

The reply of Demosthenes (*de Corona*) is mainly con-

---

[1] Plut., *Dem.*, ch. xxiii.

cerned with a defence of his own policy, the technical points on which the issue nominally depended being kept very much in the background.  It is remarkable that in dealing with the early years he makes no attempt to take credit for the great speeches by which in that time he attempted to influence his country— the *First Philippic* and the three *Olynthiacs*.  He discusses chiefly the peace negotiations.  He speaks more fully of the second period, and lays the greatest stress on the third—the years during which he was the acknowledged leader of the people, so that an eulogy of the national policy must involve a tribute to his own patriotism.  Only short allusions are made to the last period, the years since the battle of Chaeronea.

The order is not chronological, and the structure is not apparently systematic ; nevertheless the *de Corona* is the greatest of all Athenian speeches.

The speech cannot be represented by extracts ; it must be read as a whole to be appreciated.  All that a summary can do is to draw attention to the peculiarities of structure, which are possibly due in some measure to the length of the speech and the variety of the subjects which have to be treated : [1]

1. §§ 1-8.  The conventional exordium, in this case both introduced and finished by a solemn prayer.

2. §§ 9-52.  Refutation of the calumnies uttered by Aeschines.  This section consists chiefly of Demosthenes' own version of the negotiations for the peace of 346 B.C., showing that Aeschines and his associates were really guilty of treason in their dealings with Philip.

---

[1] See also *infra*, p. 253, *note* 1, and p. 254.

3. §§ 53-125.  Defence of Ctesiphon—Demosthenes undertakes to prove (*a*) that he deserved to receive a crown, (*b*) that on the legal point Ctesiphon is not to blame.  (*a*) He summarizes the condition of Greece during the years of peace, and immediately after it records his own public services and justifies his policy.  (*b*) He examines the question of legality, and proves that Ctesiphon is on the right side of the law.

4. §§ 126-159.  Invective against Aeschines.  This might be called a pseudo-epilogue, but is really only an interlude.  It deals with (*a*) the birth and life of his rival, and (*b*) in particular, his action which kindled an Amphictyonic war.

5. §§ 160-251.  Demosthenes continues the discussion of his past policy, in regard to the Theban alliance and the last war with Philip.

6. §§ 252-324.  An epilogue of exceptional length, mainly devoted to a comparison between Demosthenes and Aeschines.  The speaker closely identifies himself with the city, whose policy he has shaped; so that in attacking him, Aeschines attacks Athens.  The speech ends, as it began, with a prayer.

## § 3

For the next few years Demosthenes probably spent some of his time in composing private speeches for others, though the extant speeches of this period are mostly of doubtful authenticity.  He also remained as a prominent figure in Athenian politics.  He had not changed his views, but he seems to have been deposed from the leadership of the patriotic party by others whose patriotism was of a more violent type than his, so that he must be now counted as a moderate in opinion.   It may have been this position which brought him into danger in 324 B.C.

Harpalus, who had been left as Alexander's governor at Babylon, on receipt of a rumour of his master's death in India, made off with the royal treasure, and, accompanied by a force of six thousand men, took ship and sailed for Greece.   He appeared off Piraeus, and the fervid patriots proposed that Athens should welcome him and use his treasure and his men to help them in a revolt.

Demosthenes opposed an open breach with Alexander, and on his motion admission was refused to the flotilla.   Harpalus came a second time without his army, and was admitted.   Close on his heels came messengers from Alexander to demand his surrender, but this was resisted by Demosthenes and Phocion. On the motion of Demosthenes it was decided to temporize ; Harpalus was to be treated as a prisoner, and the treasure deposited in the Parthenon.   The amount of the treasure was declared by Harpalus as 720 talents, but it soon became known that only 350 talents had been lodged in the Acropolis.   Harpalus in the meantime had escaped from prison and disappeared, and suspicion was roused against all who had had any kind of dealings with him.   To allay the public excitement Demosthenes proposed that the Council of the Areopagus should investigate the mystery of the lost talents.   Six months later the Council gave its report, issuing a list of nine public men whom it declared guilty of receiving part of the lost money. The name of Demosthenes himself headed the list ; he

P

was charged with having received twenty talents for helping Harpalus to escape. This declaration did not constitute a judicial sentence, but in consequence of it prosecutions were instituted, ten public prosecutors were appointed, and Demosthenes was found guilty. He was condemned to pay a fine of fifty talents, and being unable to raise the money he was cast into prison. He soon escaped, and fled first to Aegina and then to Troezen, where, according to Plutarch, he sat daily by the sea, watching with sad eyes the distant shores of Attica.

The whole affair is obscure ; we do not know how Demosthenes defended himself, but we possess two of the speeches for the prosecution, by Hyperides and Dinarchus. Neither is explicit. The report of the Areopagus was held to have established the facts, so that no further evidence was required ; it was the business of the court only to interpret motives and decide the degree of each defendant's guilt.

Hyperides [1] affirms that Demosthenes began by admitting the receipt of the money ; but he afterwards denied it, declaring that he was ready to suffer death if it could be proved that he had received it.[2] It was certainly Demosthenes who proposed that the Areopagus should investigate the affair.

Two details in the case give rise to perplexity : the fine inflicted—two and a half times the amount involved—was light, considering that the law demanded ten-fold restitution ; secondly, it is difficult to see when Demosthenes can have received the money. Harpalus could not pay him at the time of his escape,

---

[1] Hyp., *Against Dem.*, fr. 3, col. xiii.
[2] Dinarchus, *Against Dem.*, § 1.

or indeed at any time subsequent to his arrest, for he did not take the money to prison with him. It seems improbable that the money should have been paid earlier, for Demosthenes was acting against Harpalus all the time. Professor Butcher supposed that payment might have been made when Demosthenes resisted the surrender of Harpalus to Alexander.[1]

Two theories have been proposed with a view to the complete or partial exculpation of the orator—one, that he was absolutely innocent, but became the victim of a combination of his political enemies, the extreme patriots, who were dissatisfied with his moderate policy, and his ancient foes the Macedonian party. The other view is that he received the money and spent it, or intended to spend it, on secret service of the kind on which every State spends money, though it is generally impossible to give a detailed account of such expenses. Even if he could not prove such a use, the offence of receiving bribes was a venial one, as even his prosecutor Hyperides admits, if they were not received against the interests of the State. In Demosthenes' favour we have the late evidence of Pausanias, who affirms that an agent of Harpalus, when examined by Alexander with regard to this affair, divulged a list of names which did not contain that of Demosthenes.

A minor charge of bribery is brought by Dinarchus, who asserts that Demosthenes received 300 talents from the Great King to save Thebes in 335 B.C., but sacrificed Thebes to his own avarice because he wished to keep ten talents which had been promised to the Arcadians for their assistance. The story is ridiculous.

[1] Butcher, *Dem.*, pp. 124-127.

In 323 B.C. Alexander died; the hope of freedom revived, and Demosthenes started at once on a tour of the Peloponnese to urge on the cities the need of joint action. He was reconciled with the party of Hyperides and recalled from exile. He was fetched home in a trireme, and a procession escorted him from the harbour to the city. By a straining of the law, the public paid his fine. The Lamian war opened successfully under Leosthenes, but at the battle of Crannon Antipater crushed the Greek forces. Athens was forced to receive a Macedonian garrison, to lose her democratic constitution, and to give up her leaders to the conqueror's vengeance. Demades carried a decree for the death of Demosthenes and Hyperides. Demosthenes had already escaped and taken sanctuary in the temple of Posidon on the island of Calauria. Here he was pursued by an agent of Antipater, one Archias, known as the exile-hunter, who had been an actor. This man tried to entice him forth by generous promises, but Demosthenes answered, ' Your acting never carried conviction, and your promises are equally unconvincing.' Archias then resorted to threats, but was met by the calm retort, ' Now you speak like a Macedonian oracle; you were only acting before; only wait a little, so that I may write a few lines home.' While pretending to write he sucked poison from the end of his pen, and then let his head sink on his hands, as if in thought. When Archias approached again he looked him in the face and said, ' It is time for you to play the part of Creon, and cast out this body unburied. Now, adored Posidon, I leave thy precinct while yet alive; but Antipater and his Macedonians have left not even thy shrine undefiled.' He essayed to walk out, but fell and died upon the steps of the altar.[1]

Lucian, in his *Encomium of Demosthenes*, has given a fanciful account of Antipater receiving the news from Archias ;  these are the concluding words :

' So he is gone, either to live with the heroes in the Isles of the Blest or along the path of those souls that climb to Heaven, to be an attendant spirit on Zeus the giver of Freedom ;  but his body we will send to Athens, as a nobler memorial for that land than are the bodies of those who fell at Marathon.' [2]

### § 4.   *Literary Reputation*

The verdict of antiquity, which has generally been accepted in modern times, ranked Demosthenes as the greatest of orators.  In his own age he had rivals : Aeschines, as we have seen already, is in many respects worthy of comparison with him ;  of his other contemporaries Phocion was impressive by his dignity, sincerity, and brevity—' he could say more in fewer words ' ;  the vigorous extemporizations of Demades were sometimes more effective than the polished subtleties of Demosthenes ;  Aeschines claims to prefer the speaking of Leodamas of Acharnae, but the tone in which he says so is almost apologetic, and the laboured criticism to which Aeschines constantly subjects his rival practically takes it for granted that the latter was reckoned the foremost speaker of the time.

Later Greek authorities, who are far enough removed to see in proper perspective the orators of the pre-Macedonian times, have an ungrudging admiration for Demosthenes.  The author of *The Sublime* saw in him

---

[1] This account is taken from Plutarch (*Dem.*, ch. xxix.).
[2] Lucian, *Dem. Enc.*, § 50.

many faults, and admitted that in many details Hyperides excelled him.[1] Nevertheless he finds in Demosthenes certain divine gifts which put him apart from the others in a class by himself ; he surpasses the orators of all generations ; his thunders and lightnings shake down and scorch up all opposition ; it is impossible to face his dazzling brilliancy without flinching. But Hyperides never made anybody tremble.

In later times we find Demosthenes styled ' The Orator,' just as Homer is ' The Poet.' Lucian, whose literary appreciations are always worthy of attention, wrote an *Encomium of Demosthenes*, containing an imaginary dialogue, in which Antipater is the chief speaker. He pays a generous tribute to his dead enemy, who ' woke his compatriots from their drugged sleep ' ;[2] the *Philippics* are compared to battering-rams and catapults, and Philip is reported to have rejoiced that Demosthenes was never elected general, for the orator's speeches shook the king's throne, and his actions, if he had been given the opportunity, would have overturned it.

Of Roman critics, Cicero in many passages in the *Brutus* and *Orator* expresses extreme admiration for the excellence of Demosthenes in every style of oratory ; he regards him as far outstripping all others, though failing in some details to attain perfection. Quintilian's praise is discriminating but sincere ; in fact we may say that the Greek and Roman worlds were practically unanimous about the orator's merits.

It is difficult to take a general view of the style of Demosthenes, from the mere fact that it is extremely

---

[1] *de Sublimi*, ch. xxxiv.
[2] § 36, οἷον ἐκ μανδραγόρου καθεύδοντας.

varied ; the three classes of speeches—the forensic speeches in private and public suits, and the public harangues addressed to the assembly, all have their particular features : nevertheless there are certain characteristics which may be distinguished in all classes.

First of these is his great care in composition. Isocrates is known to have spent years in polishing the essays which he intended as permanent contributions to the science of politics ; Plato wrote and erased and wrote again before he was satisfied with the form in which his philosophy was to be given to the world ; Demosthenes, without years of toil, could produce for definite occasions speeches whose finished brilliancy made them worthy to be ranked as great literature quite apart from their merits as contributions to practical policy.

It is a well-known jest against him that his speeches smelt of midnight oil, but he must have had a remarkable natural fluency to be able to compose so many speeches so well. It is quite possible, on the other hand, that the speeches which survive are not altogether in the form in which they were delivered. It seems to have been a habit among orators of this time to edit for publication their speeches delivered in important cases, in order that a larger audience might have an opportunity of reading a permanent record of the speakers' views on political or legal questions which had more than a transitory interest.

We have indirect evidence that Demosthenes was in the habit of introducing corrections into his text. Aeschines quotes and derides certain expressions, mostly exaggerated metaphors, which do not occur in the speeches as extant to us, though some of them evidently should, if the text had not been submitted to a recension.[1]  We may note the remark of Eratosthenes [2] that while speaking he sometimes lost control of himself, and talked like a man possessed, and that of Demetrius of Phaleron, that on one occasion he offended against good taste by quoting a metrical oath which bears the stamp of comedy :

'By earth and fountains, rivulets and streams.'[3]

This quotation is not to be found in any extant speech, but it is noticeable that formulae of the kind, typically represented by the familiar ὦ γῆ καὶ θεοί—'Ye Earth and Gods '—are commonly affected by Demosthenes, as indeed they are to be found in his contemporary Aeschines.

Evidently the Attic taste was undergoing a modification ; such expressions are foreign to the dignified harmonies of Isocrates and of rare occurrence in the restrained style of Lysias ; but they begin to appear more frequently in Isaeus, whose style was the model for the early speeches of Demosthenes.  Certain other expressions belonging to the popular speech, and probably avoided by Isocrates as being too colloquial, are found in Demosthenes' public speeches—e.g. ὁ δεῖνα and ὦ τᾶν.

Under the same heading must come the use of coarse expressions and terms of personal abuse.  In many of the speeches relating to public law-suits Demosthenes allows himself all the latitude which was

---

[1] Aesch., *Ctes.*, §§ 72, 166 ; *de Leg.*, § 21 ; *Ctes.*, §§ 84, 209.
[2] Plut., *Dem.*, ch. ix., παράβακχον.
[3] ἐνθουσιῶντα.  Cf. Aristophanes, *Clouds*, 194 :
μὰ γῆν, μὰ παγίδας, μὰ νεφέλας, μὰ δίκτυα.

sanctioned by the taste of his times.  In the actual use of abusive epithets—θηρίον, κατάρατος, and the like—he does not go beyond the common practice of Aeschines, and is even outstripped by Dinarchus ; but in the accumulation of offensive references to the supposed private character of his political opponents he condescends to such excesses that we wonder how a decent audience can ever have tolerated him.[1]  Evidently an Athenian audience loved vulgarity for its own sake, apart from humour.

In the private speeches there is at times a certain coarseness—inevitably, since police-court cases are often concerned with sordid details.  Offensive actions sometimes have to be described ;[2] but this is a very different matter from the irrelevant introduction of offensive matter.

In the speeches delivered before the ecclesia Demosthenes set himself a higher ideal.  Into questions of public policy, private animosities should not be allowed to intrude, and throughout the *Philippics* and *Olynthiacs* Demosthenes observes this rule.  Under no stress of excitement does he sink to personalities ; his political opponents for the time being are not abused, not even mentioned by name.  The courtesies of debate are fully and justly maintained.

---

[1] Notably the caricatures of Aeschines' private life and family history in the *de Corona*, §§ 129-130, 260.  Mr. Pickard-Cambridge makes it clear that the habitual members of the law-courts would be of a lower average socially than the ecclesia.  The pay in either case was not enough to attract any but the unemployed, but whereas members of the leisured classes would have sufficient motives for attending the ecclesia, and well-to-do business-men might sacrifice valuable time unselfishly for the good of the State, there would be little inducement to such people to endure the wearisome routine of the law-courts (see *Demosthenes*, ch. iii.).

[2] *E.g. Conon*, § 4.

### § 5.  *Style and Composition*

Though Demosthenes wrote in pure Attic Greek, it is to Lysias and Isocrates rather than to him that Dionysius assigns praise for the most perfect purity of language.  It is probable that Demosthenes was nearer to the living speech.  Even in his deliberative speeches he can use such familiar expressions as ὦ τᾶν, ὁ δεῖνα and such expletives as νὴ Δία, the frequent use of which would have seemed to Isocrates to belong to the vocabulary of Comedy.  The epideictic style would also have shunned such vigorous touches as λαγὼ βίον ἔζης—' you lived a hare's life,' or, to give the proper equivalent, ' a dog's life,' [1] or the famous κακῶν Ἰλιάς— ' Twenty-four books of misery.' [2]  Colloquial vigour is apparent in some metaphorical uses of single words, *e.g.* ἕωλα καὶ ψυχρά—' stale and cold ' (applied to crimes),[3] προσηλῶσθαι—' to be pinned down,' [4] or the succession of crude metaphors in the account of how Aristogiton, in prison, picked a quarrel with a newcomer ; ' he being newly caught and fresh, was getting the better of Aristogiton, who had got into the net some time ago and been long in pickle ; so finding himself getting the worst of it, he ate off the man's nose.' [5] There is bold personification of abstractions in ' Peace, which has destroyed the walls of your allies and is now building houses for your ambassadors,' [6] and such phrases as τεθνᾶσι τῷ δέει τοὺς τοιούτους ἀποστόλους

---

[1] *de Cor.*, § 263.    [2] *de Falsa Leg.*, § 148.
[3] *Midias*, § 91.    [4] *Ibid.*, § 105.
[5] On the other hand he often apologizes for metaphors by ὥσπερ or οἷον—ἦν τοῦθ' ὥσπερ ἐμπόδισμά τι τῷ Φιλίππῳ——though ἐμπόδισμα is probably as natural a form of expression as our ' obstacle.'
[6] *de Falsa Leg.*, § 275.

—' they are frightened to death of so and so,' are more vigorous than literary.[1]

Demosthenes seems to discard metaphor in his most solemn moments. In a spirit of sarcasm he can use such expressions as those quoted above about the disorderly scene in prison, and in an outburst of indignation he can speak of rival politicians as ' Fiends, who have mutilated the corpses of their fatherlands, and made a birthday present of their liberty first to Philip, and now again to Alexander ; who measure happiness by their belly and their basest pleasures ' ;[2] but on grave occasions, whether in narrative or in counsel, he reverts to a simplicity equal to that of Lysias. The plainness of the language in which he describes the excitement caused by the news of Philip's occupation of Elatea is proverbial ;[3] and the closing sentences of the *Third Philippic* afford another good example :

' If everybody is going to sit still, hoping to get what he wants, and seeking to do nothing for it himself, in the first place he will never find anybody to do it for him, and secondly, I am afraid that we shall be forced to do everything that we do not want. This is what I tell you, this is what I propose ; and I believe that if this is done our affairs may even yet be set straight again. If anybody can offer anything better, let him name it and urge it ; and whatever you decide, I pray to heaven it may be for the best.'

The simplicity of the language is only equalled by the sobriety of tone. The simplest words, if properly used, can produce a great effect, which is sometimes heightened by repetition, a device which Demosthenes

[1] I *Phil.*, § 45 ; cf. τεθνάναι τῷ φόβῳ Θηβαίους, *de Falsa Leg.*, § 81.
[2] *de Cor.*, § 296.  [3] *de Cor.*, § 169.

finds useful on occasion—ἀλλ' οὐκ ἔστιν, οὐκ ἔστιν ὅπως ἡμάρτετε—'But surely, *surely* you were not wrong.'[1] We realize a slight raising of the voice as the word comes in for the second time. Dinarchus, an imitator of Demosthenes, copies him in the use of this 'figure,' but uses it too much and inappropriately. In this, as in other details, his style is an unsuccessful parody of the great orator.

Dionysius compares Demosthenes to several other writers in turn. He finds passages, for instance, which recall the style of Thucydides.[2] He quotes the first section from the *Third Philippic*, and by an ingenious analysis shows the points of resemblance. The chief characteristic noticed by the critic is that the writer does not introduce his thoughts in any natural or conventional sequence, but employs an affected order of words which arrests the attention by its avoidance of simplicity.

Thus, a parenthetical relative clause intrudes between the subject and the verb of the chief relative clause, while we are kept in long suspense as to what the verbs are to be, both in relative clauses and in the main clause itself. The peculiar effects which he notices cannot be reproduced in a non-inflexional language such as English.

At other times, especially in narrative, Demosthenes emulates the lucidity of Lysias at his best. Dionysius quotes with well-deserved approval the vivid present-ment of the story on which the accusation against Conon is based. As the speech gives us an excellent picture of the camp life of an undisciplined militia, it will be worth while here to quote some extracts :

[1] *de Cor.*, § 208.      [2] *de Thucyd.*, ch. 53.

' Two years ago, having been detailed for garrison-duty, we went out to Panactum.  Conon's sons occupied a tent near us ;  I wish it had been otherwise, for this was the primary cause of our enmity and the collisions between us. You shall hear how it arose.  They used to drink every day and all day long, beginning immediately after breakfast, and this custom they maintained all the time that we were in garrison.  My brothers and I, on the contrary, lived out there just as we were in the habit of living at home.  So by the time which the rest of us had fixed for dinner, they were invariably playing drunken tricks, first on our servants, and finally on ourselves.  For because they said that the servants sent the smoke in their faces while cooking, or were uncivil to them, or what not, they used to beat them and empty the slops over their heads . . . and in every way behaved brutally and disgustingly.  We saw this and took offence, and first of all remonstrated with them ;  but as they jeered at us and would not stop, we all went and reported the occurrence to the general—not I alone, but the whole of the mess.  He reprimanded them severely, not only for their offensive behaviour to us, but for their general conduct in camp ;  however, they were so far from stopping or feeling any shame that, as soon as it was dark that evening, they made a rush on us, and first abused us and then beat me, and made such a disturbance and uproar round the tent that the general and his staff and some of the other soldiers came out, and prevented them from doing us any serious harm, and us from retaliating on their drunken violence.'[1]

Another passage quoted from the same speech gives a companion picture of the defendant's behaviour in civil life :

' When we met them, one of the party, whom I cannot identify, fell upon Phanostratus and held him tight, while

---

[1] *Against Conon*, §§ 3-5.

the defendant Conon and his son and the son of Andromenes fell upon me, and first stripped me, and then tripped me up, and dashed me down in the mud.  There they jumped upon me and beat me, and so mishandled me that they cut my lip right through, and closed up both my eyes. They left me in such a weak state that I could neither get up nor speak, and as I lay on the ground I heard them uttering floods of abominable language.  What they said was vilely slanderous, and some of it I should shrink from repeating, but I will mention one thing which is an example of Conon's brutality, and proves that he was responsible for the whole incident—he began to crow like a game-cock after a victory, and the others told him to flap his arms against his sides in triumph.  After this I was carried home naked by some passers-by, while the defendants made off with my coat.' [1]

Dionysius observes that the ecclesia and the courts were composed of mixed elements ; [2] not all were clever and subtle in intellect ;  the majority were farmers, merchants, and artisans, who were more likely to be pleased by simple speech ;  anything of an unusual flavour would turn their stomachs :  a smaller number, a mere fraction of the whole, were men of high education, to whom you could not speak as you would to the multitude ;  and the orator could not afford to neglect either section.  He must therefore aim at satisfying both, and consequently he should steer a middle course, avoiding extremes in either direction.

In the opinion of Dionysius both Isocrates and Plato give good examples of this middle style, attaining a seeming simplicity intelligible to all, combined with a subtlety which could be appreciated only by the expert ;  but Demosthenes surpassed them both in the

---

[1] *Against Conon*, §§ 8-9.          [2] *de Demos.*, ch. xv.

perfection of this art. To prove his case he quotes first the passage from *The Peace* which Isocrates himself selected for quotation, as a favourable example of his own style, in the speech on the *Antidosis*. With this extract a passage from the third *Olynthiac* is contrasted, greatly to the advantage of Demosthenes, who is found to be nobler, more majestic, more forcible, and to have avoided the frigidity of excessive refinement with which Isocrates is charged.

The criticism professes to be based on an accumulation of small details, but there is no doubt that Dionysius depended, in the main, not upon analysis, but upon subjective impressions. After enumerating the points in which either of the writers excels or falls short, he describes his own feelings :

' When I read a speech of Isocrates, I become sober and serious, as if I were listening to solemn music ; but when I take up a speech of Demosthenes, I am beside myself, I am led this way and that, I am moved by one passion after another : suspicion, distress, fear, contempt, hate, pity, kindliness, anger, envy—passing successively through all the passions which can obtain a mastery over the human mind ; . . . and I have sometimes thought to myself, what must have been the impression which he made on those who were fortunate enough to hear him ?  For where we, who are so far removed in time, and in no way interested in the actual events, are led away and overpowered, and made to follow wherever the speech leads us, how must the Athenians and other Greeks have been led by the speaker himself when the cases in which he spoke had a living interest and concerned them nearly ? . . .'[1]

Dionysius, as we know from many of his criticisms, had a remarkably acute sense of style ; he had also a

[1] *Demos.*, ch. **xxii.**

strong imagination. In this same treatise he recounts how the forms of the sentences themselves suggest to him the tone in which the words were uttered, the very gestures with which they were accompanied.[1]

Though we modern students cannot expect to rival him in these peculiar gifts, it is still possible for us to sympathize with his feelings. We cannot fail, in reading a speech like the *Third Philippic*, for instance, to appreciate how fully Demosthenes realizes the Platonic ideal, expressed in the *Gorgias*, that rhetoric is the art of persuasion. We need not pause to analyse the means by which he attains his end ; he may resemble Lysias at one moment in a simple piece of narrative, at another he may be as involved and antithetical as Thucydides, or even florid like Gorgias ; he can be a very Proteus, as Dionysius says, in his changes of form ; but in whatever shape he appears, naive, subtle, pathetic, indignant, sarcastic, he is convincing. The reason is simple : he has a single purpose always present to his mind, namely, to make his audience feel as he feels. Readers of Isocrates were expected, while they followed the exposition of the subject-matter, to regard the beauties of the form in which it was expressed ; in Demosthenes there is no idea of such display. A good speech was to him a successful speech, not one which might be admired by critics as a piece of literature. It is only incidental that his speeches have a literary quality which ranks him among the foremost writers of Attic prose ; as an orator he was independent of this quality.

---

[1] *Demos.*, chs. liii., liv. So Aeschines, after reading aloud some extracts from Demosthenes, and observing their effect on his hearers, exclaimed, ‘ But what if you had heard the brute himself ? ’

The strong practical sense of Demosthenes refused to be confined by any theoretical rules of scholastic rhetoricians. He does not aspire to the complexity of periods which makes the style of Isocrates monotonous in spite of the writer's wonderful ingenuity. Long and short, complex and simple sentences, are used in turn, and with no systematic order, so that we cannot call any one kind characteristic; the form of the sentence, like the language, is subordinate to its purpose.[1]

He was moderately careful in the avoidance of hiatus between words, but in this matter he modified the rule of Isocrates to suit the requirements of speech; he was guided by ear, not by eye; thus we find that hiatus is frequently omitted between the *cola* or sections of a period; in fact any pause in the utterance is enough to justify the non-elision of an open vowel before the pause. Isocrates, on the contrary, usually avoids even the appearance of hiatus in such cases.

There is one other formal rule of composition which Demosthenes follows with some strictness; this is the avoidance of a succession of short syllables. It is notable that he very seldom admits a tribrach (three short syllables) where a little care can avoid it, while instances of more than three short vowels in succession are very exceptional.[2] An unusual order of

---

[1] *de Chersoneso*, §§ 69-71, gives an example of a sentence of about twenty-seven lines in the Teubner edition.

[2] *Timocrates*, § 217, οὐδ' ὁτιοῦν ἂν ὄφελος εἴη is a case in point— (◡ ◡ ◡ ◡ – –); in this instance no other arrangement of the words was possible; οὐδ' ὁτιοῦν ἂν εἴη ὄφελος would give a harsh hiatus. Cf. also *First Olynthiac*, § 27, ἡλίκα γ' ἐστὶ τὰ διάφορ' ἐνθάδ' ἢ 'κεῖ πολεμεῖν, where five shorts appear in sequence.

Q

words may often be explained by reference to this practice.[1]

We know from Aristotle and other critics that earlier writers of artistic prose, from Thrasymachus onwards, had paid some attention to the metrical form of words and certain combinations of long and short syllables. Thrasymachus in particular studied the use of the *paeonius* (– ◡ ◡ ◡ or ◡ ◡ ◡ –) at the beginning and end of a sentence.[2]

The effect of increasing the number of short syllables, whether in verse or prose, is to make the movement of the line or period more rapid. The frequent use of tribrachs by Euripides constantly produces this impression, and an extreme case is the structure of the Galliambic metre, as seen, for instance, in the *Attis* of Catullus.[3] Conversely the multiplication of long syllables makes the movement slow, and produces an effect of solemnity.[4]

Demosthenes seems to have been the first prose-writer to pay attention to the avoidance of the tribrach; Plato seems to have consciously preferred a succession of short syllables where it was possible. The difference between the two points of view is probably this—that Plato aimed at reproducing the natural rapidity of conversation, Demosthenes aimed

---

[1] *E.g. de Falsa Leg.*, § 11, διεξιὼν ἡλίκα τὴν Ἑλλαδα πᾶσαν, οὐχὶ τὰς ἰδίας ἀδικοῦσι μόνον πατρίδας οἱ δωροδοκοῦντες. The position of ἀδικοῦσι is peculiar, but the sentence already contains a preponderance of short syllables, and any other arrangement would give more of them together: *e.g.* the more natural orders τὰς ἰδίας μόνον πατρίδας ἀδικοῦσι (– ◡ ◡ ◡ ◡ – ◡) or ἰδίας μόνον ἀδικοῦσι πατρίδας (◡ ◡ – ◡ ◡ ◡ ◡ – ◡ – ◡ ◡).

[2] Arist., *Rhet.*, iii. 8. 4.

[3] Super alta vectus Attis celeri rate maria, etc. The ending with five short syllables gives an impression of headlong speed.

[4] Cf. the ' spondaic ' hymn, Ζεῦ πάντων ἀρχά, πάντων ἅγητορ, Ζεῦ σοὶ σπένδω ταύταν ὕμνων ἀρχάν.

at a more solemn and dignified style appropriate to impressive utterance before a large assembly.

This is the only metrical rule which Demosthenes ever observed, and one of the soundest of modern critics believes that even this observance was instinctive rather than conscious.[1] He never affected any metrical formula for the end of sentences comparable to Cicero's famous *esse videatur*, or the double trochee $(-\cup-\cup)$ at the beginning of a sentence, approved by later writers. An examination shows that he has an almost infinite variety both in the opening and the close of his sentences. He seems never to follow any mechanical system.

Much labour has been expended, especially in Germany, on the analysis of the rhythmical element in Demosthenes' style. There is no doubt that many orators, from Gorgias onwards, laboured to produce approximate correspondence between parallel or contrasted sections of their periods. In some cases we find an equal number of syllables in two clauses, and even a more or less complete rhythmical correspondence. Such devices serve to emphasize the peculiar figures of speech in which Gorgias delighted, and may have been appropriate to the class of oratory intended primarily for display, but it is hard to believe that such elaboration was ever consciously carried through a long forensic speech.

The appendix to the third volume of Blass' Attic oratory is a monumental piece of work. It consists of an analysis of the first seventeen sections of the *de Corona*, and the whole of the *First Olynthiac* and *Third Philippic* speeches, and conveys the impression that

---

[1] Croiset, *Hist. de la Litt. Gr.*, tome iv., pp. 552-553.

this Demosthenic prose may be scanned with almost as much certainty as a comparatively simple form of composition like a Pindaric ode.  It is hard to pronounce on such a matter without a very long and careful study of this difficult subject ; but the theory of rhythmical correspondence seems to have been worked out far too minutely.  In many cases emendation is required ; we have to divide words in the middle, and clauses are split up in an arbitrary and unnatural way. I am far from believing that analysis can justifiably be carried to this extent ; it is more reasonable to suppose that Demosthenes had a naturally acute ear, and that practice so developed his faculty that a certain rhythm was natural to all his speech.  I am not convinced that all his effects were designed.[1]

### § 6. *Rhetorical Devices*

Isaeus, the teacher of Demosthenes, was a master of reasoning and demonstration ; Demosthenes in his earliest speeches shows strong traces of the influence of Isaeus, but in his later work he has developed varied gifts which enable him to surpass his master.  Realizing the insufficiency, for a popular audience, of mere reasoning, he reinforced his logic by adventitious aids, appealing in numerous indirect ways to feeling and prejudice.  One valuable method of awakening interest was his striking use of paradox :

' On the question of resources of money at present at our disposal, what I have to say will, I know, appear paradoxical, but I must say it ; for I am confident that, considered in the proper light, my proposal will appear to be the only true and right one.  I tell you that we need not raise the question of money at all : we have great resources

_______

[1] See *ad hoc*, Croiset, iv. 553. 1.

which we may fairly and honourably use if we need them. If we look for them now, we shall imagine that they never will be at our disposal, so far shall we be from willingness to dispose of them at present ; but if we let matters wait, we shall have them. What, then, are these resources which do not exist at present, but will be to hand later on ? It looks like a riddle. I will explain. Consider this city of ours as a whole. It contains almost as much money as all other cities taken together ; but those individuals who possess it are so apathetic that if all the orators tried to terrify them by saying that the king is coming, that he is near, that invasion is inevitable, and even if the orators were reinforced by an equal number of soothsayers, they would not only refuse to contribute ; they would refuse even to declare or admit the possession of their wealth. But suppose that the horrors which we now talk about were actually realized, they are none of them so foolish that they would not readily offer and make contributions. . . . So I tell you that we have money ready for the time of urgent need, but not before.' [1]

Similarly in the *Third Olynthiac* he rouses the curiosity of the audience by propounding a riddle, of which, after some suspense, he himself gives the answer. The matter under discussion is the necessity of sending help to Olynthus. There is, as usual, a difficulty about money.

' " Very well," you may say ; " we have all decided that we must send help ; and send help we will ; but how are we to do it ; tell me that ? " Now, Gentlemen, do not be astonished if what I say comes as a surprise to most of you. *Appoint a legislative board.* Instruct this board not to pass any law (you have enough already), but to repeal the laws which are injurious under present conditions. I refer to the laws about the Theoric Fund.' [2]

<hr>

[1] *de Symmor.*, §§ 24-26.     [2] *Third Olynthiac*, §§ 10-11.

This mention of the Festival Fund suggests some reflections on the orator's tenacity and perseverance. He is not content to say once what he has to propose, and leave his words to sink in by their own weight. Like a careful lecturer he repeats his statement, emphasizing it in various ways, until he perceives that his audience has really grasped its importance. The walls which he is attacking will not fall flat at the sound of the trumpet ; his persistent battering-rams must make a breach, his catapults must drive the defenders from their positions. Such is the meaning of Lucian's comment in the words attributed to Philip.[1]

The speech *On the Chersonese*, for instance, may be divided into three parts, dealing successively with the treatment of Diopeithes, the supineness of Athens, and the guilt of the partisans of Philip ; but in all parts we find emphatically stated the need for energetic action. This is really the theme of the speech ; the rest is important only in so far as it substantiates the main thesis.

The extract last given [2] shows with what adroitness he introduces dialogues, in which he questions or answers an imaginary critic. This is a device frequently employed with considerable effect. The following shows a rather different type :

' If Philip captures Olynthus, who will prevent him from marching on us ?   The Thebans ?   It is an unpleasant thing to say, but they will eagerly join him in the invasion. Or the Phocians ?—when they cannot even protect their own land, unless you help them.   Can you think of any one else ?—" My dear fellow, he won't want to attack us." It would indeed be the greatest surprise in the world if he

---

[1] Quoted above, p. 230.

[2] *Supra*, p. 245.

did not do it when he got the chance ; since even now he is fool enough to declare his intentions.' [1]

Narrative, too, can take the place of argument ; a recital of Philip's misdeeds during the last few years may do far more to convince the Athenians of the necessity for action than any argument about the case of a particular ally who chances to be threatened at the moment.[2]

Demosthenes' knowledge of history was deep and broad. The superiority of his attainments to those of Aeschines is shown in the more philosophic use which he makes of his appeals to precedent ; his examples are apposite and not far-fetched ; he can illuminate the present not only by references to ancient facts, but by a keen insight into the spirit which animated the men of old times.[3]

The examples already quoted of rhetorical dialogue with imaginary opponents will have given some idea of his use of a sarcastic tone. Sarcasm thinly concealed may at times run through a passage of considerable length, as in the anecdote which follows. We may note in passing that he is usually sparing in the use of anecdote, which is never employed without good reason. Here it may be excused by the fact that it figures as an historical precedent of a procedure which he ironically recommends to his contemporaries.

---

[1] *First Olynthiac*, §§ 25-26.

[2] *Chersonese*, §§ 61-67. The recital of the present condition of Phocis is a simple but impressive piece of argument by description : ' It was a terrible sight, Gentlemen, and a sad one; when we were lately on our way to Delphi we were compelled to see it all, houses in ruins, walls demolished, the country empty of men of military age ; only a few poor women and little children and old men in pitiable state—words cannot describe the depth of the misery in which they are now sunk ' (*de Falsa Leg.*, § 65).

[3] Cf. *Third Olynthiac*, §§ 24-26.

Inveighing against the reckless procedure of the Athenian politicians, who propose laws for their own benefit almost every month,[1] he recounts the customs of the Locrians, and, with an assumption of seriousness, implies a wish that similar restrictions could be imposed at Athens :

' I should like to tell you, Gentlemen, how legislation is conducted among the Locrians. It will do you no harm to have an example before you, especially the example of a well-governed State. There men are so convinced that they ought to keep to the established laws and cherish their traditions, and not legislate to suit their fancy, or to help a criminal to escape, that any man who wishes to pass a new law must have a rope round his neck while he proposes it. If they think that the law is a good and useful one, the proposer lives and goes on his way ; if not, they pull the rope and there is an end of him. For they cannot bear to pass new laws, but they rigorously observe the old ones. We are told that only one new law has been enacted in very many years. Whereas there was a law that if a man knocked out another man's eye, he should submit to having his own knocked out in return, and no monetary compensation was provided, a certain man threatened his enemy, who had already lost an eye, to knock out the one eye he had left. The one-eyed man, alarmed by the threat, and thinking that life would not be worth living if it were put into execution, ventured to propose a law that if a man knocks out the eye of a man who has only one, he shall submit to having both his own knocked out in return, so that both may suffer alike. We are told that this is the only law which the Locrians have passed in upwards of two hundred years.' [2]

This, however, occurs in a speech before the law-

---

[1] Viz., on every meeting of the ecclesia at which legislation was possible.

[2] *Timocrates*, §§ 139 *sqq.*

courts ; it is excellent in its place, but would have been unsuitable to the more dignified and solemn style in which he addresses the assembly. Equally unsuitable to his public harangues would be anything like the virulent satire which he admits into the *de Corona*, the vulgar personalities of abuse and gross caricatures of Aeschines and his antecedents.[1] For these the only excuse is that, though meant maliciously, they are so exaggerated as to be quite incredible. They may be compared to Aristophanes' satire of Cleon in the *Knights*, which was coarse enough, but cannot have done Cleon any serious harm. Demosthenes indeed becomes truly Aristophanic when he talks about Aeschines' acting :

' When in the course of time you were relieved of these duties, having yourself committed all the offences of which you accuse others, I vow that your subsequent life did not fall short of your earlier promise. You engaged yourself to the players Simylus and Socrates, the " Bellowers," as they were called, to play minor parts, and gathered a harvest of figs, grapes, and olives, like a fruiterer getting his stock from other people's orchards ; and you made more from this source than from your plays, which you played in dead earnest at the risk of your lives ; for there was a truceless and merciless war between you and the spectators, from whom you received so many wounds that you naturally mock at the cowardice of those who have never had that great experience.' [2]

He is generally described as deficient in wit, and he seems in this point to have been inferior to Aeschines,

---

[1] In particular *de Corona*, §§ 129-130, 258-262. Cf. *supra*, p. 164.
[2] *de Corona*, §§ 261-262.

though on one or two occasions he could make a neat repartee.[1]    As Dionysius says :

' Not on all men is every gift bestowed.'[2]

If, as his critic affirms,[3] he was in danger of turning the laugh against himself, he had serious gifts which more than compensated this deficiency.

It must not be supposed that he was entirely free from sophistry.  Like many good orators in good or bad causes he laboured from time to time to make a weak case appear strong, and in this effort was often absolutely disingenuous.  The whole of the *de Corona* is an attempt to throw the judges off the scent by leading them on to false trails.  It may be urged in his defence that on this occasion he had justice really on his side, but finding that Aeschines on legal ground was occupying an impregnable position, he practically threw over the discussion of legality and turned the course of the trial towards different issues altogether. In this case, admittedly, the technical points were merely an excuse for the bringing of the case, and were probably of little importance to the court.  The trial was really concerned with the political principles and actions of the two great opponents, while Ctesiphon was only a catspaw.  But a study of other speeches results in the discovery of many minor points in which, accurately gauging the intelligence of his audience, he has intentionally misled them.  Thus, his own knowledge of history was profound ; but experience has proved that the knowledge possessed by any audience

---

[1] *Vide supra*, pp. 170, 177.
[2] οὐ γάρ πως ἅμα πάντα θεοὶ δόσαν ἀνθρώποισι.
[3] *de Sublimi*, ch. xxxiv.

of the history of its own generation is likely to be
sketchy and inaccurate. Events have not settled
down into their proper perspective ; we must rely
either on our own memories, which may be distorted
by prejudice, or on the statements of historians who
stand too near in time to be able to get a fair view.
This gives the politician his opportunity of so grouping
or misrepresenting facts as to give a wrong impression.

Instances of such bad faith on the part of Demosthenes are probably numerous, even if unimportant.

In the speech on the *Embassy*[1] he asserts that
Aeschines, far from opposing Philip's pretension to be
recognized as an Amphictyon, was the only man who
spoke in favour of it ; yet Demosthenes himself had
counselled submission. In the speech *Against Timocrates* there are obvious exaggerations to the detriment
of the defendant. Timocrates had proposed that certain debtors should be given time to pay their debts ;
Demosthenes asserts that he restored them to their full
civic rights without payment.[2] Towards the end of
the speech a statement is made which conflicts with
one on the same subject in the exordium.[3]

But such rhetorical devices are only trivial faults
to which most politicians are liable.[4] The orator him-

---

[1] *de Falsa Leg.*, §§ 112-113, with Weil's note.          [2] § 90.

[3] §§ 9, 196. Weil remarks truly, ' Les orateurs ne se piquent
pas d'être exacts : ils usent largement de l'hyperbole mensongère.'

[4] Mr. Pickard-Cambridge (*Demos.*, p. 80) observes : ' Men who
are assembled in a crowd do not think. . . . The orator has often
to use arguments which no logic can defend, and to employ methods
of persuasion upon a crowd which he would be ashamed to use
if he were dealing with a personal friend.' This is partly true, but
should be accepted with reservations. The arguments in the
harangues of Demosthenes will generally bear the light, and the
public speeches by distinguished statesmen of this country on the
causes of the Great War have frequently appealed to the *higher*
nature of their audiences.

self would probably feel that even more doubtful actions were justifiable for the sake of the cause which he championed. We must remember that all the really important cases in which he took part had their origin on political grounds, and during his public career he never relaxed his efforts for the maintenance of those principles which he expounded in his public harangues. Until the end he had hopes for Greek freedom, freedom for Athens, not based on any unworthy compromise, but dependent on a new birth of the old Athenian spirit. The regeneration which he pictured would be due to a revival of the spirit of personal self-sacrifice. Every man must be made to realize first that the city had a glorious mission, being destined to fulfil an ideal of liberty based on principles of justice ; secondly that, to attain this end, each must live not for himself or his party but wholly for the city. It is the consciousness that Demosthenes has these enlightened ideas always present in his mind which makes us set him apart from other orators. Lycurgus, a second-rate orator, becomes impressive through his sincerity and incorruptibility ; Demosthenes, great among orators, stands out from the crowd still more eminently by the nobleness of his aspirations.

### § 7. *Structure of Speeches*

The structure of the speeches will give us a last example of the versatility of the composer and his freedom from conventional form.

We find, indeed, that he regularly has some kind of exordium and epilogue, but in the arrangement of other divisions of the speech he allows himself perfect freedom ; we cannot reckon on finding a statement of the case in one place, followed regularly by evidence, by refutation of the opponent's arguments, and so forth. All elements may be interspersed, since he marshals his arguments not in chronological nor even, necessarily, in logical order, but in such an arrangement as seems to him most decisive. He is bound by no conventional rules of warfare, and may leave his flanks unprotected while he delivers a crushing attack on the centre. In some cases it is almost impossible to make regular divisions by technical rule ; thus, in the *de Corona* there is matter for dispute as to where the epilogue really begins.[1]

The majority of the speeches actually end, according to the Attic convention which governed both Tragedy and Oratory, in a few sentences of moderate tone contrasting with the previous excitement ; a calm succeeds to the storm of passions. In the forensic speeches there is usually at the very end some appeal for a just verdict, or a statement of the speaker's conviction that the case may now be safely left to the court's decision ; thus the *Leptines* ends with a simplicity worthy of Lysias :

' I cannot see that 1 need say any more ; for I conceive there is no point on which you are not sufficiently instructed ' ; the *Midias* more solemnly, ' On account of all that I have laid before you, and particularly to show respect to the god whose festival Midias is proved to have profaned,

---

[1] There is a pseudo-epilogue, §§ 126-159, devoted chiefly to the birth and life of Aeschines. Here the speech might have ended, but the orator reverts in § 160 to an examination and defence of his own political life. The real epilogue is contained in §§ 252-324. The disorder is undoubtedly due in part to the peculiar facts of the case, namely, that the issues of the trial were much wider than might have appeared. Demosthenes is not so much concerned to prove the legality of Ctesiphon's decree as to offer an *apologia* of his own political conduct during many years.

punish him by rendering a verdict in accordance with piety and justice.'

In the *de Falsa Legatione* there is more personal feeling : ' You must not let him go, but make his punishment an example to all Athens and all Greece.' The *Timocrates* is rather similar : ' Mercy under these circumstances is out of place ; to pass a light sentence means to habituate and educate in wrong-doing as many of you as possible.' The *Androtion* ends with a personal opinion on the aspect of the offence, and the *Aristocrates* is in a similar tone. The (first) speech against Aristogiton appeals directly to the personal interests of all the jurors : ' His offence touches every one, every one of you : and all of you desire to be quit of his wickedness and see him punished.'

The *de Corona* is remarkable in every way ; this great speech, which, arising from causes almost trivial, abandons the slighter issues, and is transformed into a magnificent defence of the patriotic policy, begins with a solemn invocation : ' I begin, men of Athens, with a prayer to all the gods and goddesses that you may show me in this case as much good-will as I have shown and still show to Athens and to all of you.' It ends in an unique way with an appeal, not to the court but to a higher tribunal, an appeal which is all the more impressive as its language recalls the sacred formulas of religious utterance. ' Never, ye gods of heaven, never may you give their conduct your sanction ; but, if it be possible, may you impart even to my enemies a sounder mind and heart. But if they are beyond remedy, hurl them to utter and absolute destruction by land and sea ; and to the rest of us grant, as quickly as may be, release from the terrors which hang over us, and salvation unshakable.'

The speeches before the assembly are naturally different in their endings from the judicial speeches; there is no criminal to attack, and no crime to stigmatize; the hearers themselves are, as it were, on their defence, and Demosthenes freely points out their faults, but, as has been noticed, individual opponents escape; if there have been evil counsellors, the responsibility for following bad advice rests with the public, and they can only be exhorted to follow a better course. The speeches on the *Symmories* and on *Megalopolis* end with a summary of the speaker's advice. So, too, does that *On the Freedom of Rhodes*, the last words containing a fine appeal to the lesson of antiquity. 'Consider that your forefathers dedicated these trophies not in order that you might gaze in admiration upon them, but in the hope that you might imitate the virtues of those who dedicated them.'

Several of the speeches dealing with the Macedonian question end with a short prayer for guidance: thus, the *First Philippic*, 'May that counsel prevail which is likely to be to the advantage of all'; the *First Olynthiac*, 'May your decision be a sound one, for all your sakes'; the *Third Philippic*, 'Whatever you decide, I pray to heaven it may be to your advantage'; the *Third Olynthiac*, 'I have told you what I think is to your advantage, and I pray that you may choose what is likely to be of advantage to the State and all yourselves.'

Sometimes there is a greater show of confidence, as in the *Second Olynthiac*: 'If you act thus, you will not only commend your present counsellor, but you will have cause to **commend** your own conduct later on, when you find a general improvement in your prospects.'

The *Second Philippic* ends with a prayer rather similar to that in the *de Corona*, though less emphatic ; the speech *On the Chersonese* with a reproof and a warning.[1] *The Peace* contains no epilogue at all, but breaks off with a sarcasm.

An indication of the nature of the subjects of the genuine speeches may be useful for reference. They may be taken in their three groups : A. Private, B. Public, C. Deliberative speeches.

### A.—Speeches in Private Causes

*Against Aphobus*, i. and ii., 363 B.C., delivered in the action which Demosthenes brought against his guardian for the recovery of his property.

*For Phanos against Aphobus*, 363 B.C. Aphobus, convicted in the former case, accused a witness, Phanos, of perjury : Demosthenes defends the latter.

*Against Onetor*, i. and ii., 362 B.C. Another case arising out of the guardianship. When Aphobus was convicted it was found that he had made over some of the property to his father-in-law Onetor, against whom Demosthenes was forced to bring a δίκη ἐξούλης.

*On the Trierarchic Crown*, between 361-357 B.C. Apollodorus, having been awarded the crown given each year to the trierarch who first had his ship in commission, claims a second crown for having given the best equipped ship.

*Against Spudias* (date unknown). One Polyeuctus died, leaving his property equally to his two daughters. The husband of the elder claims that the dowry promised with her was never paid in full, and that Spudias,

---

[1] Quoted *supra*, p. 216.

the husband of the younger daughter, has consequently no right to half of the *gross* estate. The debt to the complainant should be discharged first.

*Against Callicles* (date unknown). Callicles, a farmer, alleges that the defendant's father built a wall stopping a water-course; consequently the plaintiff's land was flooded in rainy weather. The defendant denies the charge, and ridicules it on the ground that the high-road was the natural water-course.[1]

*Against Conon* (possibly 341 B.C., see Paley and Sandys' edition). Ariston prosecutes Conon for assault. The quarrel dated from a time when the two parties were on garrison duty, and Conon and his sons deliberately annoyed Ariston and his friends. Subsequently the defendant, aided by his sons and others, members of a disreputable ' Mohock ' club called the ' Triballi,' violently assaulted the speaker.[2]

*For Phormio*, 350 B.C. Phormio, chief clerk to Pasion, the famous Athenian banker, succeeded him in the business. Some years later Apollodorus, Pasion's elder son, claimed a sum of money, said to be due to him under his father's will ; Phormio, however, proved that a compromise had been made which rendered the present action invalid.

*Against Stephanus*, i., 349 or 348 B.C. Apollodorus accuses Stephanus, a witness for Phormio in the previous case, of perjury. It is noticeable that Demosthenes, the professional speech-writer, has now changed sides, an action of rather dubious morality if judged by strict standards.

---

[1] A plausible answer. In Greece at the present day water-courses are used as roads, and the same is true of the south of Spain. At Malaga, a few years ago, the tram-line actually crossed the river-bed. [2] *Vide supra*, p. 237.

R

*Against Boeotus*, i., 348 B.C. Mantias, an Athenian politician, had three sons, Mantitheus (legitimate), and Boeotus and another illegitimate. Boeotus laid claim to the name Mantitheus, and the true Mantitheus brought an action to restrain him from using the name.

*Against Pantaenetus*, 346 B.C. A plea ($\pi\alpha\rho\alpha\gamma\rho\alpha\phi\acute{\eta}$) by one Nicobulus against Pantaenetus, who had charged the former with damaging his mining property. The case is hard to follow, since the mine in question was held in succession by no less than six different parties, whether as owners, mortgagees, or lessees.

*Against Nausimachus* (about 346 B.C.). Nausimachus and Xenopeithes, orphans, brought an action against their guardian Aristaechmus with regard to their estate, but agreed to compromise for three talents, which was duly paid. After his death they brought an action against his four sons, renewing their original claim. The sons put in a $\pi\alpha\rho\alpha\gamma\rho\alpha\phi\acute{\eta}$ to stop the action on the ground of the compromise.

*Against Eubulides*, 345 B.C. Euxitheus, who has been ' objected to ' at the revision of the list of citizens, claims that he is a citizen by rights, but has been removed from the roll maliciously by Eubulides. The present case is his appeal ($\H{\epsilon}\phi\epsilon\sigma\iota\varsigma$) to the court against the decision.

The remaining private speeches were quite possibly not composed by Demosthenes, though proof is generally impossible. They seem, however, to be genuine speeches, composed for delivery by some author or authors of the Demosthenic period, and are of extreme interest and importance to all students of private life at Athens.

*Against Callippus*, 369 B.C. An $\H{\epsilon}\phi\epsilon\sigma\iota\varsigma$ or appeal to a court from an arbitration which, according to the plaintiff Apollodorus, Pasion's son, was informal, as the arbitrator had not taken the oath. The case arises from a claim made by Callippus for money deposited with the banker Pasion, and by him paid out to one Cephisiades.

*Against Nicostratus*, 368-365 B.C. Apollodorus had declared that Arethusius, a debtor to the State, possessed two slaves, who were liable to be confiscated in payment of the debt. Nicostratus, brother of Arethusius, declared that the slaves were his. Apollodorus in this speech has to prove that the claim is false.

*Against Timotheus*, 362 B.C. Apollodorus claims from Timotheus money which, he affirms, the latter borrowed from Pasion.

*Against Polycles*, 358 B.C. Apollodorus was forced to act at trierarch beyond the appointed time, as Polycles, his successor, was not ready to take over the duty. The former claims damages.

*Against Stephanus*, ii. See *Against Stephanus*, i., to which this is a supplement.

*Against Euergus and Mnesibulus*, 356-353 B.C. A prosecution for perjury of witnesses in a case of ex-trierarchs who are state-debtors.

*Against Zenothemis*, date unknown. An intricate story of fraud and collusion in connexion with money borrowed on the security of a ship and an attempt to scuttle the ship.

*Against Boeotus*, ii., 348-346 B.C. (see the first speech *Against Boeotus*). Mantitheus claims from his brothers the payment of his mother's dowry in addition to his share of his father's inheritance.

*Against Macartatus*, c. 341 B.C.  A case dealing with a forged will and conflicting claims to an inheritance.

*Against Olympiodorus*, c. 341 B.C.  Olympiodorus and Callistratus, brothers-in-law, obtained the inheritance of Conon.  Their title being questioned, judgment went against them by default.  They brought a fresh action, Olympiodorus claiming the whole and Callistratus half, but they had secretly agreed to divide the booty equally.  Olympiodorus was awarded the whole, and kept it, so Callistratus brought an action on the ground of their agreement.

*Against Lacritus*, date unknown.  Lacritus disclaims responsibility for the debts of his brother Artemon, whose property he has inherited.

*Against Phaenippus*, 330 B.C. (?).  The petitioner, chosen for the trierarchy, claimed that Phaenippus was better able to afford it, and should submit to *antidosis*, or exchange of property.  He accuses Phaenippus of making a false declaration.

*Against Leochares*, date unknown ; another case of disputed inheritance.

*Against Apaturius*, 341 B.C. (?).  Apaturius claims that the speaker has certain liabilities towards him in accordance with an agreement which he has lost.  The speaker affirms in a παραγραφή that the contract was fulfilled some time ago and the document torn up.

*Against Phormio*, c. 326 B.C.  Phormio having borrowed money on the security of a ship's cargo in a voyage to the Bosporus and back, shipped no cargo on the return journey, but as the ship was lost, evaded his liabilities.  When Chrysippus, the debtor,

claimed repayment, Phormio put in a παραγραφή
stating that he had fulfilled his contract.

*Against Dionysodorus*, 323-322 B.C. Another action
for breach of contract in a similar case.

## B.—SPEECHES IN PUBLIC CAUSES

*Against Androtion*, 355 B.C., written for Diodorus.
Androtion had proposed the bestowal of a golden crown
on the Boulé for their services during the year.
Euctemon and Diodorus attacked the proposal as
illegal because the navy had not been increased during
the year. Demosthenes in this speech attacks the
retrograde naval policy, pointing out by historical
argument the importance of the navy, and inveighs
generally against the corruptness of the party which
Androtion represents, as well as his personal character.

*Against Leptines*, 354 B.C. This is the first appearance of Demosthenes in a public court. Leptines had
proposed the abolition of hereditary immunities from
taxation (ἀτέλειαι) granted to public benefactors.
It was a salutary measure in view of the existing
financial embarrassment, but Demosthenes opposed
it as being a breach of faith. ' You must take care
not to be found guilty of doing, as a State, the sort of
thing that you would shrink from as individuals.' [1]
This debasement of the State is compared to a debasement of the coinage,[2] which is a capital offence.[2]

*Against Timocrates*, 353 B.C. Another speech written
for Diodorus, contains several passages repeated from
the *Androtion*. This man and others, having failed
to repay certain moneys which they had embezzled,
were liable to imprisonment. Timocrates proposed

[1] § 136.                                   [2] § 167.

an extension of the time within which they might pay. Demosthenes maintains that the law was informally passed and was unconstitutional. Many of the arguments are sophistical or trivial, but some are weighty, and on general grounds, that retrospective legislation in the interests of individuals is bad, this speech is very sound. The peroration contains an eulogy on the laws of Athens.[1]

*Against Aristocrates*, 352 B.C., is an important authority for the Athenian law of homicide. Aristocrates had carried a resolution making the person of Charidemus inviolable. This man, an Euboean by birth, was a mercenary leader, who having helped to lose Amphipolis, was now proposing to recover it. He was at present commanding the forces of the Thracian chief Cersobleptes. Demosthenes wrote this speech for Euthycles, who impeached the proposal. It contains an unusually careful arrangement in three divisions : (1) The proposal is illegal, (2) it is against our interest, (3) Charidemus is an unworthy person. Demosthenes is seen at his best in his appeal to legislative principle, his use of historical argument, and his description of the conditions of mercenary service and the politics of the barbarian fringe. The case against Charidemus is strong ; he has been in the service of Athens, Olynthus, Asia, and Thrace, and has played fast and loose with all.

*Against Midias*, 347 B.C. A fine speech on a trivial subject, which all the eloquence of Demosthenes cannot dignify. Strong emotion is evident all through, the tone is exalted, there are pathetic and humorous passages, and all about a box on the ear !

[1] §§ 210 *sqq.* ' A State's character is reflected in its laws ' (νόμους . . . ὑπειλήφασι . . . τρόπους τῆς πόλεως.).

Midias, who had a long-standing personal grudge against Demosthenes, was also his political opponent. When Demosthenes undertook to furnish the chorus for his tribe at the greater Dionysia in 348 B.C., Midias did all that he could to ruin the performance. On the day itself he slapped Demosthenes in the face in the presence of the whole people in the theatre.[1] Demosthenes laid a complaint, and Midias was declared guilty of ' contempt ' in a religious sense (ἀδικεῖν περὶ τὴν ἑορτήν). This preliminary vote involved no penalty, and Demosthenes was determined to push the case to extremes. Midias, having assaulted an official in discharge of his duty, and, further, committed sacrilege in so doing, might be condemned to death or confiscation of property. In the end, however, as we learn from Aeschines,[2] a compromise was made, and Demosthenes accepted half a talent as compensation for his injuries. This sum was quite inadequate, but there is good reason to believe that Demosthenes gave way for political reasons, since at the end of this year we find there is an understanding between him and the party of Eubulus, to which Midias belonged.

*On the Embassy (de Falsa Legatione), 344 B.C.*

We come now to the two great speeches arising out of the political hostility of Demosthenes and Aeschines, the speeches *On the Embassy*, 344 B.C., and *On the Crown*, 330 B.C. The history of the quarrel has been given in earlier chapters, and the speeches themselves to some extent described, since an account of the lives of the two orators must have been very incomplete without a full reference to their antagonism.[3] A few supplementary remarks may, however, be in place here.

---

[1] *Vide supra*, p. 190.          [2] *Ctes.*, § 52.

In the *Embassy* Demosthenes has to fight an uphill fight; he accuses Aeschines of having, from corrupt motives, concluded a dishonourable and fatal peace. He can bring no direct evidence of the guilt of his rival, but his presumptive evidence is strong. He has one undisputed fact to work upon: Aeschines, on his return from the second embassy, made certain statements and promises which misled the people, and resulted in the occupation of Thermopylae and the ruin of Phocis. Aeschines himself must either have been duped or bribed by Philip, and as he has never admitted that he was a fool, it becomes certain that he was a knave. A long section of the speech (§§ 29-97) is devoted to a description of the effects of Aeschines' policy, and another (§§ 98-149) infers his guilt on the lines indicated and from other incidents in his career. A presumption of guilt had already been reached in the opening sections (§§ 9-28) where the sudden change of front of Aeschines is described. The impression is strengthened by a review of the events of the second embassy (§§ 150-178). The charge has now been established as far as circumstances permit; the remainder of the speech, almost as long as this first part, is really a supplement. It is more discursive, and in some places, by its enunciation of general principles, recalls the tone of deliberative oratory.

The speech *On the Crown*,[1] 330 B.C., surpasses even the preceding speech in the appearance of disorder, which is probably due to deep design. The unity and consistency of the whole is preserved by the thought, which pervades every section, that the speaker must identify himself with the city; his policy has been

---

[1] Cf. *supra*, p. 223.

hers ; personal interests are merged in those of the community, and the case is to be won not on technical points of law but by a justification of the broader principles which have underlain all actions of the State.

The speeches *Against Aristogiton*, 325-4 B.C.,[1] are generally considered spurious ; Weil, however, defends the authenticity of the first, while abandoning the second. The process is an attempt to crush a malicious and dangerous sycophant.

Two more public speeches by contemporary writers are included wrongly in editions of Demosthenes : *Against Neaera*, written for Apollodorus between 343 and 339 B.C., on a question of the legal status of a *hetaira*, and *Against Theocrines*, about 340 B.C. Theocrines was another sycophant, whom Demosthenes branded for ever by using his name as a term of abuse, referring to Aeschines as ' a Theocrines with the bearing of a tragic actor.'[2]

## C.—Deliberative Speeches

*On the Symmories*, 354 B.C., deals with a rumour that Persia intended to invade Greece. Demosthenes points out that this apprehension is unfounded, and discourages any rash steps ; but admits that trouble is to be anticipated in the future, and so finds an opportunity for introducing a scheme of naval reform. The money could be obtained when the danger was imminent ;[3] it was necessary now to perfect the machinery. The style is Thucydidean.

---

[1] We know from Dinarchus, *Aristogiton*, § 13, that this trial shortly preceded the affair of Harpalus.

[2] *de Cor.*, § 313, τραγικὸς Θεοκρίνης.     [3] *Vide supra*, pp. 244-245.

*For the people of Megalopolis*, 353 B.C.   Megalopolis, the city of the Arcadian league, instituted by Epaminondas, was threatened with disruption by Sparta, and appealed to Athens.   Sparta sent an embassy at the same time.   Demosthenes, professing neutrality, really supported the Arcadians, wishing to preserve their integrity for the sake of the balance of power.   He failed in his object.

*First Philippic*, 351 B.C., *vide supra*, pp. 206-210.

*For the Liberty of the Rhodians*, 351 B.C., supports the claim of the islanders against oppression by Artemisia, widow of Mausolus of Caria.   Demosthenes failed again, chiefly through the prejudice against Rhodes, which had revolted against Athens in 357 B.C.

*First, Second*, and *Third Olynthiacs*, all in 349 B.C., *vide supra*, p. 210.

*On the Peace*, 346 B.C., *vide supra*, p. 212.

*Second Philippic*, 344 B.C., *vide supra*, pp. 213-214.

*On the Chersonese*, 341 B.C., *vide supra*, pp. 215-216.

*Third Philippic*, 341 B.C., *vide supra*, pp. 216-218.

The spurious *Fourth Philippic* (341-340 B.C.) has been discussed (*supra*, p. 218).   The speech on *Halonnesus* (342 B.C.) is attributed to Hegesippus.   It is a reply to an offer on the part of Philip to present to Athens the island of Halonnesus which he had seized, after clearing out the pirates who occupied it.[1]

---

[1] This Hegesippus, an orator of secondary importance, was an ardent supporter of the patriotic party.   In 357 B.C. he had brought an accusation against one Callippus in connexion with the affairs of Cardia (*de Halon.*, § 43, and the hypothesis to the speech).   In 343 B.C. he was one of an embassy sent to Philip (Demos., *de Falsa Leg.*, § 331).   He was still alive in 325 B.C. (Croiset, vol. iv. p. 621). The extant speech consists of a clear and straightforward discussion of the various points in Philip's proposal; the style is easy, but without distinction, and Dionysius, who did not doubt that it was the work of Demosthenes, remarks that the orator has reverted

*On the Treaty with Alexander*, date uncertain, probably 335 B.C., is also by a contemporary of Demosthenes. The theme is,—Treaties should be observed by all, but Macedon has broken promises, so this is an opportunity for Athens to recover her freedom.

The *Answer to Philip's Letter* and the speech περὶ συντάξεως (on financial organization) are generally regarded as rhetorical forgeries.

Two epideictic speeches, the *Epitaphius* and *Eroticus*, are almost certainly not by Demosthenes, and the six *Letters* are doubtful. The fifty-six *prooemia*, or introductions to speeches, are probably genuine exercises of the orator's early days.

to the style of Lysias (*de Demos.*, ch. ix.). Hiatus is frequent and there are some monotonous repetitions. Critics were somewhat shocked by the concluding phrase of § 45—'If you carry your brains in your heads, and not in your heels so as to walk on them.' Aeschines calls the orator κρώβυλος, from his affected way of wearing his hair in a ' bun ' on the top of his head.

# CHAPTER X

## PHOCION, DEMADES, PYTHEAS

THOUGH as a rule an orator could not hope to be successful in fourth-century Athens without a professional training, yet there were at times men who, either through strength of character or natural gifts, could dispense with a rhetorical education.

Foremost among the men of the peace party was Phocion, an aristocrat by instinct if not by birth ; a man admired alike for ability and integrity, so that, though he was no great orator, his speeches always commanded respect. He aspired, like Pericles, to be both a statesman and a general, and in the former capacity had at times to speak in the assembly. Various anecdotes in Plutarch point to his efforts to attain a conciseness which was almost laconic. His utterance was as trenchant as it was brief—Demosthenes called him ' the knife that cuts my speeches down ' ; and he had a lively wit, which must have pleased his hearers even though his policy was unpopular. On one occasion, when the people applauded him—which was rare, for he neither courted nor expected popularity—he paused in his speech and asked, ' Have I said something absurd ? '

An unsparing critic of the democracy, as he was nevertheless their faithful servant, he continued, from the purest motives, to urge peace, though the best years of his life were spent in war. He was respected for his high character by Philip and Alexander, and acquiesced in the government instituted by Antipater in 322 B.C., but fell a victim to the hatred of the extreme democrats, and was forced to drink hemlock, at the age of eighty years, in 317 B.C.

Demades, his contemporary, and a member of the same political party, is a perfect type of the vulgar demagogue. He depended for his success on a lively wit and a never-failing flow of words. After the battle of Chaeronea, where he was taken prisoner, he became an avowed agent of Philip and Alexander.[1] In consequence of his supposed services to Athens after the destruction of Thebes, he attained great popularity, his statue was erected in the market-place, and the more material benefit of perpetual meals in the Prytaneum was decreed to him. He was put to death by Cassander, the son of Antipater; his fellow-citizens melted down his statues and applied the metal to even baser purposes.[2] His recorded sayings show imagination—'Alexander is not dead; if he were, the whole world would stink of his corpse'; or again, 'Macedon without Alexander would be like the Cyclops without his eye';[3] finally, Athens is to him 'not the sea-fighter whom our ancestors knew, but an old woman, wearing slippers and supping barley-water.'[4] For the high opinion entertained of his eloquence we may refer to the verdict of Theophrastus—'Demosthenes is an orator worthy of Athens; Demades is on a higher

[1] Dinarchus, *Demos.*; § 104, ὁμολογῶν λαμβάνειν καὶ λήψεσθαι.
[2] Plut., *Moralia*, 820 F, κατεχώνευσαν εἰς ἀμίδας.
[3] Demetrius, *de Elocutione*, §§ 282, 284.          [4] *Ibid.*, § 286

plane than Athens.'[1]   We have no further means of forming any conception of his style.

Pytheas, another orator who raised himself by his talents from a humble position, was much younger than the previous two, who were about contemporary with Demosthenes.[2]  He was one of the prosecutors of Demosthenes in the affair of Harpalus in 324 B.C. Soon after the death of Alexander he was banished, took service with Antipater, and worked as his agent in the Peloponnese, using his influence to thwart the efforts of Demosthenes towards united resistance. After this we lose sight of him.  He is said to have had talent, but to have been handicapped by lack of education.  He was the coiner of the famous phrase about the speeches of Demosthenes, that they 'smelt of the lamp,' and another equally apt, though less familiar, that Demosthenes 'had swallowed Isaeus whole.'[3]

[1] For this and other judgments, see Plut., *Demos.*, chs. viii.-x.
[2] *Ibid.*, ch. viii.                [3] Dionysius, *Isaeus*, ch. iv.

# CHAPTER XI

## LYCURGUS, HYPERIDES, DINARCHUS

### § 1.  *Life*

LYCURGUS, according to Libanius, was older than Demosthenes,[1] though they were practically contemporaries.  He belonged to the illustrious house of the Eteobutadae, who traced their descent from one Butes, brother of Erechtheus.  The priesthood of Posidon-Erechtheus, and other religious offices, were hereditary in this family.

The grandfather of the orator, also called Lycurgus, was put to death by the Thirty ; his father, Lycophron, is known only by name.

In the orator's extant speech, and in his recorded actions, we find abundant proof of a sincere piety and deep religious feeling, which were natural in the true representative of such a family.  The traditions of his house may well have turned his thoughts to the stern virtues of ancient days, the days of Athenian greatness, when self-sacrifice was expected of a citizen. He expresses a friendly feeling towards Sparta.

Of his earlier political life we know only that he was an ally of Demosthenes.[2]  He came into greater prominence after Chaeronea, and was one of the ten orators whose surrender was demanded by Alexander after the destruction of Thebes.

---

[1] Hypothesis to Demos., *Against Aristogiton.*

[2] In some MSS. of Demosthenes (*Phil.*, iii., § 72) his name occurs as a member of an embassy which made a tour of the Peloponnese in 343 B.C. to rouse opposition against Philip.

In 338 B.C., when the war party came into power, he succeeded Eubulus, the nominee of the peace party, in an important financial office. In the decree quoted by the Pseudo-Plutarch he is called ' Steward of the public revenue ' (τῆς κοινῆς προσόδου ταμίας), which is probably not his correct title, though it fairly represents his appointment.[1] He kept this office for twelve years. His long administration, which was characterized by absolute probity, brought the finances of Athens to a thoroughly sound condition. During his office he built a theatre and an odeon, completed an arsenal, increased the fleet, and improved the harbour of Piraeus. He also embellished the city with works of art—statues of the great poets erected in the public places, golden figures of Victory and golden vessels dedicated in the temples. His respect for the poets was further shown by his decree that an official copy should be made of the works of the three great tragedians—a copy which afterwards passed into the possession of the Alexandrine library.[2]

He conceived it as his mission to raise the standard of public and private life. Himself almost an ascetic,[3] he enacted sumptuary laws ; as a religious man by instinct and tradition, he built temples and encouraged religious festivals ; an ardent patriot by conviction,

---

[1] See (Aristotle) Ἀθηναίων πολιτεία, ch. 43, with Sandys' notes. He must have been either ταμίας τῶν στρατιωτικῶν or president of οἱ ἐπὶ τὸ θεωρικόν, or perhaps he held both these appointments, as the scope of his work seems to imply. Ps.-Plutarch says πιστευσάμενος τὴν διοίκησιν τῶν χρημάτων.

[2] Ptolemy Philadelphus borrowed it in order to have it copied. He deposited a large sum as security, but in the end he sacrificed the deposit, kept the original, and presented Athens with his new copy.

[3] He wore the same clothes in summer and winter, and shoes only in very severe weather (*Ps.-Plut.*).

he thought it his duty to undertake the ungrateful
part of a public prosecutor, pursuing all who failed in
their sacred duty towards their country. In this way
he conducted many prosecutions, which were nearly
all successful. He was never a paid advocate or a
writer of speeches for others; indeed he would have
thought it criminal to write or speak against his convictions.[1] His indictments were characterized by
such inflexible severity that his contemporaries compared him to Draco, saying that he wrote his accusations with a pen dipped in death instead of blood.[2]

He died a natural death in 324 B.C.,[3] and was
honoured by a public funeral. His enemy Menesaechmus, who succeeded to his office, accused him of
having left a deficit, though, according to one story,
Lycurgus, on the point of death, had been carried into
the ecclesia and successfully defended himself on that
score. His sons were condemned to make restitution,
and, being unable to pay, were thrown into prison, in
spite of an able defence by Hyperides. They were
released on an appeal by Demosthenes, then in exile.[4]

## § 2. *Works*

Fifteen speeches of Lycurgus were preserved in antiquity, nearly all accusations on serious charges. He
prosecuted Euxenippus, whom Hyperides defended;
he spoke against the orator Demades, and, in alliance
with Demosthenes, against the sycophant Aristogiton.
Other speeches known to us by name are *Against Auto-
lycus, Against Leocrates*, two speeches *Against Lycophron*,

---

[1] See his condemnation of the advocates of Leocrates, § 135.

[2] οὐ μέλανι ἀλλὰ θανάτῳ χρίοντα τὸν κάλαμον κατὰ τῶν πονηρῶν (*Ps.-Plut.*).　　[3] Suidas.

[4] Assuming (with Blass) the authenticity of the third letter of Demosthenes, which is doubtful.

S

*Against Lysicles, against Menesaechmus,* a *Defence of himself against Demades, Against Ischyrias,* πρὸς τὰς μαντείας (obscure title), *Concerning his administration, Concerning the priestess,* and *Concerning the priesthood.*[1]

Only one speech is now extant, the impeachment of Leocrates.

Leocrates, an Athenian, during the panic which succeeded the battle of Chaeronea, fled from Athens to Rhodes, and thence migrated to Megara, where he engaged in trade for five years. About 332 B.C. he returned to Athens, thinking that his desertion would have been forgotten ; but Lycurgus prosecuted him as a traitor.

Only a small part of the speech is really devoted to proving the charge. By § 36 Lycurgus regards it as generally admitted. The remaining 114 sections consist mostly of comment and digressions which aim at emphasizing the seriousness of the crime and produce precedent for the infliction of severe punishment in such cases.

*Analysis*

1. *Introduction.* Justice and piety demand that I should bring Leocrates to trial (§§ 1-2) ; the part of a prosecutor is unpopular, but it is my duty to undertake it (§§ 3-6). This is a case of exceptional importance, and you must give your decision without prejudice or partiality, emulating the Areopagus (§§ 7-16).
2. *Narrative.* The flight of Leocrates to Rhodes. *Evidence* (§§ 17-20). His move to Megara and occupation there. *Evidence* (§§ 21-23).

---

[1] This list is taken from Suidas. The list compiled by Blass, from various sources, is different in some details.

3. *Argument*. Comments on the narrative. Possible line of defence (§§ 24-35). The case is now proved. It remains to describe the circumstances of Athens at the time when Leocrates deserted her (§ 36).

4. The panic after the battle of Chaeronea (§§ 37-45). Praise of those who fell in the battle there (§§ 46-51). Acquittal is impossible (§§ 52-54). Another ground of defence cut away (§§ 55-58). Further excuses disallowed (§§ 59-62). Attempt of his advocates to belittle his crime refuted by appeal to the principles of Draco (§§ 63-67). They appeal to precedent—the evacuation of the city before the battle of Salamis: this precedent can be turned against them (§§ 68-74). The sanctity of oaths and punishment for perjury. Appeals to ancient history. Codrus (§§ 75-89). Leocrates says he is confident in his innocence—*quem deus vult perdere, prius dementat* (§§ 90-93). Providence (§§ 94-97). Examples of self-sacrifice ; quotations from Euripides and Homer (§§ 97-105). Praise of Sparta. Influence of Tyrtaeus on patriots. Thermopylae (§§ 106-110). Severity of our ancestors towards traitors (§§111-127). Sparta was equally severe (§§ 128-129). Due severity will discourage treachery, and the treachery of Leocrates is of the basest sort (§§ 130-134). His advocates are as bad as he is (§§ 135-140). Appeal to the righteous indignation of the judges (§§ 141-148).

*Epilogue* (§§ 149-150) :

' I have come to the succour of my country and her religion and her laws, and have pleaded my case straightforwardly and justly, neither slandering Leocrates for his general manner of living, nor bringing any charge foreign to the present matter ; but you must consider that in acquitting him you condemn your country to death and slavery. Two urns stand before you, the one for betrayal, the other for salvation ; votes placed in the former mean the ruin of your fatherland, those in the latter are given for civil security and prosperity. If you let Leocrates go, you will be voting for the betrayal of Athens, her religion, and her ships ; but if you put him to death, you will encourage others to guard and secure your country, her revenues, and her prosperity. So imagine, Athenians, that the land and its trees are supplicating you, that the harbours, the dockyards, and the walls of the city are imploring you ; that the temples and holy places are urging you to come to their help ; and make an example of Leocrates, remembering what charges are brought against him, and how mercy and tears of compassion do not weigh more with you than the safety of the laws and the commonwealth.' [1]

### § 3.  *Style, etc.*

Lycurgus is called a pupil of Isocrates ; whether he was actually a student under the great master we cannot be sure, but undoubtedly he had studied the master's works. The influence of the *Panegyric* may be traced here and there in the forms of sentences and in certain terms of speech which are characteristic of the epideictic style. Blass and others have drawn attention to isolated sentences in the speech against Leocrates which might have been deliberately modelled, with only the necessary changes of words for the different circumstances, on sentences in Isocrates.[2] The employment of a pair

---

[1] §§ 149-150.

[2] *E.g.* cf. § 3, ἐβουλόμην δ' ἄν, ὥσπερ ὀυφέλιμόν ἐστι, etc., with Isocr. viii. (*de Pace*), § 36, ἠβουλόμην δ' ἄν, ὥσπερ προσῆκόν ἐστιν, etc. also § 7 with Isocr. vii. (*Areopagiticus*), § 43, etc.

of synonyms, or words of similar sense, where one would suffice, also belongs to this style [1]—*e.g.* safeguard and protect, § 3; infamous and inglorious, § 91; greatheartedness and nobility, § 100.

With these we must class such phrases as τὰ κοινὰ τῶν ἀδικημάτων for τὰ κοινὰ ἀδικήματα [2] (§ 6), and the employment of abstract words in the plural, as εὔνοιαι, φόβοι, § 48, 43.

Lycurgus is very variable with regard to hiatus. In some instances he has deliberately avoided it by slight distortions of the natural order of words; [3] in some passages he has been able to avoid it without any dislocation of order—a work of greater skill; [4] but again there are sentences where the sequences of open vowels are frequent and harsh. [5] Other instances of careless writing may be found in the inartistic joining of sentences and clauses, for instance in §§ 49-50, where several successive clauses are connected by γάρ, [6] or in the clumsy accumulation of participles, as in § 93. [7] We must conclude that Lycurgus, though so familiar with the characteristics of Isocratean prose as to reproduce them by unconscious imitation, was too much interested in his subject to care about being a stylist; and that

---

[1] Cf. *supra*, p. 134.

[2] This circumlocution may have been employed originally for the avoidance of hiatus, as in the example quoted, and in § 111, τὰ καλὰ τῶν ἔργων; it is, however, also used in cases where no such consideration enters, *e.g.* § 48, τοὺς ποιητοὺς τῶν πατέρων.

[3] E.g. § 7, οὐ μικρόν τι μέρος συνέχει τῶν τῆς πόλεως, οὐδ' ἐπ' ὀλιγὸν χρόνον, where συνέχει | οὐδ' is deliberately avoided.

[4] E.g. §§ 71-73.

[5] E.g. § 143, καὶ αὐτίκα μάλ' ὑμᾶς ἀξιώσει ἀκούειν αὐτοῦ ἀπολογουμένου. § 20, πολλοὶ ἐπείσθησαν τῶν μαρτύρων ἢ ἀμνημονεῖν ἢ μὴ ἐλθεῖν ἢ ἑτέραν πρόφασιν εὑρεῖν.

[6] See the translation on p. 278.

[7] φυγόντα, καὶ . . . ἀκούσαντα . . ., ἀφικόμενον καὶ . . . καταφυγόντα, καὶ οὐδὲν ἧττον . . . ἀποθανόντα.

though, like Demosthenes, he wrote his speeches out, he really belongs rather to the class of improvisatory speakers like Phocion.

His tendency towards the epideictic style is also seen in his treatment of his subject-matter; thus §§ 46-51 are nothing but a condensed funeral speech on those who died at Chaeronea. It is introduced with an apology (§ 46); it may seem irrelevant, he says, but it is frankly introduced to point the contrast between the patriot and the traitor. The concluding sections of the eulogy are as follows:

' And if I may use a paradox which is bold but nevertheless true, they were victorious in death. For to brave men the prizes of war are freedom and valour; for both of these the dead may possess. And further, we may not say that our defeat was due to them, whose spirits never quailed before the terror of the enemy's approach; for to those who fall nobly in battle, and to them alone, can no man justly ascribe defeat; for fleeing from slavery they make choice of a noble death. The valour of these men is a proof, for they alone of all in Greece had freedom in their bodies; for as they passed from life all Greece passed into slavery; for the freedom of the rest of the Greeks was buried in the same tomb with their bodies. Hence they proved to all that they were not warring for their personal ends, but facing danger for the general safety. So, Gentlemen, I need not be ashamed of saying that their souls are the garland on the brows of their country.' [1]

This, with the exception of a slight imperfection of style already noticed, is good in its way, in the style which tradition had established as appropriate to such subjects. It is less conventional and, in spite of its bold metaphors, less insincere than Gorgias, avoiding as it does the extravagance of his antithetical style.

[1] §§ 49-50.

But in spite of the speaker's apology we feel that it is out of place, and its effect is spoiled by the use to which it is put in the argumentative passage which immediately follows :

' And because they showed reason in the exercise of their courage, you, men of Athens, alone of all the Greeks, know how to honour noble men. In other States you will find memorials of athletes in the market-places ; in Athens such records are of good generals and of those who slew the tyrant. Search the whole of Greece and you will barely find a few men such as these, while in every quarter you will easily find men who have won garlands for success in athletic contests. So, as you bestow the highest honours on your benefactors, you have a right to inflict the severest punishments on those by whom their country is dishonoured and betrayed.' [1]

His use of examples from ancient history is similar to that of Isocrates, *e.g.* in the *Philip* and the *Panegyric* ; but many of these episodes are forcibly dragged into a trial of the kind with which Lycurgus was concerned, whereas those of Isocrates always help to convey the lesson which he is trying to enforce. Thus the following passage, which succeeds a quotation from Homer, leads up to a digression on Tyrtaeus, accompanied by a lengthy quotation from his works. There is only a bare pretence that all this has anything to do with the case :

' Hearing these lines and emulating such actions, our ancestors were so disposed towards manly courage that they were content to die not only for their own fatherland but for all Greece, as their common fatherland. Those, at any rate, who faced the barbarians at Marathon, conquered the armament of all Asia, by their individual sacrifice gain-

[1] § 51.

ing security for all the Greeks in common, priding themselves not upon their fame but on doing deeds worthy of their country, setting themselves up as champions of the Greeks and masters of the barbarians ; for they made no nominal profession of courage, but gave an actual display of it to all the world.' [1]

Here Lycurgus has reverted to the antithetical style of Antiphon, the opposition of ' word ' and ' deed,' ' private ' and ' public,' and the like. We are also from time to time reminded of Antiphon by the prominence given in the *Leocrates* to religious considerations. The digressions may be partly explained by the speaker's avowed motive in introducing some of them —his wish to be an educator. He introduces a very moral tale of a young Sicilian who, tarrying behind to save his father, on the occasion of an eruption of Etna, was providentially saved while all the others perished. This is his excuse—' The story may be legendary, but it will be appropriate for all the younger men to hear it now ' ; [2] and the manner of the lecturer is evident elsewhere—' There are three influences above all which guard and protect the democracy and the welfare of the city,' etc. ' There are two things which educate our youth :—the punishment of evil-doers and the rewards bestowed on good men.' [3]

Quite apart from these decorative digressions, Lycurgus admits into his ordinary discourse poetical phrases and metaphors which the stricter taste of Isocrates would have excluded. The bold personifications in his epilogue and elsewhere are cases in point :

' So imagine, Athenians, that the land and its trees are supplicating you ; that the harbours, the dockyards, and

<hr>

[1] § 104.    [2] § 95.    [3] §§ 3, 10 ; cf. also § 79.

the walls of the city are imploring you ; that the temples and holy places are urging you to come to their help.' [1]

Lycurgus must have tried the patience of his hearers by his lengthy quotations from the poets. No other orator, perhaps, would have dared to recite fifty-five lines of Euripides and to follow them, after a short extract from Homer, with thirty-two lines of Tyrtaeus. Aeschines, no doubt, was fond of quoting, but his extracts are comparatively short and generally to the point ; he can make good use of a single couplet. Demosthenes too, in capping his great adversary's quotations, observed moderation and season. But the long quotations in Lycurgus are superfluous ; that from Euripides is a mere excrescence, for he has already summarized in half a dozen lines the story from which he draws his moral ; and the only purpose in telling the story at all is to introduce the refrain ' Leocrates is quite a different kind of person.'

In this matter Lycurgus lacks taste—that is to say, he lacks a sense of proportion ; but for all that he is felt to be speaking naturally quite according to his own character ; he is attaining the highest *ethos* by being himself. We know his interest in the tragedians from the fact that he caused an official copy of the plays to be preserved ; and though religious motives would suffice to account for this decree, probably personal feeling, the statesman's private affection for the works which he thus perpetuated, to some degree influenced his judgment.

[1] § 150, cf. also § 43. ' He contributed nothing to the nation's safety, at a time when the country was contributing her trees, the dead their sepulchres, and the temples their arms.' And § 17, οὔτε τοὺς λιμένας τῆς πόλεως ἐλεῶν ; § 61, πόλεώς ἐστι θάνατος ἀνάστατον γενέσθαι. Hyperides has a similarly bold expression, ' Condemning the city to death.'

Though he may be unskilful, if judged by technical standards, Lycurgus impresses us by his dignified manner. He will not condescend to any rhetorical device which might detract from this dignity. He has no personal abuse for his opponent ; he promises to keep to the specific charge with which the trial is concerned,[1] and at the end of the speech can justly claim that he has done so.[2] Though it may lay him open to the suspicion of sycophancy, he disclaims any personal enmity against Leocrates ; he professes to be impelled entirely by patriotic motives, and we believe him.[3] He may seem to us excessively severe ; we may regard the crime of Leocrates as nothing worse than cowardice; but we are convinced that to Lycurgus it appeared as the greatest of all crimes ; and the Athenian assembly too was apparently so convinced.[4]

Failure in patriotism was to Lycurgus an offence against religion, and religion has the utmost prominence in his speech. There can be no doubt of his sincerity. The court of the Areopagus, which was more directly under religious protection and more closely concerned with religious questions than any other court, is mentioned by him with almost exaggerated praise.[5] The Areopagus was very highly respected by all Athenians, but it was not a democratic court ; it was a survival from pre-democratic days. An orator who only wished to propitiate the good-will of his popular audience would praise not the old aristocratic court but the modern popular assembly before which he was speaking.

---

[1] § 11.    [2] § 149.    [3] § 5.
[4] Leocrates was acquitted by one vote only.
[5] § 12. ' It is so far superior to other courts that even those who are convicted before it do not question its justice. You should take it as your model.'

Lycurgus gives praise and blame where he thinks them due.   He is by no means satisfied with the democratic courts.

' I too, shall follow justice in my prosecution, neither falsifying anything, nor speaking of matters extraneous to the case.   For most of those who come before you behave in the most inappropriate fashion ;  for they either give you advice about public interests, or bring charges, true or false, of every possible kind rather than the one on which you are to be called on to give your verdict.

' There is no difficulty in either of these courses ;  it is as easy to utter an opinion about a matter on which you are not deliberating as it is to make accusations which nobody is going to answer.   But it is not just to ask you to give a verdict in accordance with justice when they observe no justice in making their accusations.   And you are responsible for this abuse, for it is you who have given this licence to those who appear before you. . . .' [1]

The whole speech is pervaded by references to religion ; Rehdantz has noted that the word θέος occurs no less than thirty-three times ; and other words of religious import are very frequent, though the orator never uses ejaculations such as the ὦ γῆ καὶ θεοί of Demosthenes.   This reiteration is of less significance than the serious tone of the passages in which such references occur ;  his opening sentences indicate the attitude which he is to maintain :

' Justice and Piety will be satisfied, men of Athens, by the prosecution which I shall institute, on your behalf and on behalf of the gods, against the defendant Leocrates. For I pray to Athena and the other gods, and to the heroes whose statues stand in the city and in the country, that if I have justly impeached Leocrates ;  if I am bringing to

[1] §§ 11-12.

trial the betrayer of their temples, their shrines and their sanctuaries, and the sacrifices ordained by the laws, handed down to you by your forefathers, they may make me to-day a prosecutor worthy of his offences, as the interests of the people and the city demand; and that you, remembering that your deliberations are concerned with your fathers, your children, your wives, your country, and your religion, and that you have at the mercy of your vote the man who betrayed them all, may prove relentless judges, both now and for all time to come, in dealing with offenders of this kind and degree. But if the man whom I bring to trial before this assembly is not one who has betrayed his father-land and deserted the city and her holy observances, I pray that he may be saved from this danger both by the gods and by you, his judges.' [1]

Passages later in the speech deepen this impression, and contain definite statements of belief which we cannot disregard:

' For the first act of the gods is to lead astray the mind of the wicked man; and I think that some of the ancient poets were prophets when they left behind them for future generations such lines as these:

For when God's wrath afflicteth any man,
By his own act his wits are led astray,
And his straight judgment warped to crooked ways,
That, sinning, he may know not of his sin.

' The older men among you remember, the younger have heard, the story of Callistratus, whom the city condemned to death. He fled the country, and hearing the god at Delphi declare that if he went to Athens he would obtain his due, he came here, and took sanctuary at the altar of the twelve gods; but none the less he was put to death by the city.

' This was just; for a criminal's due is punishment. And the god rightly gave up the wrong-doer to be punished by

____________________
[1] §§ 1-2.

those whom he had wronged ; for it would be strange
if he revealed the same signs to the pious and the wicked.'

' But I am of opinion, Gentlemen, that the god's care
watches over every human action, particularly those concerned with our parents and the dead, and our pious duty
towards them ; and naturally so, for they are the authors
of our being, and have conferred innumerable blessings on
us, so that it is an act of monstrous impiety, I will not say
to sin against them, but even to refuse to squander our own
lives in benefiting them.' [1]

The following fragment deserves quotation as an
example of his dignified severity :

' You were a general, Lysicles ; a thousand of your fellow-
citizens met their death, two thousand were made prisoners,
and our enemies have set up a trophy of victory over Athens,
and all Greece is enslaved ; all this happened under your
leadership and generalship ; and yet do you dare to live
and face the sun's light, and invade the market-place—you,
who have become a memorial of disgrace and reproach to
your country ? ' [2]

## HYPERIDES

Hyperides, a member of a middle-class family,
was born in 389 B.C., and so was almost exactly contemporary with Lycurgus, whose political views he
shared. He too, according to his biographer, was a
pupil of Isocrates and of Plato, but the influence of the
latter can nowhere be traced in his work.

A man of easy morals and self-indulgent habits, he
presents a striking contrast to the austerity of Lycurgus.
The comic poets satirized his gluttony and his partiality
for fish, and the Pseudo-Plutarch records that he took

---

[1] §§ 92-94.                    [2] *Against Lysicles*, fr. 75.

a walk through the fish-market every day of his life ; but the pursuit of pleasure did not impair his activity.

He was at first a writer of speeches for others, as Demosthenes was at the beginning of his career ;[1] but before he reached the age of thirty he began to be concerned personally in trials of political import. He prosecuted the general Autocles on a charge of treachery, in 360 B.C. ; he appeared against the orator Aristophon of Azenia, and Diopeithes. He impeached in 343 B.C., Philocrates, who had brought about the peace with Philip.[2] He was sent as a delegate to the Amphictyonic Council,[3] and showed himself a vigorous supporter of the policy of Demosthenes ; in 340 B.C., when an attack on Euboea by Philip was anticipated, he collected a fleet of forty triremes, two of which he provided at his own cost. Shortly before Chaeronea he proposed a decree to honour Demosthenes ; after the battle he took extreme measures for the public safety, including the enfranchisement of *metoeci* and the manumission of slaves. He was prosecuted by Demades for moving an illegal decree, and retorted, ' The arms of Macedon made it too dark to see the laws ; it was not I who proposed the decree, but the battle of Chaeronea.'[4] He was able to retaliate soon afterwards by prosecuting Demades for the same offence of illegality. Demades had proposed to confer the title of *proxenos* on Euthycrates, who had betrayed Olynthus

---

[1] He could not afford to be particular as to the kind of cases which he took up ;  the affair of Athenogenes is far from respectable on either side, and several of his speeches were in connexion with *hetairai* of the less reputable sort. His defence of the famous Phryne was his masterpiece.

[2] He mentions these three among the most famous cases in which he has been concerned (*For Euxenippus*, § 28).

[3] Demos., *de Cor.*, §§ 134-135.          [4] Fr. 28.

to Philip. A fragment which remains of Hyperides'
speech on this subject shows him to be a master of
sarcasm.[1]

We know nothing for certain about the origin of the
breach between him and Demosthenes ; it may have
been due to his disapproval of the latter's policy of
inactivity when Sparta in 330 B.C. wished to fight with
Antipater ; at any rate his language in 334 B.C. shows
him to be an irreconcilable adversary of Macedon.
Nicanor had sent a proclamation to the Greeks request-
ing them to recognize Alexander as a god, and to receive
back their exiles. At the same time Harpalus, Alexander's treasurer, had deserted from the king's side
and arrived at Athens with a considerable treasure.
Demosthenes was in favour of negotiating with Alexander ; Hyperides wished to reject the proposals of
Nicanor, and use the treasure of Harpalus for continuing the war against Macedon. Harpalus was arrested, but succeeded in escaping, and many prominent
statesmen came under suspicion of having received
bribes from him. Hyperides was chosen as one of the
prosecutors, and Demosthenes was exiled.

Hyperides, after Alexander's death, took the chief
responsibility for the Lamian war, and was chosen to
pronounce the funeral oration on his friend, the general
Leosthenes, and the other Athenians who fell in the
war. Demosthenes had now returned from exile ; the
two patriots were reconciled, and persisted in the policy
of resistance from which the prudence of Phocion had
long striven to dissuade Athens. After the battle of
Crannon, Antipater demanded the surrender of the
leaders of the war party ; Hyperides fled, was captured

---

[1] *Vide infra*, p. 295.

and put to death in 322 B.C.    He is said to have bitten out his tongue for fear that he might, under torture, betray his friends.    His body was left unburied till the piety of a kinsman recovered it and gave him interment in the family tomb by the Rider's Gate.    He had proved himself consistent throughout his public life, and however mistaken his policy, especially in the latter years, may have been, honour is due to him for the unflinching patriotism which led him to martyrdom in a vain struggle to uphold his country's honour.

Until the middle of the nineteenth century, Hyperides was known to the modern world only from the criticisms of Dionysius and other ancient scholars, and from a few minute fragments preserved here and there by quotations in scholiasts and lexicographers.    A manuscript is believed to have existed in the library at Buda, but when that city was captured by the Turks in 1526 the library was destroyed or dispersed, and Hyperides was lost.

In 1847 portions of his speeches began to reappear among the papyri discovered in Egypt.    In that year a roll, containing fragments of the speech *Against Demosthenes* and of the first half of the *Defence of Lycophron*, was brought to England; a second roll discovered in the same year was found to contain the second half of the *Lycophron* and the whole of the *Euxenippus*.    In 1856 were discovered considerable fragments of the Funeral Speech.    In 1890, some fragments of the speech *Against Philippides* were acquired by the British Museum, while the most important discovery of all was that of the speech *Against Athenogenes*. The MS. was purchased for the Louvre in 1888, but the complete text was only published in 1892.    Its importance may be estimated by the fact that Dionysius couples this speech and the defence of Phryne as being the best examples of a style in which Hyperides surpassed even Demosthenes. The papyrus itself is of interest as giving us one of the very earliest classical MSS. that we possess; it dates from the 2nd century B.C.[1]

In many points Hyperides challenges comparison with Lysias. The criticism of Dionysius is well worth our consideration: ' Hyperides is sure of aim, but seldom exalts his subject; in the technique of diction he surpasses Lysias, in subtlety (of structure) he surpasses all. He keeps a firm hold throughout on the matter at issue, and clings close to the essential details. He is well equipped with intelligence, and is full of charm ; he seems simple, but is no stranger to cleverness.'[2]

The first sentence contrasts Hyperides once for all with his contemporary Lycurgus, who, while less sure of his aim, has a personal dignity which gives exaltation to every theme.

We have hardly enough of the work of Hyperides to enable us to form a first-hand judgment as to the merits of his diction compared with that of Lysias. He has, indeed, the same simplicity and naturalness, but hardly, so far as we can judge, the same felicity of expression.

Hermogenes blames him for carelessness and lack of restraint in the use of words, instancing such expressions as μονώτατος, γαλέαγρα, ἐπήβολος, etc., which seem to him unsuited for literary prose. As we have had occasion to notice already, rare and unusual words

---

[1] The agreement of Blass and Kenyon on this point may be taken as conclusive. Small fragments of another speech *For Lycophron* have been recently published (*Pap. Oxyrh.*, vol. xiii.).

[2] ἀρχαίων κρίσις, v. 6.

T

may be found occasionally in every orator, almost in every writer. Hyperides was no purist; he enlivened his style with words taken from the vocabulary of Comedy and of the streets. He did not wait for authority to use any expression which would give a point to his utterance.

Critics who expected dignified restraint in oratorical prose may have been shocked by the adjective θριπή-δεστος, 'worm-eaten,' which he applied to Greece; to us it seems an apt metaphor. Of his other colloquialisms some recall the language of Comedy—as κρόνος ('an old Fossil'), the diminutive θεραπουτίον, and ὀβολοστάτης[1] ('a weigher of small change' = 'usurer'), προσπερι-κόπτειν ('to get additional pickings'—the metaphor is apparently from pruning a tree), παιδαγωγεῖν in the sense of 'lead by the nose.' Others seem to be merely colloquial, part of that large and unconventional voca-bulary which was soon to form the basis of Hellen-istic Greek; for we must remember that we are already on the verge of Hellenism, and that the Attic dialect must soon give way before the spread of a freer language. In this class we may put ἐποφθαλμιᾶν ('to eye covetously'), ὑποπίπτειν ('to put oneself under control of somebody'), ἐνσείω ('to entrap'), κατατέμνειν ('to abuse'), ἐπεμβαίνω (poetical or colloquial, 'to trample on').

In some of his speeches relating to *hetairai* he seems to have used coarse language which offended his critics; nothing offensive is found in his extant speeches.[2]

Other metaphors and similes abound; he is fond of comparing the life of the State to the life of a man, as

---

[1] ὀβολοστατεῖν was used by Lysias also (fr. 41).
[2] Demetrius, περὶ ἑρμηνείας, § 302.

Lycurgus does also—ἐν μὲν σῶμα ἀθάνατον ὑπείληφας
ἔσεσθαι, πόλεως δὲ τηλικαύτης θάνατον κατέγνως.
' You imagine that one person (*i.e.* Philip) can live for
ever, and you passed sentence of death on a city as old
as ours.'  The Homeric phrase ἐπὶ γήρως ὁδῷ (=ἐπὶ
γήραος οὐδῷ, ' on the threshold of old age ') is curiously
introduced into a serious passage in the *Demosthenes*
without any preparation or apology.  We can only
suppose that it was so familiar to his hearers that it
would not strike them as being out of place in ordinary
speech.  It is similarly used by Lycurgus.[1]  In the
same speech (*Against Demosthenes*) Hyperides speaks of
the nation being robbed of its crown, but the metaphor is suggested by the fact that actual crowns had
been bestowed on Demosthenes.  Such metaphors as
' others are building their conduct on the foundations
laid by Leosthenes,' though less common in Greek than
in English, are perfectly intelligible.  A happy instance
of his ' sureness of aim ' which Dionysius commended
is preserved in a fragment about his contemporaries :

' Orators are like snakes ; all snakes are equally loathed,
but some of them, the vipers, injure men, while the big
snakes eat the vipers.' [2]

He uses simile, however, with varying success ;  the
following, though the conception is good, is not properly
worked out, as the parallelism breaks down :

' As the sun traverses the whole world, marking out the
seasons, and ordering everything in due proportion, and
for the prudent and temperate of mankind takes charge
of the growth of their food, the fruits of the earth and all
else that is beneficial for life ;  so our city ever continues
to punish the wicked and help the righteous, preserving
equal opportunities for all, and restraining covetousness,

______

[1] *Leoc.*, § 40.  [2] Fr. 80.

and by her own risk and loss providing common security for all Greece.' [1]

The *Epitaphios* from which the last quotation is taken is a speech of a formal kind composed in the *epideictic* style, and naturally recalls similar speeches of Isocrates and others.   Its composition shows much greater care than was taken with the other speeches ; thus there are few examples of harsh hiatus, a matter to which the author as a rule paid no attention.   All the other extant speeches have far more instances of clashing vowels.[2] The antithetical sentences are appropriate to the style, and the periodic structure is like that of Isocrates, except that the sentences are, on the whole, shorter and simpler.

In other speeches he mingles the periodic and the free styles with discretion.   The objection to a long period is that it takes time to understand it ; we cannot fully appreciate the importance of any one part until we have reached the end and are in a position to look back at the whole.   For practical oratory it is far better to make a short statement which may be in periodic form, and amplify it by subsequent additions loosely connected by καί, δέ, γάρ, and such particles.   This is what Hyperides does with success, for instance in the opening of the *Euxenippus*, an argumentative passage.[3] In narrative passages a free style is expected.[4]

---

[1] *Epitaphios*, § 5.

[2] Cf. *de Demos.*, col. xi, ἐν τῷ δήμῳ ἑπτακόσια φήσας εἶναι τάλαντα, νῦν τὰ ἡμίση ἀναφέρεις, καὶ οὐδ' ἐλογίσω ὅτι τοῦ πάντα ἀνενεχθῆναι ὀρθῶς, κ.τ.λ.   *Ibid.*, col. xiii., καὶ οἱ ἄλλοι φίλοι αὐτοῦ ἔλεγον ὅτι ἀναγκάσουσι, κ.τ.λ.   *Euxenippus*, § 19, etc.

[3] §§ 1-3, although a full stop occurs in the second line of § 3, are all really one sentence, but in spite of its length it is perfectly lucid.

[4] A good example of a story told by a succession of short sentences joined by καί is to be found in *Athenogenes*, § 5.

In contrast to this flowing style we must notice the quick abrupt succession of short sentences which he sometimes affects, either in the form of question and answer, as in the following fragment, or otherwise :

' " Did you propose that the slaves should be made free ? " " I did, to save the free men from becoming slaves." " Did you move that the disfranchised citizens should be enfranchised ? "—" I did, in order that all in harmony might fight side by side for their country." ' [1]

Still more effective is the following :

' It is on this account that you have enacted laws to deal separately with every possible offence that a citizen may commit.  A man commits sacrilege—prosecution for sacrilege before the king-archon.  He neglects his parents—the archon sits on his case.  A man proposes an illegal measure—there is the council of the Thesmothetae.  He makes himself liable to arrest—the " eleven " are permanent officials.' [2]

Hyperides possessed an active wit which enabled him on many occasions to evade an argument by making his opponent appear ridiculous.  Euthias, in prosecuting Phryne for impiety, made his audience shudder by describing the torments of the wicked in Hades.  ' How is Phryne to blame,' asked Hyperides, ' for the fact that a stone hangs over the head of Tantalus ? ' [3]  In the *Euxenippus*, he complains that the process of impeachment before the assembly has been applied to the present case :

' Impeachment has hitherto been employed against people like Timomachus, Leosthenes, Callistratus, Philon, and Theotimus who lost Sestos—some of them for betraying ships which they commanded, some for betraying cities, and one for giving, as an orator, bad advice to the

[1] Frr. 27-28.　　　[2] *Euxenippus*, §§ 5, 6.　　　[3] Fr. 173.

people. . . . The present state of affairs is ridiculous—Diognides and Antidorus are impeached for hiring flute-players at a higher price than the law allows ; Agasicles of Piraeus is impeached for being registered as of Halimus ; and Euxenippus is impeached on account of the dream which he says he dreamed.' [1]

His sarcasm is playful at times, even in serious passages ; for instance the following :

' These Euboeans Demosthenes enrolled as Athenian citizens, and he treats them as his intimate friends ; this need not surprise you ; naturally enough, since his policy is always ebbing and flowing, he has secured as his friends people from Euripus.' [2]

Another good example of his sarcastic humour appears in the defence of Euxenippus against the charge of Macedonian sympathy :

' If your assertion (the prosecutor's) were true, you would not be the only person to know it. In the case of all others who in word or deed favour Philip, their secret is not their own ; it is shared by the whole city. The very children in the schools know the names of the orators who are in his pay, of the private persons who entertain and welcome his emissaries, and go out into the streets to meet them on their arrival.' [3]

This same sarcasm is in many places a powerful weapon of offence, as in the next extract from the indictment of Demosthenes :

' You, by whose decree he was put in custody, who when the watch was relaxed did nothing to assure it, and when it was abandoned altogether did not bring the guilty to trial—no doubt it was for nothing that you turned the opportunity to such advantage. Are we to believe that

---

[1] *Euxenippus*, §§ 1-3.
[2] *Against Demos.*, fr. v., col. xv. 15. The tide in the Euripus, which ebbed and flowed nine times a day, was, of course, proverbial.
[3] *Euxenippus*, col. xxxiv., § 22.

Harpalus gradually paid out his money to the minor politicians, who could only make a noise and raise an uproar, and overlooked you, who were master of the whole situation ? ' [1]

The following fragment contains the most striking example of irony to be found anywhere in his works ; the situation explains itself :

' The reasons which Demades has introduced are not the true justification for Euthycrates' appointment, but if he must be your *proxenos*, I have composed, and now put forward, a decree setting forth the true reasons why he should be so appointed :—Resolved—that Euthycrates be appointed *proxenos*, for that he acts and speaks in the interests of Philip ;  for that, having been appointed a cavalry-leader, he betrayed the Olynthian cavalry to Philip ; for that by so doing he caused the ruin of the people of Chalcidice ; for that after the capture of Olynthus he acted as assessor at the sale of the prisoners ;  for that he worked against Athens in the matter of the temple at Delos ;  for that, when Athens was defeated at Chaeronea, he neither buried any of the dead nor ransomed any of the captured.' [2]

We have seen already how he could turn his wit against the whole class of orators, to which he belonged himself ;  it is pleasant to find him, in a speech which he wrote for a fee, thus describing Athenogenes : ' A common fellow, a professional writer of speeches.' [3]  It was the business of the *logographos* to sink his own personality in that of his client, and Hyperides, who was an artist by instinct, did so more successfully than any other speech-writer, except, perhaps, Demosthenes.  In the present instance he must have felt a peculiar satisfaction in his work.

In private speeches he introduces many matters

---

[1] *Against Demos.*, col. xii.    [2] Fr. 76.
[3] *Athenogenes*, col. 2, ἄνθρωπον λογόγραφόν τε καὶ ἀγοραῖον.

extraneous to the case ; thus in the *Athenogenes*, though the question is only about a shady business transaction, he rouses odium by references to his adversary's political offences.   No doubt many weak cases succeeded by such devices, which call forth the just indignation of Lycurgus.[1]   In public cases he has a higher ideal.   When Lycurgus was an advocate on the other side, Hyperides referred to him with all the respect due to his character.   Even the speech against Demosthenes is entirely free from personal abuse, if we except a little mild banter about Demosthenes' austere habits of sobriety.[2]   The indictment of Demosthenes' public actions is vigorous enough, but it is restrained within the limits of good taste, and this is not for the sake of ancient friendship, which Hyperides repudiates :

' After that will you dare to remind me of our friendship ? . . . (as if it were) not you yourself who dissolved that friendship, when you received money to do your country harm, and changed sides ?   When you made yourself ridiculous and brought disgrace on us who hitherto had been of your party ?   Whereas we might have been held in the highest respect by the people, and been attended for the rest of life's journey by an honourable repute, you shattered all such hopes, and are not ashamed at your age to be tried by the younger generation for receiving bribes.   On the contrary, the younger politicians ought to receive education from men like you ; if they committed any hasty action they ought to be rebuked and punished.   Things are quite different now, when it falls upon the young men to correct those who have passed the age of sixty.   And so, Gentlemen, you may well be angry with Demosthenes, for through you he has had his fair portion of wealth and renown ; and

---

[1] Lycurgus, *Leocr.*, § 11 ; cf. § 149.
[2] Col. xxxix., the last two fragments of the speech in Blass' edition.

now, with his foot on the threshold of old age, he shows that he cares nothing for his country.' [1]

Dionysius approves the diversity of Hyperides' manner in dealing with his narratives :—' He tells his story on a variety of ways, sometimes in the natural order, sometimes working back from the end to the beginning.' [2] We have no means of judging; the *Euxenippus*, the only complete forensic speech, contains practically no narrative; the story of the *Athenogenes* is, apparently, told straight through without a break, and then followed by evidence and criticism and legal arguments. Then follows the attempt to blacken the character of Athenogenes by extraneous arguments.

We may conclude this section by a few sentences from the treatise *On the Sublime*, expressing an estimate of the general character of his oratory :

' If successes were to be judged by number, not by magnitude, Hyperides would be absolutely superior to Demosthenes. He has more tones in his voice, and more good qualities. He is very nearly first-class in everything, like a pentathlete, so that, while other competitors in every event beat him for the first prize, he is the best of all who are not specialists.' . . . ' Where Demosthenes tries to be amusing and witty, he raises a laugh, but it is against himself. When he attempts to be graceful, he fails still more signally. At any rate, if he had attempted to compose the little speech about Phryne or the one against Athenogenes, he would have established still more firmly the reputation of Hyperides.' ' But . . . the beauties of the latter, though numerous, are not great ; his sobriety renders them ineffective, and leaves the hearer undisturbed—no one, at any rate, is moved to terror by reading Hyperides.' [3]

---

[1] *Demos.*, v., §§ 20-21.          [2] *de Dinarcho*, ch. 6.
[3] περὶ ὕψους, ch. 34.

And the passage concludes with a sincere tribute to the titanic force of Demosthenes.

Hyperides had seventy-seven speeches ascribed to him, of which fifty-two were thought by the Greek biographer to be genuine.[1] Blass has collected the titles of no less than sixty-five, in addition to the five which are extant in the papyri ; so that only seven are unknown by name. Some quotations have been given from the indictment of Demosthenes ;[2] the subject-matter has been explained,[3] and the treatment, so far as we can judge from the fragments, criticized.[4] The date is 324 B.C. The *Defence of Lycophron* is a speech in an εἰσαγγελία in which Lycurgus was one of the prosecutors. Lycophron, an Athenian noble, was a commander of cavalry in Lemnos, and was accused of seducing a Lemnian woman of good family, the wife of an Athenian who died before the case came on. The date is uncertain ; perhaps *circa* 338 B.C. The case of Euxenippus arises out of the fact that Philip, after Chaeronea, restored the territory of Oropus to Athens. It was divided into five lots, and one lot assigned to every two tribes. A question arose whether the portion given to the Hippothoöntid and Acamantid tribes was not sacred to Amphiaraüs, and Euxenippus and two others were deputed to sleep in the shrine of the hero and obtain from their dreams a divination on the subject. They reported a dream which could be interpreted in favour of their tribes. In the present instance they are prosecuted for having given a false report of their dreams. The defendant and another advocate had already preceded Hyperides, so that the present speech is mainly devoted to bickering with the

---

[1] *Ps.-Plut.*, § 15.  
[3] *Supra*, p. 225-227.  
[2] *Supra*, pp. 18, 294-296.  
[4] *Supra*, p. 296.

prosecutors, of whom Lycurgus was one.   Date about
330 B.C.

The speech *Against Philippides*[1] is very much mutilated.     It is a γραφὴ παρανόμων against Philippides,
otherwise unknown, who had proposed a vote of thanks
to a board of πρόεδροι or presidents of the ecclesia for
their action in passing a certain decree, which seems to
have been a vote of honour to Philip.   It was passed
under compulsion, and Philippides attempted subsequently to exonerate them from all possible blame
by a decree which is here declared illegal.

The *Epitaphios* or Funeral Speech is a composition
in a well-known conventional form.   The topics for
such a speech were already laid down by long custom.
The skill of the orator is seen in his original way of
handling the traditional commonplaces.   First of all
there is the strong personal note.   He had been associated in politics with Leosthenes, and with him was
jointly responsible for the Lamian war in which the
latter met his death.[2]   His personal feeling for the
general is very prominent in the speech ; Leosthenes
is in fact the principal theme ; he is put, as M. Croiset
remarks, almost on a level with Athens :—' Leosthenes
seeing all Greece humbled and cowering, brought to
ruin by the traitors whom Philip and Alexander had
bought ; seeing that our city wanted a man, and all
Greece wanted a city, to take the leadership, freely gave
himself for his country and gave our city for the Greeks
to win their freedom.'[3]   It is not, he says, that he
wishes to slight the other patriots, but in praising
Leosthenes he is praising all.   He draws a fancy picture
of the heroes of antiquity welcoming Leosthenes in
Hades.   It is a sign of the times that the individual

_______________
[1] Date 336-5 B.C.        [2] 322 B.C.        [3] *Epitaphios*, § 10.

should so be exalted ; we have travelled far indeed from the cold impersonality of Pericles, to whom the nameless heroes who sacrifice their lives are but part of a pageant passing before the eyes of the deathless city. The consolation to the living is remarkable for containing references to a future life, which is quite without precedent :—' It is hard to comfort those who are in such grief ; for neither speeches nor laws can send sorrow to sleep ' . . . (there follow remarks about eternal praise, which are not particularly characteristic ; but he concludes in a higher strain) :—' Furthermore, if the dead are as though they had never been, our friends are released from sickness and pain and the other misadventures which afflict mankind ; but if the dead have consciousness, and are under the care of God, as we believe, we may be sure that they, who upheld the honour of the gods when it was threatened, are now the objects of God's loving kindness.' [1] Truly Socrates had not lived in vain.

The speech *Against Athenogenes* [2] is an admirable example of the orator's lighter style. Its chief merit is the way in which the narrative of the events is delivered by the speaker.

Hyperides' client, a young Athenian, wished to obtain possession of a young slave, who was employed in a perfumery-shop. Athenogenes, the owner of the shop—' a vulgar speech-maker, and worst of all an Egyptian ' —saw his opportunity for a good stroke of business, and at first refused to sell the slave. A quarrel ensued. At this point Antigona, once the most accomplished courtesan of her day, but now retired, came and offered her services to the young man. She contrived to pick

---

[1] *Epitaphios*, §§ 41-43.    [2] Date between 328 and 323 B.C.

up for herself a gratuity of 300 drachmas, just as a proof of his good opinion.   Later, she told the young man that she had persuaded Athenogenes to release the boy, not separately, but together with his father and brother, for forty minas.   The young man borrowed the money ;  a touching scene of reconciliation followed, Antigona exhorting the two adversaries to behave as friends in future.   ' I said that I would do so, and Athenogenes answered that I ought to be grateful to Antigona for her services;  "and now," he said, "you shall see what a kindness I will do you for her sake."' He offered, instead of setting the slaves free, to sell them formally to the plaintiff, who could then set them free when he liked, and so win their gratitude.   ' As to any debts they have contracted, you can take them over ;  they are trifling, and the stock remaining in the shop will easily cover them.'   Assent having been given, Athenogenes produced a contract in these terms, which he had brought with him, and it was signed and sealed on the spot.   Within three months the unhappy purchaser found himself liable for business debts and deposits amounting to five talents.   Athenogenes made the preposterous excuse that he had not known anything about this enormous debt.   His dupe was in an awkward position, as he had formally taken over the business and its liabilities.   He tries to prove that the contract should be held not valid.   His legal claim is very slight ;  the appeal is really to equity.   The second part of the speech deals with Athenogenes in his political relations.  The epilogue exhorts the judges to take this opportunity of punishing such a scoundrel on general grounds, even if he cannot actually be brought under any particular law.

## DINARCHUS

Dinarchus, the last of the ten orators of the Alexandrian Canon, was a Corinthian by birth. He lived as a *metoecus* at Athens, but never obtained the citizenship, and was therefore unable to appear in the courts or the assembly. He was born about 360 B.C.; on coming to Athens he is said to have studied under Theophrastus, and he began to write speeches, as a professional *logographos*, about 336 B.C. He did not come into prominence till about the time of the affair of Harpalus, and his most flourishing period was after the death of Alexander, under the oligarchic constitution set up by Cassander. During these fifteen years, 322-307 B.C., he composed a large number of speeches. In 307 B.C. the democratic restoration threatened danger to all who had flourished under the oligarchy, and he retired to Chalcis in Euboea, where he lived for fifteen years.[1] He returned to Athens in 292 B.C. and stayed for a time with one Proxenos, who, taking advantage of his age and infirmity, robbed him of a large sum of money. He brought his host to justice, and, according to Dionysius and other biographers, himself spoke in court for the first time. We know nothing of the result of the case, and have no information of the rest of the life of Dinarchus or his death.[2]

---

[1] Dion. (*de Dinarcho*, ch. iv., *ad fin.*) believed that he wrote no speeches during this time, for nobody would take the trouble to go to Chalcis for a speech either in a private or public action—οὐ γὰρ τέλεον ἠπόρουν οὕτω λόγων. Dionysius consequently rejected as spurious all speeches attributed to Dinarchus which were dated between 307 and 292 B.C.

[2] Suidas says that he was appointed Commissioner of the Peloponnese (ἐπιμελητὴς Πελοποννήσου) by Antipater, but this was another Dinarchus. Demetrius Magnes, quoted by Dionysius Din., ch. i), mentions four men of this name.

Dinarchus wrote, according to Demetrius Magnes,[1] over a hundred and sixty speeches. Many of these were rejected by Dionysius, who, however, admits the authenticity of a sufficiently large number—sixty out of eighty-seven which he knew.[2] Three only have come down to us, and the authenticity of the longest of these—*Against Demosthenes*—was questioned by Demetrius. We shall, however, treat it as genuine, since in style and subject-matter it is very similar to the others. The three speeches, *Against Demosthenes*, *Aristogiton*, and *Philocles*, all relate to the affair of Harpalus. The corruption connected with this affair was so deep-rooted that it was necessary above all to find men of upright character to conduct the prosecutions, and these would not be well-known orators, since most of the prominent politicians were implicated as defendants in the case. It is hardly remarkable, therefore, that professional speech-writers should be employed or that one writer should compose speeches to be delivered in three of the many prosecutions.

Dinarchus, the last of the truly Attic orators, is of very little importance in himself, but must find a place in any history of this kind as representing the beginning of the decline of oratory. ' He flourished most of all,' says Dionysius, ' after the death of Alexander, when Demosthenes and the other orators had been condemned to perpetual banishment or put to death, and there was nobody left who was worth mentioning after them.' This contains a fairly just estimate of the merits of the man, who, according to the same critic, ' neither invented a style of his own, like Lysias and Isocrates

<hr>

[1] In Dionysius, *de Din.*, ch. i.
[2] The curious may collect the titles from Dionysius (*de Din.* chs. x.-xiii.).

and Isaeus, nor perfected the inventions of others, as, in our judgment, Demosthenes, Aeschines, and Hyperides did.'[1]   His merits and defects are very obvious.   He knows all the technique of prose composition ;  he can avoid hiatus cleverly, and writes a style which is easily intelligible, even when his sentences are inordinately long.   He has some skill in the use of new words and metaphors—μετοιωνίσασθαι τὴν τύχην, 'auspicate your fortunes anew '—ἐκκαθάρατε, 'purge him away from the State '—δευσοποιὸς πονηρία, 'ingrained wickedness.'   He has some vigour and liveliness : abrupt statements like the following are terse and graphic enough—' You chose prosecutors in due course ; he came before the court ;  you acquitted him ' ;[2] he makes good use of rhetorical questions addressed to the defendant :—' Did you propose any motion about it ?   Did you give any counsel ?   Did you contribute any money ?   Did you ever in any small matter prove serviceable to those who were working for the common safety ?   Not in the slightest degree ' . . . etc.[3]   His sarcasm, which is rare, because he is generally too directly violent to be sarcastic, is at times pointed :—' Read again the decree which Demosthenes proposed against Demosthenes.'[4]   He knows the oratorical tricks : he can flatter the jury by references to their intelligence, by praise of the Areopagus, by encomia on the virtues of their ancestors.   He can appeal to ancient and modern precedent for the impartiality of judges and their severity against evil-doers.

He is at his best in the long refutation of the defence which he anticipates from Demosthenes [5]—this is, on

---

[1] Dion., *Din.*, ch. 2.    [2] *Demos.*, § 58.    [3] *Ibid.*, § 35.
[4] *Ibid.*, 83.    [5] *Demos.*, §§ 48-63.

the whole, orderly and effective—and in short passages like the following from the speech *Against Philocles*:

' Reflecting on these facts, Athenians, and remembering the present crisis, which calls for honour, not corruption, it is your duty to hate evil-doers, to exterminate from your city such beasts, and show the world that the nation has not shared in the degradation of certain of its politicians and generals, and is not a slave to conventional opinion ; knowing that, by God's favour, with the help of justice and concord, we shall easily defend ourselves, if any enemies wrongfully attack us, but that in union with corruption and treachery and other such vices which infect mankind, no city can ever be saved.' [1]

He was, then, thoroughly competent ; but he was careless. He passes from section to section with no logical and little formal connection ; invective takes the place of argument, and even his abuse is incoherent. Everything is overdone ; other writers have produced striking effects by slight changes in the order of words ; Dinarchus disarranges his order without improving the emphasis.[2] Again, the repetition of a single word may give emphasis, as thus :—' A hireling, men of Athens, a hireling he is and has been ' ; but this device is used *ad nauseam*.[3] His sentences, great concatenations of participles and relatives, trail along like wounded snakes.[4]

Invective had its place in Athenian oratory, but when on every page we find such expressions as beast,

---

[1] *Phil.*, § 19.

[2] In such extravagances as ἡ τῶν ἐκ προνοίας φόνων ἀξιόπιστος οὖσα βουλὴ τὸ δίκαιον καὶ τἀληθὲς εὑρεῖν (*Demos.*, § 6).   Cf. also §§ 12, 23, 59, 110, and elsewhere.

[3] *Demos.*, § 28 ;  cf. §§ 10, 27, 46, 76, etc.

[4] *Demos.*, §§ 18-21 (thirty-six lines without a real stop) ; *Philocles*, §§ 1-3 (twenty-three lines).

U

foul creature, foul beast, scum, cheat, accursed, thief, traitor, perjurer, receiver of bribes, hireling, unclean, we feel that the orator is spitting rather than talking.[1] There is a similar lack of decency in his imputation of corrupt motives to all the public actions of Demosthenes, good or bad, and to his exaggeration of the latter's offences. He becomes positively ridiculous when he describes Aristogiton's first imprisonment—the first of many. Aristogiton, the worst man in Athens, or rather, in all the world . . . has spent more time in prison than out . . . the first time he went there he behaved so disgustingly that the other prisoners, the dregs of all the world, refused to have their meals with him, or associate with him on terms of equality.[2] This abuse of a man who is on trial for a merely political offence, is grossly over-coloured, and is probably as false as his description of Demosthenes' callousness :—
'He went about exulting in the city's misfortunes ; he was carried in a litter down the road to Piraeus, mocking at the miseries of the poor.' Finally, his plagiarisms from Demosthenes, Aeschines, and other orators are too numerous to record ; he borrows whole passages without skill or appropriateness.[3] He borrows even from himself.[4] The ancient nicknames for him, ἀγροῖκος Δημοσθενής, κριθινός Δημοσθενής—'the boorish Demo-

---

[1] θηρίον, μιαρός, μιαρὸν θήριον, κάθαρμα, γόης, κατάρατος, κλέπτης, προδότης, ἐπιωρκηκώς, δωρόδοκος, μισθωτός, καταπτυστός are culled without any special diligence from his elegant repertory.

[2] *Aristog.*, §§ 1, 2, 9-10.

[3] *Demos.*, § 24, description of Thebes, from Aeschines. See Weil, *les Harangues de Démosthène*, p. 338, note on *Philippic*, iii., § 41, and Din., *Aristog.*, § 24, which is borrowed from it : ' Il est à son modèle ce que la bière est au vin.' (This barley-beer was a barbarian drink.)

[4] *E.g.* the passage about Conon's son, *Demos.*, § 14, used again in *Phil.*, § 17.

sthenes,' ' the small-beer Demosthenes,' are as apt as such characterisation can be.[1]

To sum up: the very marked decline of which Dinarchus is typical, is due not to lack of technical ability, but to lack of originality on the intellectual side, and still more to moral causes :—lack of literary conscience, shown in the plagiarisms ; lack of proper care, shown in the incoherence of the whole speeches ; and lack of all sense of proportion and restraint, shown by the numerous exaggerations of various kinds which have been described above.

[1] Dion., *de Din.*, ch. viii.; Hermogenes, περὶ ἰδεῶν, Β, p. 384, iv.

## CHAPTER XII

## THE DECLINE OF ORATORY

OWING to the extraordinary success of the Macedonian arms, Hellenic culture spread rapidly over a great part of the world ; but it was beaten out thin in the process.[1]

The conditions of life in Greece underwent a great change in the generations which succeeded the death of Alexander. Athens, which had for so long been the intellectual headquarters of the world, was now only a station of secondary importance. Alexandria, founded by the king himself, became under the divine auspices of the Ptolemies not only the great mart of the world but the greatest centre of learning ; Pergamus in the course of time rivalled Alexandria, at any rate in literary resources ; while Antioch and Tarsus also became prominent in the history of learning.

From early times men of genius born elsewhere in Greece, in the Ionian cities and in Magna Graecia, had turned to Athens for appreciation of their powers. It is easy to see at a glance how much Athens owed to these aliens for her intellectual advancement—Gorgias of Leontini, Protagoras of Abdera, Anaxagoras of Clazomenae, Thrasymachus of Chalcedon. Her dramatic poets were her own, and so were her great orators,

---

[1] The general decline of taste reacted on literary style, cf. *infra*, pp. 309-10.

with the exception of Lysias ; but this is partly due to the fact that the constitution of her laws gave little opportunity for aliens to win distinction on the platform or the stage. Of her great historians, one was not of Athenian birth and even wrote in a foreign dialect ; in philosophy no true-born Athenian before Plato won real distinction. In the Macedonian era a distinguished stranger had more prospect not only of appreciation but of material advancement in one of the royal cities than in a city-state which had become little better than a minor satrapy in one of the great empires, and traded only on the fading memories of its former magnificence. Life in the great cities was very different, too, from life in democratic Athens. From the time of Pericles to that of Demosthenes, all citizens had at least a strong corporate feeling ; all citizens knew each other. The sculptor fought side by side with the tanner, the Alcmaeonid met the lamp-seller in debate ; there were many common grounds in which all could meet under conditions of equality. In the law-courts the orator must satisfy not only the learned few but the unlettered many ; in the theatre the poet and his actors appealed to all classes, from the high-priest who must not be allowed to slumber on his central throne to the people who ate sweetmeats in the back rows, and, if dissatisfied, with true Athenian spirit, threw these harmless missiles at the performers.[1] Moreover, all spoke the same language. The diction of tragedy gradually put off its artificiality, and the orators approached nearer and nearer to the idiom of common speech.

In Alexandria, on the other hand, to take one typical

---

[1] Arist., *Eth. Nic.*, x. 5. 4, οἱ τραγηματίζοντες. Demos., *de Cor.*, cf. *supra*, p. 249.

example, there was no such unity. Among the Greek inhabitants there were many classes—the court-circle, the scholars of the Museum, the merchants, the mercenary troops, all with different aims and occupations ; and these formed but a minority. In addition there would be thousands of Jews, Egyptians, Phoenicians, Mesopotamians, and others, to whom Greek was at first a foreign language, and who when they had acquired it spoke, in the κοινή, a dialect corrupted by innumerable foreign elements. Thus, though scholarship persisted and flourished, there must always have been a sharp distinction between the lettered classes and the common people.

Oratory, like all other arts, faded away in Athens after Alexander's death, partly from the general causes indicated, partly on account of the special conditions of Athenian life.

Forced to submit to Antipater in 322 B.C., Athens was allowed to exist on humiliating terms. She received a Macedonian garrison into Munychia, the democracy was overthrown ; 12,000 of the poorer citizens were not only disfranchised but expatriated, and an oligarchy was instituted. Five years later a temporary revival occurred, when Polysperchon (317 B.C.) overthrew the oligarchy ; but a few months after this Cassander obtained possession of the city and again established a government on narrower lines, installing as governor a man of great erudition and culture, Demetrius of Phalerum. This Demetrius, though practically a satrap of Cassander, governed the city wisely for ten years ; but in 307 B.C. he fled before the approach of Demetrius Poliorcetes, son of Antigonus. The Besieger made a proclamation of freedom, which the

Athenians by this time were unworthy to enjoy; they ascribed to him divine honours, and in 301 B.C. he took up his quarters in the Parthenon. No wonder that Pallas Athene fled in disgust when her shrine was polluted by the licentious orgies of this new war-god.

Phocion, Demades, and Dinarchus, from among the contemporaries of Demosthenes, lived to see their city under Macedonian rule, but they left no successors. There were few opportunities left for an orator. The ecclesia, when it met on sufferance, could debate only on matters of domestic import; and proposals to improve the water-supply, or erect statues to a tyrant, give less scope for eloquence than the great issues of peace and war which had formerly been the subject of their deliberation. Men of political ability had no scope when politics were dead. In the courts, too, there could be no public cases of great interest comparable with the case of the *Crown* or the impeachment of Demosthenes. Private cases, in which aspiring politicians had hitherto found it convenient to try their strength, were more suited to the attainments of professional lawyers, and these cases must have greatly decreased in numbers and importance when all the dependencies of Athens were taken from her.[1] The oratory of display, brought to perfection by Isocrates, had likewise but few openings. No orator could rise at the Olympic Festival to summon all Greeks to brotherhood in arms; no funeral speech could move a people to tears or exalt them to enthusiasm when battles

---

[1] *E.g.* many of the private speeches of Demosthenes refer to maritime speculations; many of these cases, under Macedon, would be settled in local courts instead of being brought to Athens, and the diminution of Athenian commerce would still further reduce their number.

were waged by mercenaries and war declared not by a nation but by a foreign prince. The art of rhetoric was still practised, but already Aristotle, by going back to first principles, had composed the first and last scientific treatise on this subject, and shown that it must be put into its true place as a branch of philosophy, to be studied in combination with its counterpart, Dialectic.[1] Political theory, which figures prominently in Isocrates and Demosthenes, had likewise become the property of the philosophical schools.

Demetrius of Phalerum, the regent of Cassander, is reckoned by Quintilian as the last of the orators. Such time as he could spare from the management of the city and the contemplation of the 360 statues erected to him by an admiring or subservient populace,[2] was devoted to the study of philosophy, history and oratory. He wrote more than any other Epicurean on record [3]— philosophical dialogues, historical works, erudite researches, literary and rhetorical studies, speeches, all testified alike to his industry and the wide extent of his interests. His *Rhetoric*, which contained personal reminiscences of Demosthenes, is quoted by Plutarch on that account ; his treatise on *Demagogy* contained his ideas of political science ; his history of his regency (περὶ τῆς δεκαετείας) might, if we could recover it, add much to our scanty knowledge of that period. So short are the fragments remaining of his work that we must turn chiefly to Cicero and Quintilian for an estimate of his value. We gather that he was an excellent example of the ' tempered style,' excelling in grace and brilliance, but deficient in vigour and in real passion. A philo-

---

[1] Arist., *Rhet.*, i. i., *ad init.*    [2] Diog. Laert., v. 75.
[3] *Ibid.*, v. 80-81.

sophical treatment of his subject-matter was one of his marked characteristics.[1]

A few facts about his life are known chiefly from Diogenes. He was the son of Phanostratus, an enfranchised slave. He studied under Theophrastus and entered political life about 324 B.C. Belonging to the Macedonian party, he took part in the negotiations after the Lamian war. In 317 B.C., when Phocion was put to death, he fled, but was chosen by the citizens, with the approval of Cassander, to be their governor, and ruled from 317 to 307, when he was superseded by Demetrius Poliorcetes. He retired to Thebes, and twenty years later went to Egypt. Exiled from Alexandria by Philadelphus, he died of a snake-bite in one of the remote demes of Egypt about 280 B.C.

Demochares and Charisius belong also to this period; the former, one of the few Athenians who retained any independence of spirit, was a nephew of Demosthenes, whose style he imitated; Charisius imitated and exaggerated the simplicity of Lysias.[2]

From this time onward, oratory is practically dead; declamations on fictitious subjects took the place of real speeches in the assembly or the courts; oratory became an element in education and nothing more. We need mention only Hegesias of Magnesia (*c.* 250 B.C.), the founder of what was subsequently known as the ' Asian ' school of rhetoric, the characteristics of which were affected expression, grotesque metaphor, plays upon words, incongruous rhythms, and general lack of ideas.[3]

---

[1] Cicero, *Brutus*, § 37 ; *Orator*, § 92 ; *de Oratore*, ii. § 95 ; Quint., x. 1, 80 ; Diog. L., v. 82.          [2] Cicero, *Brutus*, § 286.

[3] He was over-fond of the *ditrochaeus* ($-\cup-\cup$) at the end of the sentence, *vide* Cicero, *Brutus*, § 286 ; *Orator*, §§ 226, 230 ; Dion., *de Comp. Verb.*, ch. xviii.

Dionysius quotes an extract, with the remark that it looks as if it had been written for a joke. Hegesias is important only on account of the debasing influence which he exercised over his Greek and Roman followers.

For a genuine revival of oratory we must wait till the last years of the Roman Republic.